HYDROPOLITICS

HYDROPOLITICS

Conflicts over Water as a Development Constraint

Edited by
Leif Ohlsson

UNIVERSITY PRESS LTD
Dhaka

ZED BOOKS
London & New Jersey

Hydropolitics was first published in 1995 by
Zed Books Ltd, 7 Cynthia Street, London N1 9JF, UK, and
165 First Avenue, Atlantic Highlands, New Jersey 07716, USA,
and in Bangladesh by the University Press Ltd, Red Crescent Building,
114 Motijheel C/A, PO Box 2611, Dhaka 1000, Bangladesh.

Cover designed by Andrew Corbett
Cover photograph © David Reed/Panos Pictures
Typeset in Monotype Garamond by Lucy Morton, London SE12
Printed and bound in the United Kingdom
by Biddles Ltd, Guildford and King's Lynn

A catalogue record for this book is available from the British Library
US CIP data is available from the Library of Congress

ISBN 1 85649 331 8 Cased
ISBN 1 85649 332 6 Limp

In Bangladesh
ISBN 984 05 1304 4 Limp

Contents

About the Contributors

Leif Ohlsson teaches International Relations and Development Studies at Göteborg University, Sweden. His main research interest is the international management processes of global environmental problems, and he has edited several in-house volumes of case studies of regional conflicts and conflict-resolution processes.

Elisabeth Corell has studied Political Science at Uppsala University and now researches in the Department of Water and Environmental Studies at Linköping University, Sweden. In 1992 she received a Minor Field Study Scholarship from the Swedish International Development Cooperation Agency (SIDA) to study a water dispute in south India.

Jan Hultin is a lecturer in Social Anthropology at Göteborg University. He has taught at Uppsala University, Sweden, and in the Department of Peace and Development Research, Göteborg, and worked as a consultant on water development and soil conservation in Africa. His area of research is land use and culture among the Oromo of Ethiopia.

Malin Falkenmark is Professor of Applied and International Hydrology at the Natural Science Research Council in Stockholm. She is a member of the United Nations Committee on Natural Resources, and a Global 500 Laureate.

Helena Lindholm is a researcher in the Department of Peace and Development Research at Göteborg University, and a teacher in International Relations. Her research focuses on nationalism and national identity, particularly in relation to the Palestinian case, and she has edited *Approaches to the Study of International Political Economy* (1992), and *Ethnicity and Nationalism: Formation of Identity and Dynamics of Conflict in the 1990s* (1993).

Jan Lundqvist is Professor and head of the Department of Water and Environmental Studies at Linköping University. His particular field of study is water resources scarcity and management options, in which he has wide field experience; in addition to organizing and executing research projects he has increasingly been involved in water resources management policy. He is currently scientific advisor to the Comprehensive Assessment of the Freshwater Resources of the World, which is being undertaken by the UN Commission on Sustainable Development (CSD). Recent publications include *Putting Dublin/Agenda 21 into Practice*, with T. Jönch-Clausen (1994).

Joakim Öjendal is a lecturer in the Department of Peace and Development Research, Göteborg University, and is engaged in a research project on the sharing of international water resources in mainland Southeast Asia. He has previously published on regional cooperation and development processes in Cambodia.

Michael Schulz is a lecturer in International Relations and Development Studies at Göteborg University. His areas of interest are state- and nation-building in the modern Middle East, Israeli nationalism and ethnic relations, and the new Middle Eastern regionalism.

Ashok Swain is currently engaged in a research project on the Ganges river dispute at the Department of Peace and Conflict Studies at Uppsala University, with the support of the Swedish Agency for Research Cooperation with Developing Countries (SAREC).

The Role of Water
and the Origins of Conflict

Leif Ohlsson

The water management profession will face a complex challenge in the early part of the 21st century, the like of which has never been witnessed before in human history. Clearly water management practices have to become significantly more efficient in the future than they are at present. Furthermore, this change must occur within a short period, probably a decade or at most two.

(Habib N. El-Habr and Asit K. Biswas,
'Introduction', in El-Habr [ed.], 1993)

The location is Madras. You are Swaminathan Asokan, a thirty-four-year-old clerk in a finance company. The time: 3.30 a.m., the hour you get up every morning in order to secure a place in the line for the tap on the street corner before the water is shut off at 6 a.m. Your reward: five buckets of water to carry you through the day. This is nothing you dwell on for very long; it is part of life in India's fourth city, and the taps in your own house have long been dry. Instead, your thoughts are on possibilities for holding on to your job. Among your old school friends you are the exception; aspirations for most of them have been thwarted. The nation's capital, Delhi, is regularly shut down these days by massive police forces responding to violent demonstrations from frustrated people of your own background, now organizing in politicized Hindu movements. Queuing for your five buckets from the communal tap, sleep still clouding your mind, you don't see any reason for making the connection between your standing in line for water, and the turmoil presently shaking your nation.

Neither does Khalida Messauodi, a woman mathematician in hiding somewhere in Algiers, with a death warrant from a terrorist Islamic movement hanging over her head. Suave, educated and thoroughly imbued with Western ideals of democracy, political pluralism and human rights, she is as far removed as it is possible to get in Algiers today from Climat du France, the district from which the death threat most probably emanates. Here, Rachida, a housewife waking up after a night of curfew and military police patrolling the streets, fills two large buckets of water every morning in anticipation of the water in the taps being shut off at an unpredictable hour during the early afternoon. From a hole in the wall below, Rabah, the eldest son of Yasmina, a single mother of five, trundles down to the nearby butcher's shop where he may fill two plastic bottles of water free. The butcher doesn't have the heart to charge him, although water prices have risen exorbitantly lately. Recently the boy has taken to roaming the streets, sniffing glue and joining gang fights.

Is there a connection? In that case, Kamene, a ten-year-old girl from southern Kenya, should be the one most likely to perceive it. Today she is staying home from school in order to help her mother out by carrying water from the river several kilometres away from the village. Since the local well at the once-forested hillside, now planted with maize, dried out, this is where the villagers have to get their water. But for Kamene, this is normal. She is a girl; it is her duty to help her mother support the family. Her brothers will finish school eventually; she will most probably drop out in another year, in order to work the fields alongside her mother. The extra work involved in getting the water from far away is just another of a number of small changes to which the life of her family is subjected.

The illustrative examples above of ongoing global change were all inspired by magazine reports or television documentaries reflecting one of many possible perceptions of reality from the mid-1990s. What the sum of these changes for a lot of people will amount to may become visible after ten or twenty years to a social scientist studying aggregate statistics in retrospect. But by then the connection to each single factor among the myriad strands making up the web of social change will be long lost. What, then, can reliably be said about the role of water, or the lack of it, in the multitude of challenges facing people, governments and world society during the early decades of the next century; and how will it colour our changing perceptions of those challenges?

Water, Life and Global Change

No life as we know it is possible without the simple but remarkably versatile molecule H_2O, water. Life on this planet was conceived in water only half a billion years after its creation, four and a half billion years ago. For another three and a half billion years life existed solely immersed in water, slowly evolving and changing the conditions for further evolution in the process. Not until the photosynthesizing blue-green algaes had been at work for two and a half billion years in the oceans, creating an atmosphere much richer in oxygen than is chemically stable without the presence of life, and this atmosphere had changed in its upper layers to create a protective shield of ozone against the sun's deadly ultraviolet rays, could life take the step on to land.

While geological eras came and went, continents shifting and wearing down through the erosive powers of wind and water, life on land during the last 500 million years continued to be utterly dependent on water; now it depends on the single per cent of all water on Earth which is available as fresh water, continually renewed by rain from clouds borne over the oceans, transported over large, sometimes continent-wide areas by rivers, and stored for varying periods of time in aquifers underground. The single life-creating and life-sustaining process on Earth, upon which all other life-forms are in a sense parasitic, the photosynthesis taking place in a small part of the cells of green leaves on land and phytoplanktons in the oceans uses sunlight to combine the two simple molecules water and carbon dioxide to create organic matter, and water to sustain the flow of nutrients through the organism. We are creatures of water, dependent not only on ingesting water daily, even hourly, to keep up the flow of life through our own bodies, but also on safeguarding the flow of water through the structure of the societies we have built, and through the biosphere making up our only basic life-support system.

The civilizational and cultural progress we reckon with when we define man as a social animal was built on our ability to make water work for us, and to sustain those production systems. The dawn of civilization, a mere ten thousand years ago, was ushered in by people in arid areas who were able to create gardens from the desert surrounding them by intricate irrigation systems. But when glistening salt covered the fields of Ancient Babylon, the Hanging Gardens collapsed with them; and when the irrigation systems of the first great civilization on the Indian subcontinent, the people of Mohenjo Daro on the Indus, were clogged again and again by enormous flash-floods of silt, they succumbed as well. On the Nile, on the other hand, great civilizations, invading and succeeding each other, were able to survive continuously by utilizing the mighty river's gift of delivering just the right amount of nourishing silt from the yearly floods to compensate for what man removed from the soil by agriculture, at the same time flushing the accumulated salts out of the soil and into the Mediterranean.

Even the last stage of civilizational man's efforts, industrialization, was heralded, only a few hundred years ago, by the noise of myriads of water-driven mechanical hammers reverberating through European forests. And when the motive power for the machines cutting wood, moulding steel and weaving cloth was changed to water vapour, fired by coal, industrial cities still grew up on rivers. Ever larger amounts of water were necessary – for transporting raw materials and finished products, but also for the boiling, cooling, rinsing, dyeing and dissolving processes inside the factory walls. Falkenmark (1990) makes the compelling argument that no successful industrial nation came forward during the initial industrializing phase in areas where water was not relatively abundant (with the possible exceptions of South Africa and Australia, and even here industrialization was confined to the small enclaves of relative water abundance in otherwise dry areas).

Finally, only during the last century or so, and mainly in industrialized countries, water was brought into every household and a complex water-borne system was created by which a large part of our waste products are disposed of. It is generally assumed (although hard to prove) that historically no single factor, not even antibiotics or vaccines, has contributed more to general health and shrinking infant mortality figures than people being offered access to clean water and sanitation.

At the end of this century, as groundwater tables in many parts of the world are declining, great rivers are utilized to the point where they no longer reach the ocean, more soils are taken out of production due to erosion, waterlogging and salinization than virgin soils are brought under the plough, and clean water, free from industrial pollution or disease-carrying organisms, is a scarce resource, we have come to a point where water scarcity is increasingly perceived as an imminent threat, sometimes even the ultimate limit, to development, prosperity, health, even national security. How close are we to those limits?

How Much Water Is There, and Where Does It Come From?

Viewed from space, Earth is a planet of shimmering blue and glistening white, much more so than green. What you see from an astronaut's viewpoint are the enormous expanses, more than 70 per cent of the Earth's surface, covered by seas, and the complex patterns of cloud, carrying water from the oceans and precipitating it far inland over the brownish continents with their sparse patches of green. A fair argument might indeed be put forward for changing the planet's name to Water instead of Earth.

The total volume of water on Earth would cover the globe to a height of 2.7 kilometres if it were spread evenly over its surface, but more than 97 per cent is sea water. The 3 per cent of fresh water would still make up a layer 70 metres high if it were spread evenly, but two-thirds are locked in icecaps and glaciers, and a large proportion of the remaining 1 per cent lies too far underground to exploit. Only 0.3 per cent of the 3 per cent fresh water – less than a per cent of a per cent of all water – is found in the rivers and lakes that constitute the bulk of our usable supply (Postel, 1992; Gleick, 1993).

Every year 500,000 cubic kilometres of moisture evaporates into the atmosphere, 86 per cent from the oceans and 14 per cent from land. All of it is precipitated, but more so over land than over sea, so that continents gain 40,000 cubic kilometres annually from the oceans. This amount constitutes the world's renewable fresh water supply. Two-thirds runs off in floods, leaving about 12–14,000 cubic kilometres as a relatively stable source of supply in rivers and lakes (Postel, 1992; Golubev, 1993).

These rivers and lakes are in fact only the visible part of the great hydrological cycle. Part of the runoff will have spent a longer or shorter time underground in aquifers before finally returning to the ocean. All too often we seem to forget that water taken out of the ground and consumed will not necessarily enter rivers, and vice versa. A sustainable use of rivers, reservoirs and lakes, as well as aquifers, ultimately depends on keeping annual consumptive water withdrawal within the limits of the yearly precipitation a particular watershed receives from the oceans. The inability to treat water problems within the totality of the hydrological cycle has led Falkenmark (e.g. 1990) and others to coin the phrase 'water blindness' to describe the particular engineering culture which has grown out of areas with a comparative abundance of water.

The world's annual societal withdrawal of water is presently slightly more than 4,000 cubic kilometres, which would seem to leave ample reserves, compared to the renewable supply in rivers and streams of 12–14,000 cubic kilometres. The problem, of course, is the uneven distribution of the readily available water, particularly when compared to areas with rapidly rising demands. More than half the global runoff occurs in Asia (31 per cent) and South America (25 per cent), while Europe accounts for just 7 per cent and Australia for only 1 per cent. The runoff from the Amazon River alone amounts to 20 per cent of global average runoff and 80 per cent of South America's. Thirty per cent of the total runoff in Africa comes from a single river basin, the Congo/Zaire. More than 80 per cent of the runoff is concentrated in the northern and equatorial zones, which have fairly small populations. In the temperate zones that are most suitable for agriculture and where most of the earth's population lives, flowing water resources are extremely limited. Large areas of the globe are semi-arid, arid or deserts. Dry regions occupy 33 per cent of Europe, 60 per cent of Asia, a large fraction of Africa, the southwestern regions of North America, about 30 per cent of South America, and the overwhelming majority of Australia. On the other hand, on all these continents there are also wet regions with abundant water resources (Shiklomanov, 1993; Gleick, 1993).

It is exactly this uneven distribution of water supply and demand that makes comparisons at the global or continent level, or even within a single large country, highly misleading. One conclusion would be that water problems are predominantly *local* in their effects, and at the most regional in origin. When we try to deal with global water problems, therefore, they should always be understood as an amalgam of a large number of such local problems (Golubev, 1993). Unfortunately, as we shall see, this aggregate view is all too often highly misleading.

How Is the Available Water Used?

On a global scale agriculture makes up for 69 per cent of water withdrawal, industry 21, municipal water works 6 and reservoirs 4 per cent. Much of this water is returned to rivers and used again and again by consumers downstream. Of the purely consumptive use (not available for other users) agriculture makes up for 89 per cent, industry 3, municipal water 2 and reservoirs 6 per cent (Shiklomanov, 1993).

Particularly noteworthy in these figures is agriculture's high consumption. In arid and semi-arid countries the figure is even higher – for instance 98 per cent in Egypt (Golubev, 1993). The consumptive use of reservoirs comes from evaporation and leakage to the ground. (We will return to the seemingly low consumptive use of industry below.)

In northern and western Europe farmers benefit from perhaps the greatest gift of all from God, as it were: an abundance of rainfall. Although 84 per cent of the world's cropland is watered by nothing but rain (Postel, 1992), only rarely does it fall as opportunely and in such precisely adequate amounts as here, making these areas some of the world's best farmland. (Incidentally, it is also the main reason for the water blindness in this part of the world.) All too often the story, as in Ethiopia and the 'hunger belt' of Africa's Sahel area, is one of the yearly rains failing. Traditional subsistence systems may have been able to cope with these dry spells by stocking a year's supply of grain locally. Today, when they are increasingly caught up in the restructuring process of adjusting to the modern global economy, a year of drought will spell immediate disaster for tens of millions of people.

The food aid flown or shipped in will most probably come from the 'breadbasket of the world', the western plains of the USA, where farmers largely benefit from the greater control over crop results afforded by irrigation. Although irrigated fields make up only 16 per cent of the world's farmland, they contribute 36 per cent of the crop results. Without irrigation the critical grain-growing areas of northern China, northwest India, and the western US Great Plains would drop by a third to a half. Many countries, including China, Egypt, India, Indonesia, Israel, Japan, North and South Korea, Pakistan and Peru, rely on such land for more than half their domestic food production (Postel, 1992).

Agriculture's water use has increased fivefold over the course of the century, particularly during the period since 1950, coinciding with the era of the Green Revolution. The hybrid varieties of maize, wheat and rice planted on an increasing number of fields all over the world during this period demand three major inputs to yield their record harvests: fertilizers, pesticides, and large amounts of water. The important fact to remember here is that agricultural output is roughly proportional to the amount of water supplied.

Between 1950 and 1985 the world's population doubled from 2.5 to 5 billion, but agricultural production increased 2.6-fold, more than enough to keep pace with population increases. But the mid-1980s also marked the culmination of this agricultural feat; since 1984 *per capita* grain production has fallen roughly 1 per cent a year, with the drop concentrated in developing countries. This historically new and alarming trend coincides with a drop of the *per capita* area of irrigated land, which reached its all-time high a few years earlier, in 1978 (Postel, 1992).

Although the debate on the reasons for this double drop is far from settled, there are many reasons for believing that it will be a permanent feature for a considerable time. The cost of new irrigation works has proved prohibitive, particularly when it is viewed as an economic investment and compared to other more lucrative areas. There is a shortage of new land suitable for irrigation, since nearly all suitable sites have been used during the expansion so far. When irrigation depends on the pumping of groundwater, all too often the consequence is an alarmingly rapid decline of water tables. There are huge problems with irrigation *per se*: waterlogging, salinization and the spread of parasites and epidemics, to name but a few. Finally, in an increasing number of countries, governments and the public have begun to realize the enormity of the social and environmental costs involved; the controversies over the Narmada Dam and the Aral Sea catastrophe are but two blatant examples.

The very inefficiency of irrigation (average figures cited in the literature vary considerably: from about 50 per cent down to as low as 37 per cent) is in fact a sign of hope, since it means that there is considerable room for improved efficiency. Some of the unused water is not lost but will seep down, replenishing groundwater, or flow back into rivers, as will the ground leakage of reservoirs (Golubev, 1993; Pearce, 1992; Postel, 1992).

It was stated above that industry has surprisingly low rates of global water use: 21 per cent of total withdrawal and only 3 per cent of consumptive withdrawal. The misleading character of such aggregate figures is immediately apparent if we break them down on a country basis. In developed countries where irrigation is not widespread, such as Germany, the UK and France, industry comes to the fore as the great consumer of supplied (as distinct from totally available) water: between 71 and 87 per cent of total water use in those countries. In industrialized countries where irrigation does play an important part in agriculture, such as the USA, Japan and the former USSR, industry's share of consumption still remains high: between 31 and 46 per cent.

Per capita industrial withdrawal of water varies from 995 cubic metres per year in the USA to between 305 and 584 cubic metres per year in the other industrial countries mentioned. The amount of water consumed per unit of industrial product also varies by more than ten times, indicating that there is plenty of room for improved efficiency. Every unit of water withdrawn for industrial purposes in the USA in 1978 was used 3.4 times. By the year 2000 this ratio is expected to increase to 17 times. US industry would then use 45 per cent less water than in 1978, despite considerable growth in production (Golubev, 1993; Postel, 1992).

Industrial water use reflects the double face of water problems. In arid or semi-arid areas, as in most agricultural areas, water scarcity remains a real lack of the physical resource; in northern and industrial areas it more often reflects a lack of clean water. Whenever water passes through industry or other sectors and goes back to a river without proper treatment, it creates great problems for the third large sector of water consumers: municipal water works.

Although the urban population of the world uses less than a tenth of all water withdrawn, this is the most expensive water, owing to the need to build and maintain complex systems. It is also one of the most inefficient ways to use water. As much as half of the water in the pipes is lost through underground leakage in the cities of the world, not counting the multitude of leaking taps, toilets and other household water devices. The leakage of sometimes century-old underground systems is very difficult to cure; as for the household fixtures, a number of more efficient alternatives are coming on to the market, some of which may cut water use by 50–70 per cent. Using less water in the household does not necessarily mean sacrificing hygiene, particularly in industrialized countries. The three million inhabitants of present-day Rome use less water per person than the 1,000 litres a day provided by aqueducts to their one million ancestors in ancient days (Golubev, 1993; Postel, 1992).

The review of societal water usage so far has been one of a traditional engineering management process. Aggregate demand from different sectors has to be reconciled with aggregate available supply; if the figures don't match, conservation measures must be applied, while existing sources are developed to their limits, preferably on a sustainable basis. In many parts of the world this old paradigm now increasingly has to be replaced by a new one, reflecting the stark reality of absolute scarcity: the amount of available water cannot be increased; instead the task is to determine how it should best be utilized.

This grim task is further complicated by a factor that has not come to the fore until recent years: the water needs of ecosystems themselves. When the Rhine's flow was constrained to its present almost wholly artificial river bed, during a period coinciding with the rise of the German nation, great forest and wetland areas which not only sustained a diversity of life but were of vital importance for regulating the supply of groundwater were lost forever. The same sequence of events took place when the East Anglian fens were dyked and laid dry (Pearce, 1992). Slowly, and mostly in advanced industrial nations, a re-evaluation of the importance of restoring natural wetlands is now taking place, for the services they provide in preserving biodiversity and their crucial role in the hydrological cycle. The global aspect of this issue is that the countries which have the most to gain from such protective and restorative measures are the very ones that are squeezed hardest by the people's demands for water and land.

When areas of former water abundance, which once attracted and were able to sustain large populations, find themselves hard pressed to meet the needs of ecosystems on the one hand, and the combined demands for water by agriculture, industry, and cities with growing populations with rising expectations on the other, a large part of the problem lies with the rapidity of social change. Nowhere is this squeeze felt more than in Third World cities, where the two faces of water scarcity merge: an absolute lack of water, and a lack of clean water.

How Many People Are Still Without Clean Water and Sanitation?

Despite herculean efforts during the UN Water Decade (the 'International Drinking Water Supply and Sanitation Decade', 1981–90), a large and – particularly in Third World cities – increasing number of people are still without clean water and sanitation. The programme's goal was to provide safe water for another 500,000 people every day during the entire decade of the 1980s. It failed to achieve this ambitious goal, but was a major success in that daily, over an eight-year period, almost 200,000 additional people were supplied with water (Falkenmark, 1990). Nash (1993) cites figures showing that 1.2 billion people were without a safe water supply and 1.7 billion without adequate sanitation at the end of the decade, although significant improvements were made, especially in rural water supply, where the number of people served increased by 240 per cent globally, while the number of people with access to rural sanitation increased by 150 per cent. The number of urban dwellers with access to a water supply rose by 150 per cent as well, as did the number with access to sanitation; however, this still translated into an increase in the number of urban dwellers without access to services. In Latin America and Asia, the percentage of the urban population with access to sanitation remained essentially unchanged. Globally, the percentage of town dwellers with sanitation services increased only marginally, from 69 per cent to 72 per cent. This is a reflection of the rapid growth of cities. By the year 2000, according to UNFPA (1991) estimates, 77 per cent of Latin America's population, 41 per cent of Africa's population and 35 per cent of Asia's population will be city dwellers. While the urban population is growing by only 0.8 per cent per year in the developed countries, the growth rate in the developing regions is 3.6 per cent.

The important lesson to be learnt from this exercise with proportions and absolute numbers is that a comparatively large proportional increase of people with access to clean water and sanitation may still translate into an increase of the absolute number *without* these amenities, at a time when the population is growing rapidly and simultaneously migrating to cities. Another way of putting this is to say that present efforts will have to be not only continued but further intensified just to keep up with the challenges posed by population increase, particularly in the Third World, where 96 per cent of the projected increase of 3.6 billion people between 1990 and 2030 will occur (Brown, 1994).

The question (confronted by Falkenmark and Lundqvist in the concluding chapter of this volume) is, of course, in what areas, and when, will the increased demand for water from one sector – for example, the urban population – come into conflict with the increasing demands from the other sectors, agriculture or industry; and what solutions are there when aggregate demand surpasses available supply?

How Imminent is Water Scarcity, and Where Will It Strike First?

The map is an attempt to illustrate what the looming water crisis looks like for Europe and Africa. At an immediate glance, the only countries not likely to hit the water barrier on a national scale in the

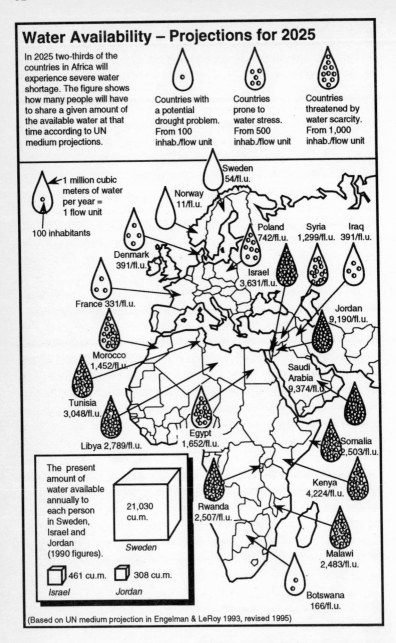

Water Availability – Projections for 2025

In 2025 two-thirds of the countries in Africa will experience severe water shortage. The figure shows how many people will have to share a given amount of the available water at that time according to UN medium projections.

Countries with a potential drought problem. From 100 inhab./flow unit

Countries prone to water stress. From 500 inhab./flow unit

Countries threatened by water scarcity. From 1,000 inhab./flow unit

← 1 million cubic meters of water per year = 1 flow unit

100 inhabitants

Sweden 54/fl.u.

Norway 11/fl.u.

Poland 742/fl.u.

Syria 1,299/fl.u.

Iraq 391/fl.u.

Denmark 391/fl.u.

Israel 3,631/fl.u.

France 331/fl.u.

Jordan 9,190/fl.u.

Morocco 1,452/fl.u.

Saudi Arabia 9,374/fl.u.

Tunisia 3,048/fl.u.

Egypt 1,652/fl.u.

Somalia 2,503/fl.u.

Libya 2,789/fl.u.

Kenya 4,224/fl.u.

The present amount of water available annually to each person in Sweden, Israel and Jordan (1990 figures).

21,030 cu.m.

Sweden

Rwanda 2,507/fl.u.

461 cu.m.

308 cu.m.

Israel

Jordan

Malawi 2,483/fl.u.

Botswana 166/fl.u.

(Based on UN medium projection in Engelman & LeRoy 1993, revised 1995)

Map I.1 Graphic representation of areas of impending water stress and crisis in Europe and Africa. The threat of absolute water shortage (represented here by drops with more than ten dots) will spread throughout northern and southern Africa over the next decade, due to population increases.

foreseeable future are the northern Scandinavian countries. South of the Baltic the situation is already more precarious, as it is in the rest of Europe, although water problems here are more often pollution problems than an absolute lack of water resources. The extreme water stress experienced by the core Middle East countries is treated in separate case studies in this volume. What is not so generally discussed is the precarious situation for North and West African countries (among them Morocco, Algeria, Tunisia, Libya and Egypt), where population increases during the next decade will bring them very close to the barrier of absolute water shortage.

The map cites figures of available water per person per year for Sweden (21,030 cubic metres), Israel (461 cubic metres) and Jordan (308 cubic metres) as illustrative examples (1994 figures).

For a better understanding of what the figures really mean we have to compare them to what are generally agreed to be acceptable levels. As a rule of thumb, hydrologists use the level of 1,000–2,000 cubic metres per person per year to designate danger of water stress. When the figure drops below 1,000 cubic metres per year per person, nations are considered water-scarce, which means that lack of water becomes a severe constraint on food production, economic development, and protection of natural systems. Today, 26 countries with 232 million people belong to this group – in Europe the Netherlands, Belgium and Hungary; in the Middle East Israel, Jordan, Syria and the whole Arabian peninsula; in Africa Egypt, Algeria, Libya, Tunisia, Kenya, and others (Postel, 1992).

Obviously, some of the countries mentioned have managed to cope with their water problems (e.g. the European countries, although signs of scarcity are beginning to show there also). The apparent anomaly is explained by the fact that figures used for designating a country as water-stressed or water-scarce are sometimes based on *internal* renewable water supplies, and do *not* include water flowing in from neighbouring countries. The figures in the map for Sweden, Israel and Jordan, however, *include* rivers flowing in, and thus mark the absolute upper limit of sustainable water withdrawal for these countries. The very low figures (below 500 cubic metres per year per person) for Israel and Jordan in fact designate them as suffering from what hydrologists call absolute water scarcity. Yet Israel's annual water withdrawal (447 cubic metres per person per year; the corresponding figure for Jordan is 173) is actually very close to the Swedish level (479 cubic metres per person per year). The difference, of course, is that

the Swedes use only a tiny fraction of their huge available water supply, and their agriculture is amply rainfed (only 9 per cent of the
renewable supply is used for agriculture), while Israel and Jordan use
up almost their entire renewable supply, and have to allot 85 and 65
per cent respectively to irrigation (figures from Gleick, 1993: 374 ff.).
Given regional and seasonal imbalances and the difficulties of utilizing
the renewable supply to its theoretical maximum, it is no wonder that
the precarious water balance of these two countries have led them,
and others in the same plight, to extreme overutilization on two counts:
groundwater is often pumped at a higher rate than it is replenished;
and rivers shared with other states, often water-stressed themselves,
are exploited – sometimes to the brink of war, as the case studies in
this volume show.

The most extreme example of unsustainable groundwater pumping
is probably Saudi Arabia, where a fossil aquifer (built up during geological eras but no longer replenished) is used for growing wheat in
what would otherwise be a desert, turning the country into a major
wheat exporter. Seventy-five per cent of Saudi Arabia's water supply
is taken from this source, which will dry up or be inundated with salt
water within fifty years at the present rate of depletion, or sooner by
the higher rates projected for the next century. In Libya, the first part
of a gigantic project called 'the world's largest man-made river' (in
fact, pipelines large enough to drive a truck through) has been in-
augurated. It will sustain Libya's coastal agricultural area with water
pumped up deep from the interior of the Sahara, also for a period of
forty to sixty years, after which the wells will run dry for ever. This
practice, however, is not restricted to desert countries. The farmers of
the southwestern USA have for a long time been depleting the gigantic
Ogallala fossil aquifer, which supplies 30 per cent of the groundwater
used for irrigation in the United States. Widespread conservation
measures have slowed the depletion rate in later years, but it still
remains a prime example of water shortsightedness. (Pearce, 1992;
Postel, 1992; Clarke, 1991).

Israel has often been cited as an innovator when it comes to water
conservation measures. 'Making the desert bloom', however, is a miracle
that has been repeated in many parts of the world (e.g. Libya, Saudi
Arabia and California). The real miracle would consist in doing it
without overtaxing renewable water supplies. Pressed by the strategic
necessity to maximize the use of available water, Israeli experts have
developed a number of intensive irrigation methods, whereby water is

injected almost drop by drop into the root-zones of plants. Research on ancient methods of 'rain harvesting' from the Negev desert, whereby a large area is set aside expressly for collecting the extremely sparse precipitation and funnelling it down to a field several times smaller, where a crop is grown on the collected water from a single rainfall, has been made good use of in arid and semi-arid African countries. A large proportion of Israel's waste water, which would otherwise have ended up in the Mediterranean, is reused for agriculture. Despite what are probably the most intensive conservation measures on record for a single country, Israel today seems to have come to the end of its tether; groundwater tables are diminishing and filling with sea water, and it now seems that they have in fact been overpumped for at least ten years (Pearce, 1992; Clarke, 1991; the case of Israel is treated extensively by Lindholm in this volume, Chapter 2).

The figure used here for assessing present and potential water scarcity, the amount of fresh water available *per capita*, is misleading in several respects. It leaves regional differences within a country, as well as widely differing rainfall patterns over the year, out of the balance. Chile may get enough water on a country basis, but it also contains some of the driest areas on Earth. On the Indian subcontinent life over large areas is regimented to periods of either too much (monsoons and floods from May to September) or too little water (droughts during long periods of the rest of the year). In large parts of Africa evaporation exceeds annual precipitation because of the hot climate, leaving countries in arid or semi-arid areas dependent on what flows into them from rivers in other countries. Altogether, therefore, it is estimated that some eighty countries with 40 per cent of the world's population already suffer from serious water shortages in some regions or at some times during the year (Gleick, 1993; Falkenmark and Lindh, 1993).

The most serious mistake of all, however, is to look at water problems as a static phenomenon, while they are in fact in constant flux, due to population increases, rising expectations from a growing population, and concurrent increasing demands for more water from agriculture and industry. By the end of this century, only a few years away, a large number of countries will enter the category of water-scarce nations. In Africa alone 300 million people, a third of the continent's projected population, will live under such conditions by the year 2000. Nine out of fourteen countries in the Middle East already face water-scarce conditions, and populations in six of them are projected to double within twenty-five years. China, with 22 per cent of the world's people and only 8 per cent of its fresh water, is in serious trouble as it is, particularly in and around its big cities and industrial centres. Water tables beneath Beijing have been dropping 1–2 metres a year, and a third of its wells are reportedly going dry. Some one hundred Chinese towns, mostly in the northern and coastal regions, have suffered shortages in recent years (Postel, 1992). What remedies, if any, are being discussed to meet these challenges?

What about the Icebergs of the Antarctic and Desalination of Sea Water?

Whenever water scarcity on a global level is discussed on a popular level, two questions immediately crop up: What about those plans to capture icebergs in the Antarctic and tow them to places that need water? And how is desalination of sea water coming along? These are legitimate questions, and deserve better than a peremptory brush off, not least because of the lessons that can be learnt from trying to answer them.

The iceberg notion has been around for some fifty years, and still no icebergs have been towed. Interestingly, the idea has cropped up again in a somewhat different form. Clarke (1991) reports plans to export water from Turkey in gigantic plastic bags to be towed across the Mediterranean to Israel. This method was used by the military during both the Falklands War and the Gulf War. Private firms now apparently offer the same services on a much larger scale. Prospective customers are thought to be Southern California (buying water from Alaska), the Gaza Strip (water from Turkey) and Saudi Arabia (transporting water from their desalination plants on the Red Sea coast to cities without such plants). It is even hoped that these water bags might help to depoliticize water issues ('The Middle East', May 1994). So far, however, almost any other solution has proved more attractive, including conduits hundreds of miles long across deserts and gigantic pumps to bring the water across mountain ridges. Israel currently uses a fifth of its available electricity to transport water through its National Water Carrier from the Sea of Galilee to cities and farms all the way to the south. Through an intricate pattern of dams, conduits and canals California is sucking the Colorado River, on the other side of the Rocky Mountains, dry to the extent that it no longer enters the Gulf of Mexico.

In spite of mighty waterworks such as these, water problems continue to be predominantly local or, at the most, regional. One important reason is the sheer volumes required, particularly so for agriculture. The 4,000 cubic kilometres withdrawn annually from the stable 12–14,000 renewable supply makes water the most widely used natural resource, and also one of the most highly mobilized by man: a third of the naturally available stable supply. The use of other voluminous, but still transportable, natural resources, such as coal or oil, is about three orders of magnitude less. It is exactly this 'bulkiness' of water that makes any solution to water problems on a continent-wide basis, or even from one end of a large country to another, unviable, at least within the foreseeable future (Golubev, 1993).

Desalination of sea water in fact takes place in 7,500 plants around the world. Production amounts to one–tenth of one per cent of total water use, but if the need is great enough and you are endowed with a lot of capital, technical expertise, and preferably also large amounts of fossil fuel at low or no cost, it is apparently a viable local option, at least for household and industry use. Not surprisingly, 60 per cent of the installed capacity is found in the oil-rich countries around the Persian Gulf, 30 per cent of it in Saudi Arabia alone. A few island nations in the Caribbean and arid regions in Australia and Spain account for most of the rest. The two principal methods used are distillation by boiling sea water and cooling the steam (the same process the sun accomplishes on a much greater scale turning sea water into clouds and transporting the water inland through the climatic processes) and reverse osmosis, which means filtering salty water under pressure through special membranes. Turning ocean water into drinking water in this way typically costs four to eight times the price of city water today, and at least ten to twenty times what farmers pay for water (Postel, 1992).

Relying on methods such as these obviously will not suffice to meet the challenges ahead. So what is left? A look at other sectors of modern society, which have recently gone through perceived squeezes of the same type, may be instructive. Only twenty years ago energy issues were discussed almost solely in terms of the need for increased production in order to meet projected increases in demand. Yet today, this supply-side-orientated way of thinking has given way almost wholly to demand-side regulation. The cheapest way of getting more available electricity is always to save some. More energy-efficient devices will almost always pay for themselves because they obviate the need to install new, and expensive, extra production capacity. What is required for the new energy-efficient devices to come into their own is 'getting the prices right'.

To a large extent this goes for water too. The possible savings in agriculture – which, as we have seen, claims at least two-thirds of present water withdrawal – constitutes the biggest pool in what Postel (1992) has aptly termed the 'last oasis'. Despite impressive savings in, for example, US agriculture in recent years, the full potential of this largely unexploited reserve will not be realized until governments stop subsidizing irrigation for farming, in both industrialized and developing countries. Until the mid-1980s farmers in California's Central Valley had repaid no more than 4 per cent of the capital costs for the massive irrigation projects they benefit from. In India, the world's third largest food producer, government irrigation projects are running at large deficits, and prices are so low – typically 2–5 per cent of the harvest's value – that no incentive for improving irrigation efficiency exists. In Mexico farmers pay just 11 per cent of the full cost of their water; those in Indonesia and Pakistan about 13 per cent. Egyptian farmers are not charged directly for their irrigation water at all.

Correcting these economic disincentives will be a herculean task, given the strong and entrenched position agriculture traditionally occupies in all economies. Concrete methods of improving irrigation efficiency will have to be worked out and implemented. Finally, some strategic decisions concerning which way irrigation should go are still unresolved.

Should the Building of Large Dams Continue?

Although there are historical exceptions (most notably ancient agriculture along the Nile, utilizing the natural flooding of the river, which flushed out accumulated salts), irrigation as such irrevocably tends to destroy farmland. No water is completely free from salts; through evaporation from fields and the plants' evapotranspiration, salt slowly concentrates in the soil, until crops will no longer grow. The typical short-term solution is to pour more water on. Even with proper drainage there is a very high risk of groundwater tables finally rising so high that water reaches the root-zone of the crops, making them rot, and the fields become waterlogged. The runoff from irrigated fields is regularly more salty than the water poured on to them, which aggravates the problem for farmers further downstream (even in another country, as is the case between the USA and Mexico). The only way of prolonging the life-term of irrigated fields is to apply the water more sparingly, but also more effectively. Great strides have been made here with both relatively simple means and high-technology methods. The end result to date, however, is that more irrigated farmland is currently taken out of production due to salinization and waterlogging, than is brought under the plough (Postel, 1992, 1994).

The majority of the world's large dams were built between 1950 and 1975. Since then the rate of dam construction has halved (Postel, 1992). The generous funding policy from the World Bank and others for the building of large dams, either for purposes of generating electricity or to provide irrigation, has been a fiasco, as admitted by the Bank itself in a candid in-house report. Almost none of the goals of alleviating rural poverty had been met. The dislocation of large masses of people necessary when dams are built has provoked so much popular resistance that many projects have been halted. Dam-building in tropical areas, such as the Amazon rainforest, brings large environmental problems when unfelled forests covered by water start to rot. It also frequently threatens indigenous peoples' livelihood (Pearce, 1992). In India, the widespread walling-in of flood-prone rivers has in many cases exacerbated the problem and created new ones (CSE, 1991).

On the other side of the argument, Biswas and El-Habr (1993) maintain that environmental assessments of dams and irrigation projects tend to focus almost exclusively on the negative aspects of development, leaving out the fact that almost any large development project will have both positive (otherwise why build them?) and negative impacts. Taking the much-abused Aswan Dam on the Nile as an example, they maintain that the dam has been remarkably successful, and that without it Egypt would have suffered badly during the years in the 1980s when the Nile ran low, and would in fact be facing a state of continuing catastrophe even now. Irrigation, in their view, should also be judged by its secondary, non-intended, good effects (increased nutritional level, new employment opportunities, new schools, improved position for women, etc.). Citing the Bhima project in India, they note that before irrigation was brought in, landless labourers could afford to educate only one son, housed with a relative while the rest of the family travelled in search of work. Daughters were never sent to school. When irrigation employment opportunities near the villages increased significantly, families could stay in one place, and for the first time daughters were sent to school.

Nevertheless, as we approach the turn of the century the fate of several big dams, irrigation projects, and flood-control plans seems to hang in the balance. From the point of view of food-production requirements this poses a great dilemma. Some of the slowdown in grain production during recent years may certainly be market-related, but not all of it. Far more important in the long run is farmland being taken out of production because of erosion or salinization, and the constraints on expanding irrigation. In *per capita* terms, grain production reached its all-time high in 1984, and had declined 11 per cent by 1993. Since ocean fishing may not be able to sustain a harvest higher than that of recent years (*per capita* fish catches peaked in 1989 and had declined 7 per cent by 1993) and rangeland (a major world source of animal protein) may be at maximum carrying capacity, any substantial increases in fish, beef and mutton production will have to come from fish-farming or feedlots, which in turn will depend on grain production and, ultimately, the availability of water (Brown, 1994).

So the fate of future big dams and irrigation works seems increasingly to be decided by the stark necessity perceived by governments to harvest, stock and funnel an ever larger part of the rain falling over their own as well as other countries' territories. The race for the rains is on. In fact, in many parts of the world it has been on for quite some time now.

Will There Be Water Wars, and If So, Where?

The case studies in this volume will show that conflicts over the rains funnelled by shared water resources, aquifers as well as rivers and lakes, have already been a major contributing cause of war and annexation of territories in at least one case: the 1967 war when Israel occupied the West Bank, the Golan Heights and the Gaza Strip (see Chapter 2). In 1975 Iraq, Syria and Turkey almost went to war over the waters of the Euphrates. Today water harvesting by Turkey threatens the common security of these countries (see Chapter 3). Even during the celebrated Camp David peace agreement Egyptian leaders made war threats in another direction: over the waters of the Nile (see Chapter 1). On the Indian subcontinent conflict over rivers deadlocked relations between India and Pakistan for more than a

Table I.1 Examples of Unresolved International Water Issues, Mid-1990s

Rivers	Countries involved in dispute	Subject of dispute
Nile	Egypt, Ethiopia, Sudan	Siltation, flooding, water flow/diversion
Euphrates, Tigris	Iraq, Syria, Turkey	Dams, reduced water flow, salinization, hydroelectricity
Jordan, Yarmuk, Litani, West Bank aquifer	Israel, Jordan, Syria, Lebanon, Palestinians on the West Bank	Water flow/diversion, allotment of water from common aquifers, water-titles
Indus, Jhelum, Chenab, Ravi, Beas, Sutlej	India, Pakistan	Irrigation (conflict mediated in 1960 with the help of the World Bank, but tension remains)
Brahmaputra, Ganges	Bangladesh, India	Siltation, flooding, water flow/diversion
Salween/Nu Jiang	Burma, China	Siltation, flooding
Mekong	Kampuchea, Laos, Thailand, Vietnam	Water flow, flooding, irrigation, hydroelectricity
Paraná	Argentina, Brazil	Dam, land inundation
Lauca	Bolivia, Chile	Dam, salinization
Rio Grande, Colorado	Mexico, United States	Salinization, water flow, agrochemical pollution
Great Lakes	Canada, United States	Water diversion
Rhine	France, Netherlands, Switzerland, Germany	Industrial pollution
Maas, Schelde	Belgium, Netherlands	Salinization, industrial pollution
Danube	Austria, Slovakia, Hungary	Water diversion, hydroelectricity
Szamos	Hungary, Romania	

Sources: This volume; Gleick, 1993; Pearce, 1992; Renner, 1989.

decade, and continue to do so between India and Bangladesh. In Karnataka, a military guard has been posted over dams on the Cauvery threatened by guerrillas from a thirsty state of the same country, downstream Tamil Nadu (see Chapter 4). In Indochina, for several decades, war prevented the development of the Mekong. Now that it is over, new conflicts over the best way to utilize the waters of the river emerge (see Chapter 5).

What we have here is the classic riparian problem. A river knows no boundaries. What happens at its source will reverberate all through its course until it reaches the ocean. Problems at the mouth may be unsolvable if you cannot control what happens at the source, and developments on the upper part cannot be made without considering effects further downstream. Almost none of the world's major rivers, however, is contained within the borders of a single state. Nearly 40 per cent of the world's people live in river basins shared by more than two countries. Africa alone contains fifty-seven river and lake basins shared by at least two nations (Postel, 1992). The India–Bangladesh Joint Rivers Commission has identified more than 140 water systems common to both countries. The disruption of, for example, the former Soviet Union has created an as yet unchartered number of new internationally shared watercourses. These examples alone will add up to more than the often-quoted total figure of 214 international rivers and lake basins (which stems from a highly misleading 1978 UN desk study, made from maps on a very small scale, and unfortunately referred to ever since); obviously the correct figure is much larger (Biswas, 1993).

So the potential for conflict over water seems to be large (see Table I.1). As the case studies will also try to show, however, so is the potential for conflict resolution and peace. Conflict over and violent annexation of common water resources is a viable strategy only so long as more water in the hands of one country is perceived by another as a loss of the same amount. Soften that notion, and the first ground for co-operation, leading to more water for all, is laid. Storing the Nile's water at the springs of the Blue Nile, in the deep mountain gorges at Lake Kana, Ethiopia, would lead to less evaporation loss, and more water, than dams on the desert plains of Sudan and Egypt. Completion of the Jonglei Canal, bypassing the Sudd marches, would have the same effect (Pearce, 1992; Clarke, 1991).

There are many complications, however. Egypt fears that Ethiopia will not just store the water, but withdraw a sizeable portion of the present Egyptian share for internal Ethiopian use. Present FAO plans for Uganda on the White Nile would similarly imply less water for downstream Sudan and Egypt. Ethiopia, on the other hand, may rightly fear that the decrease of evaporation caused by the Jonglei project will lead to less rain over the Ethiopian mountains. (The main reason for the present deadlock over the Jonglei Canal, however, is civil war in Sudan, which is largely unrelated to the Jonglei issue.) Similar examples will be found in other chapters of this book.

The degree of justification for the persistence with which many governments continue to regard international water bodies as the ultimate zero-sum game is therefore difficult to determine. Only one thing is clear: it is an age-old habit. The English words river and rival in fact have the same root, *rivus*, meaning stream in Latin, from which is derived *rivalis*, which means sharing the same stream (Biswas, 1993). Even if it were possible to show that common management of a shared water resource would in some cases lead to more water for all, it is very difficult to build up the confidence in a long-standing adversary necessary to embark on that road. One reason for this might be that living along the same large river unavoidably spelled conflicts for other reasons long before the issue at hand could possibly, by any stretch of the imagination, have been scarcity of the physical resource in common, water, as such. It is quite possible, therefore, that the inherent conflict potential of shared rivers might be not so much the very real contemporary scarcity of and competition for the waters of the river, but, rather, the ease with which today's water conflicts along rivers seem also to become pervaded by controversies of unrelated, often age-old origin, now invested with the very physical presence of the river.

Conversely, and in the light of what has been said so far, the equally real peace potential of water issues would seem to be that since water is such an essential necessity for which there is no substitution, countries perceiving an increased scarcity of water will opt for a negotiated solution of differences over water allocation rather than unilateral annexation, because continued conflict is at best a zero-sum game, while negotiations would in most cases lead to more of a scarce resource for all; and a successful peaceful resolution of the differences should initiate a positive spiral whereby a number of other ingrained conflict patterns could start to dissolve.

Far from being a mere idealistic dream, this is exactly what has happened in some places. A more than century-old conflict between the provinces of Sind and Punjab in Pakistan over the allotment of water from the Indus was finally resolved in 1990 – a feat which neither British colonialism nor later authoritarian regimes were able to achieve. In the wake of the agreement, several other conflicts between the provinces were resolved (*Far Eastern Economic Review*, 4 April 1991). Although the massive floods in 1992 seem to have rekindled conflicts over water management, the 1990 conflict resolution process still seems to have worked as a catalyst for unravelling a whole complex of conflicts.

Obviously, behind a breakthrough like this lies a lot of patient work, often initiated on a low-key, technical and administrative level. From the report of such a closed meeting of Middle East water managers the impressions given are those of constructive talks, relatively unhindered by political barriers (El-Habr, ed., 1993), mirroring the perhaps paradoxical fact that the best chances of realizing the peace potential of shared water resources will be where the conflicts are most acute – if all countries involved perceive a shortage, the stakes for developing the common resource by co-operation become very high. What is clear is that such talks will generally have to take as their point of departure the only natural unit for river management, a river basin or an aquifer in its entirety, and would thus entail regional cooperation of some sort. What fora are there for such deliberations in the world today?

Where Are Water Issues Handled Within the International System?

A systematic index prepared by the FAO contains more than 2,000 instruments relating to international watercourses, some of them dating back to the eleventh and twelfth centuries, and most of them bilateral agreements relating to rivers and lakes that form or cross boundaries. The still small, but growing, number of multilateral agreements nearly always concern specific watercourses or drainage basins. None of them contains general principles that are immediately applicable to international law. The search for such principles is carried out in three major institutions: the Institut de Droit International (Institute of International Law), the International Law Association (ILA), and the International Law Commission (ILC) of the United Nations. The Institut de Droit International has produced, among other things, the 1979 Athens Resolution on the Pollution of Rivers and Lakes and International Law; and the ILA the so-called 1966 Helsinki Rules.

The most general principle emerging from this work seems to be the one of *equitable* use and benefit of a specific watercourse. The meaning of 'equitable' must be determined in each specific case, and some crucial differences in interpretation have emerged at various stages in the work. The commentaries to the Helsinki Rules make it explicitly clear that an existing use of a river (for example, downstream agriculture in Egypt or Iraq) would have to give way to a new use (such as Ethiopian or Turkish upstream water development) in order to reach an equitable apportioning, although the new user would have to pay compensation. ILC, on the other hand, which is bound by directives from the UN General Assembly, stresses the principle of not inflicting harm on present users (building on principles from the 1972 UN Conference on the Human Environment in Stockholm), thus unfortunately leaving equitable use out of the picture (McCaffrey, 1993; Biswas, 1993). The latter approach would seem to encourage a 'race for the river', where the first user will possess all rights. The differences are still unresolved, which is one reason why water negotiations generally proceed at a painfully slow pace.

The UN system in general has been slow in reacting to water issues. The Mekong Committee dates back to 1957. Basic research on water issues was initiated by UNESCO in the 1960s, leading to the first UN world water conference (1977) in Mar del Plata, Argentina. Apart from the Water Decade 1981–90 mentioned above, and the problems with international rivers, work on water issues in the wider sense lacks an effective forum (Clarke, 1991). Falkenmark (1990) is particularly critical of the way water issues were neglected by the Brundtland Commission, leading up to the 1992 Rio Conference. One explanation may be that water issues, due to their locality and diversity, will not easily fit into a convention on the lines of, for example, the successful Montreal Protocol against ozone-depleting substances (Biswas, 1993).

Attempts to implement the Mar del Plata decisions are still being made in the 1990s by the new FAO plan for water and sustainable agriculture. In 1986 UNEP (United Nations Environmental Programme) launched a programme for Environmentally Sound Management of Inland Water Resources (EMINWA), which has resulted in a pilot project for the Zambesi River, shared by eight African countries. Similar action plans for the Lake Chad Basin and the Damman aquifer under the Arabian peninsula are under way (Mageed, 1993; Clarke, 1991).

Will There Be Enough Water for a Doubling of the Present Population?

Will there be a global water crisis, similar to the oil crisis of the 1970s, during the early decades of the next century? The short answer is no. To a large extent water, unlike oil, wheat and minerals, is not a globally tradeable commodity, in the sense that it is needed in quantities too large to make it practical to transport long distances. There will be no 'water-dollars' accumulating in the hands of some well-endowed country, or floating around to create havoc with currency markets. It will not be possible to pass 'water-relief' from the rich world to the poor. As our case studies show, some countries may be tempted to use a privileged position along a shared water resource as a lever to better their position in a regional power game. Conflicts around such shared water resources will certainly intensify, but so will conflict-resolution processes.

Still, the water crisis is obviously here to stay. But what form will it take? Some answers may be attempted. First of all, it will be local in its effects, and regional in its political and security-related implications. Second, it will affect those countries, or regions within countries, in arid and semi-arid areas with high population growth. Third, it will be a multifaceted crisis: in rapidly growing Third World cities it will aggravate health problems; in other sectors it will mean opportunities lost for creating food security, generating export incomes, or developing industry. Fourth, the transition from a situation of earlier relative water sufficiency to rising and conflicting demands on a now increasingly scarce resource will mean great social changes, and put enormous strain on the capability of the societies involved to manage the almost unavoidable internal conflicts such a process will entail. Finally, there will be no way of predicting the exact forms these conflicts will take. What social scientist will stake his or her reputation on an attempt to show the links between water scarcity in large Indian cities and the rise of Hindu fundamentalism? On the other hand, who can deny the role of water scarcity as an important part of the multitude of social strains those cities are subjected to, leading to frustrated expectations of a better life, and ultimately to social unrest?

What we are dealing with here, on the most aggregate global level, are perceptions of limits to societal growth. The oil crisis of the 1970s marked the beginning of the end of one such perception, prevalent at least since the end of World War II: scarcity of non-renewable resources, most easily identified in the popular mind as 'we will run out of oil'. Coinciding with the rise and fall of the era of the Cold War and the institutions of the Bretton Woods world order, it has been marked by traditional geopolitics, Great Power bloc struggles, and the expansion of the world economic system.

But the oil never ran out, nor did scarce metals. The economists predicting that substitution and price mechanisms would solve the problem seem to have won the day. Today, in a situation of virtual oil glut, we are instead seriously discussing the very real possibility that most of the oil, even in known and prospected reserves, will have to be left in the ground, on account of the greenhouse effect. We are in fact well into the era where limits to growth are increasingly defined by the environmental effects of the industrial mode of production, identified in the popular mind as 'we must save the environment'. On the global level it has been marked by a growing number of international negotiating processes, sometimes leading to conventions along the lines of the successful Montreal Protocol against ozone-depleting substances, and culminating so far in the 1992 Rio Conference. In this process, the need for new supra-national organs has been increasingly felt, but not so far realized.

Global climate change due to the greenhouse effect, which is the archetypal global environmental problem of the present era, will in fact show up mostly as water-related problems, which, as we have seen, are typically local problems. It is thought that areas of the world prone to droughts and floods will become increasingly so; this is one reason why climate change will take its greatest toll in agriculture, and mainly within Third World agricultural economies. In the decades to come, global climate change will thus be a test case of how the international community can handle a problem which can be ameliorated only by concerted action on a global scale, but has its most serious effects on a very local level.

Almost before we have settled into this new perception of limits to growth, however, water scarcity heralds yet another change. *Per capita* figures for the most important food-producing sectors are declining. We are witnessing what may be the beginning of the era of competition for the very resources that have so far always been advocated as the alternative during both the earlier eras; the renewable resources (Homer-Dixon *et al.*, 1993; Harrison, 1993), be they sunlight converted into biomass or rains funnelled into rivers. Rather than being merely one scare succeeding another, this is a case of a new societal constraint coming to the fore sooner than expected. In the popular mind the coming era will probably be identified with 'how shall we feed the Earth's people', and it will overlap with rather than supersede the previous environmentally orientated era, in the sense that the main strategy for response will still be sustainability in all its aspects.

But there will be some important shifts of focus. In the process it will be increasingly realized that the 3.6 billion people projected to be added to the world's population in another thirty-five years, and the doubling of 1985 levels by 2050, is not to a large extent a variable, due to the inertia of population dynamics. Almost whatever we accomplish in the way of making family planning a viable option for people who now traditionally have large families, some five billion-plus new people, another Earth, will be there by that time, and 96 per cent of them will be in the Third World. The challenge this imposes on world society will not go away; meeting it may mean that environmental concerns *per se* will have to take a back seat to concerns for human survival and welfare. No doubt there will be irreparable losses of natural wealth. More probably, however, it will turn out to be a case of preserving the productivity and diversity of natural systems *precisely because this is the only viable way of safeguarding human welfare*. Learning to handle the diversity of problems encountered – water issues being a prime example – will most probably turn into more of an art than just another managerial skill.

1

The Nile:

Source of Life, Source of Conflict

Jan Hultin

The Nile is the world's longest river, flowing south to north over 6,800 kilometres over 35 degrees of latitude until it reaches the Mediterranean. Its basin includes nine states: Rwanda, Burundi, Zaire, Tanzania, Kenya, Uganda, Ethiopia, Egypt and the Sudan. In the arid lands of the Sudan and Egypt its waters provide the basis for human life: without soil and water, there can be no cultivation. The annual flood of the river has provided both the alluvial soils and the water on which the irrigated agriculture of Egypt has been based. For thousands of years man has watched the flow of its brown waters, and measured its rise and fall in order to determine when to plant and how much to cultivate. Too much water, or too little, might spell disaster and famine (Collins, 1990: 1–3). Since ancient times, religion and science have been concerned with the problem of securing a regular seasonal rhythm in the flow of the Nile. Throughout history man's greatest fear was that this source of life would cease to flow.

In contemporary Egypt this fear is still a living reality, haunting peasants and political leaders alike. Today, however, the root of the anxiety relates not to the work of gods, but to the work of economic men and political leaders in the riparian states to the south of Egypt: it relates to the politics of water in the Nile basin. The completion of the Aswan Dam in 1970 provided over-year storage of water and eliminated the old problem of the seasonal variation in the flow. The fear that the flow to this vital reservoir may decrease, however, remains. Therefore, every attempt at development planning among any of the eight southern riparian states involving the regulation of the flow of the Nile or its major tributaries will be the cause of great

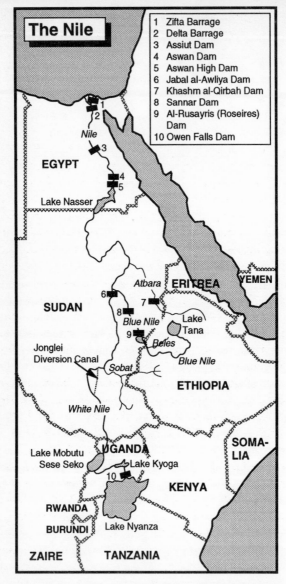

Map 1.1 The map of the Nile, with existing and projected dams and water-diverting projects, illustrates the classic riparian problem: what happens with water upstream affects countries downstream. Egypt is totally dependent on the Nile for her agricultural production. The rate of population growth is high, but the flow of the Nile is constant or diminishing. The fear of Ethiopian plans of diverting water from the Blue Nile for its own purposes is so great that Egypt has threatened to go to war with Ethiopia if the water flow of the Nile is seriously impeded. This fear, however, may in fact be exaggerated.

concern in Cairo. Egyptian leaders have stated on several occasions that they are prepared to go to war over the use of the waters of the Nile.

Water Stress

Egypt's fear and consequent aggressive rhetoric stem from the fact that the country is threatened by acute water shortage. Water, however, is a scarce resource not only in Egypt. In many countries in the Nile basin population growth, often at about 3 per cent per annum, is on a collision course with water resources. Falkenmark (1989a) talks of *water stress* when annual renewable water supplies approach 2,000 cubic metres per person. By the end of the century five countries of the East African Nile basin – Tanzania, Burundi, Rwanda, Kenya and Ethiopia – will exceed this measure of water scarcity. Egypt, together with her Mediterranean neighbours to the west, Libya, Tunisia, Algeria and Morocco (as well as Egypt's Middle Eastern neighbours), will face the same situation. Many countries will have less than 1,000 cubic metres per person. This water, then, will be needed for industrial expansion, for irrigated agriculture and for human consumption in rapidly growing cities.

At present, all the North African countries with the exception of Morocco import half or more of their grain, and this dependence on imported food will increase during the next decades (Falkenmark, 1989a; Postel, 1989: 24 ff.). In most of these countries there can be no expansion of rainfed agriculture, and definitely not in Egypt. Moreover, the need for water for the expansion of irrigated agriculture will have to compete with the need for water for other purposes. In Egypt the threat of water stress is increasing every month. The population is now 54 million, and is projected to reach 75 million by the year 2000 (Starr, 1991). With 98 per cent of the country being desert, the growing population is concentrated in 2 per cent of the land. The gross irrigated area is 3.2 million hectares, the same as Thailand; this is a little more than Italy, Japan and Romania, with 3 million hectares each, but less than Mexico, Spain and Turkey, with 3.3 million each (Postel, 1989: 8). As a comparison, it is far less than India, with 55 million hectares of irrigated farmland (one-fifth of the world's total irrigated area); China has 46 million hectares; the Soviet Union 21 million; the United States 19 million; and Pakistan 16 million.

No country in the world, however, is more dependent on irrigated agriculture than Egypt, where *all* cropland (100 per cent) is irrigated, and all future expansion must be based on either of two water sources: the Nile or underground reservoirs beneath the Sahara (Pugh, 1990). The development of the latter, however, is limited by serious constraints. First, the recharge rates are so slow that these aquifers can be mined only once: like oil, the water will not last for ever. Second, the investment costs are colossal, as Libya's 'Great Man-Made River Project' shows. Here, some 200,000–240,000 hectares are to be irrigated with water drawn from such underground, 'fossil' sources at an estimated total cost of $25 billion (Postel, 1989: 20). The cost of food produced on land irrigated by such methods is likely to be prohibitive in relation to the current world market prices. Third, ecological risks, salinization in particular, are not sufficiently considered, as the case of the Aral Sea disaster, for example, shows (Precoda, 1991; Postel, 1989: 20 ff.). Hence the Nile will be the main source for all future expansion of water use in Egypt.

From Comprehensive Planning to Nationalist Assertiveness

During the colonial era Great Britain was the dominant power in the region, and controlled the major part of the basin of the Nile and the White Nile. The Ethiopian highlands, however, with the sources of the Blue Nile, were outside British control. After the abolition of the Protectorate in 1922, Egyptian governments repeatedly asserted their aspirations concerning the Sudan. From that time on the Sudan and the use of the Nile waters emerged as a serious issue in Anglo–Egyptian relations. British engineers, however, continued to work both in the colonial administration in the Sudan and in the irrigation service of the Egyptian Ministry of Public Works, and planning and use of the Nile water were regulated by the Nile Water Agreement in 1929 (Collins, 1990: 148 f.).

After the Second World War, friction between the Sudan government and Egypt continued. Egypt's plans for the High Dam at Aswan had far-reaching consequences for the Sudan and implied, *inter alia*, the politically and economically difficult problem of resettling some 50,000 Nubians whose homelands were to be flooded (Collins, 1990: 272). When the Sudanese presented a plan for a dam on the Blue Nile at Roseires in 1954 (Al-Rusayris, see map) for the extension of the irrigation in the Gezira and to provide hydroelectric power for the Khartoum–Omdurman area (*ibid.*: 22), this provoked a hostile debate with the Egyptians, who saw the Roseires Dam as interfering with their own plans regarding the construction and full use of the High Dam at Aswan. The problem continued to affect relations between the two countries for some time after Sudan's independence in 1956. The disagreements were resolved, however, in 1959, when the two governments signed an agreement for 'full utilization of the Nile waters' (*ibid.*: 269 *et passim*). The two countries also established a joint committee which would be responsible for the supervision of all working arrangements for future conservation projects in the Nile basin; for the first time since 1921 there was now a body responsible for directing Nile water projects (*ibid.*: 273). The Sudan received financial assistance from the World Bank and West Germany for Roseires, and the dam was completed in 1966. Since its construction the dam has been subjected to very heavy silting. This, in turn, is a result of deforestation and soil erosion in Ethiopia (*ibid.*: 22).

In 1946 the Equatorial Nile Project, of which the Jonglei Canal was an important part, was presented. At that time the principal part of the Upper Nile basin was still under British administration, and this made possible a comprehensive hydrological planning of the region. In 1958 British consultants published a *Report on the Nile Valley Plan* in Khartoum. The report, the culmination of fifty years of studies of Nile hydrology, was the most comprehensive Nile plan that had ever been devised. The pioneering computer studies and technical planning notwithstanding, its most important contribution was an insistence that the whole of the Nile valley should be treated as a hydrological unity. The key to control of the Nile was not a technological problem but a political one: the newly independent states would have to look beyond their immediate national interests and work together for the control and optimal use of the river. In the last days of Empire, however, there was no time for patronizing advice to the new nationalist elites (Collins, 1990: 259 f.).

The Egyptian Ministry of public works immediately dismissed the plan as unacceptable (Collins, 1990: 259 f.). A few years later, after the independence of Tanganyika, her government made a statement that became known as the Nyerere doctrine:

> Former colonial countries had no role in the formulation and conclusion of treaties done during the colonial era, and therefore they must not be assumed to automatically succeed to those treaties. (Collins, 1990: 275)

In 1962 the government of Tanganyika informed the governments of Great Britain, Egypt and the Sudan of its position, and declared that it regarded the 1929 agreement regarding the Nile basin as not binding for Tanganyika, since it was no longer a British territory. Egypt, on the other hand, officially replied that she still regarded the 1929 agreement as valid and in full force. After independence in 1963 Kenya also invoked the Nyerere doctrine, while Uganda simply stated that her government now regarded all former British treaties as obsolete. The other riparian states in the Upper Nile basin (Zaire, Rwanda and Burundi) had not been bound by the 1929 agreement, since it had never been signed by Belgium (Collins, 1990: 275).

Thus it was evident by the first half of the 1960s that the colonial era, as well as the era of comprehensive planning of the Nile basin and the equatorial lake region, was gone: from now on any new schemes would have to be negotiated bilaterally or among the states concerned. Later, the many years of political terror and civil war in Uganda made it clear to Egypt and the Sudan that there was little hope in the foreseeable future of conserving additional water in the equatorial lakes. Therefore the Jonglei Canal in southern Sudan, which will decrease the enormous evaporation losses in the swamps of the Sudd, will be of critical importance for the future provision of water to the Sudan and Egypt. Yet even more important are the waters of Ethiopia, which provide 86 per cent of the total Nile flow (Collins, 1990: 276–7).

Egyptian leaders and planners have been particularly worried about the fact that the Blue Nile basin, which provides more than 80 per cent of the Nile flow, is outside their control (Collins, 1990: 277, 279 f. *et passim*). Throughout this century Ethiopia has been the silent partner in many Anglo–Egyptian plans concerning the regulation of Lake Tana and the Blue Nile. During the colonial era British and Egyptian engineers had free access to the Sudan and Uganda, and were able to survey the basin of the White Nile, but they were never allowed to make any comparable studies of the basin of the Blue Nile – that is, of the areas controlled by Ethiopia. The imperial government refused even to discuss many of the British and Egyptian proposals. In February 1956, one month after the independence of the Sudan, the government paper *Ethiopian Herald* asserted Ethiopia's right to use the Nile waters within her territory for her own benefit. Some months later, in the midst of the Suez crisis, Ethiopia declared in official notes to Cairo that the country 'reserved its right to utilize the water resources of the Nile for the benefit of its people, whatever might be the measure of utilization of such waters sought by riparian states' (Collins, 1990: 277 f.).

Moreover, in subsequent years the old Anglo–Egyptian dream was realized by the USA – or, more specifically, by its Bureau of Reclamation of the Department of the Interior: the Bureau developed a master plan for the Ethiopian part of the Blue Nile and its tributaries that included twenty-nine irrigation and hydroelectric projects. If the scheme were ever to materialize (so far only one hydroelectric power station on a tributary of the Blue Nile has been constructed), the flow of the Nile would be affected: the annual flood of the Blue Nile would be eliminated, and its total quantity would be reduced by 8.5 per cent. If all the projects were completed, the amount of land put into irrigated cultivation would be equal to 17 per cent of the land under cultivation in Egypt (Collins, 1990: 278 ff.).

Sixteen years of military dictatorship, however, with a disastrous combination of Stalinist agricultural policy, civil war and massive military expenditure, destroyed Ethiopia's economy and turned all development plans into illusions (World Bank, 1987a, b; Hansson, 1989). The major attempt to develop irrigated agriculture in the Nile basin took the form of resettlement schemes along some of the tributaries of the Blue Nile and along the Baro–Sobat River (a tributary of the White Nile). In 1984, at the height of the famine, the Ethiopian government drew up an action plan for a two-year programme in which 1.5 million people were to be moved from their dispersed homesteads in the central highlands and resettled in collective villages in the southwestern lowlands. Within days of the launching of the plan the first 15,000 were moved, and in the following fifteen months over half a million people were resettled (Pankhurst, 1992: 53, 55 f.) The programme was much criticized in the international press, especially for its hasty and incompetent planning and implementation, which caused unnecessary suffering and death; and for its arbitrariness and coercion in the selection of people for resettlement (*ibid.*: 55–77, 111–45, *et passim*).

During its early years the military junta regarded resettlement as a means of solving a wide range of problems: relieving population pressure, helping famine victims, providing land to the landless and settling pastoralists. By 1984, however, it was clear that the settlements were not economically viable: the policy was an economic and social disaster, and had to be revised (Pankhurst, 1992: 17–18). Yet resettlement, instead of being quietly discarded, was suddenly proclaimed to be a national priority: at the height of the famine the government declared that it intended to move ten times more people within the following two years than it had done in the previous ten.

The logic behind this juggernaut policy was simple. In 1984 the junta was celebrating the tenth anniversary of the 'revolution', the overthrow of Haile Selassie's government. Famine was linked with the *ancien régime* and its demise. At the time of the celebration, famine was again ravaging the country. The government saw the country as being reduced to poverty and at the mercy of Western donor countries that were hostile to its professed socialism. The frustrated and humiliated junta presented resettlement as a nationalist venture to reduce reliance on foreign aid and provide a means of livelihood for famine victims. It presented an image of Ethiopia not as famine-stricken badlands but as a country with vast expanses of unused virgin land waiting to be developed (Pankhurst, 1992: 52–5).

The belief in the existence of vast expanses of 'virgin' land is typical of the traditional 'frontier-cast' ideology (Kopytoff, 1987: 7–10) of Abyssinian or Ethiopian rulers and their followers. It is an ideology based on the ethnocentric self-perception of a 'core group' which considers itself surrounded by large tracts of land that are politically and physically 'open' to exploitation and inhabited by people who are considered 'inferior' in that they belong to an 'other' (i.e. different and thus lower) social order (Triulzi, 1994: 236). Historic Abyssinia was centred around a core group of Christian Tigre-Amhara highlanders and plough cultivators who saw themselves as the 'original' settlers and 'God-chosen' people entrusted with the mission to 'colonize' and 'uproot' the country, and to fertilize it with their labour (*ibid.*: 236). To the Abyssinian warlords and their clients the southern marches were there to conquer and to colonize; their modernizing, quasi-socialist successors had similar imaginations:

> Resettlement was … portrayed as a way of exploiting hitherto underdeveloped fertile-looking areas of the country. The belief in the existence of vast expanses of 'virgin' land was based on the assumption that lush-looking uncultivated lands were unused. This ignored the fact that dozens of small ethnic groups had survived in such lands for millennia by practising careful resource exploitation, involving shifting hoe agriculture, pastoralism, gathering and hunting. The existence of dense vegetation was also taken as evidence that continuous cultivation was possible, an assumption which … experience showed was not always valid. (Pankhurst, 1992: 54).

The Ethiopian resettlement policy was not only criticized by human rights organizations and Western donor countries but proved, in addition, to be an organizational and economic failure (Pankhurst, 1992). As the planning of the schemes was poor (*ibid.*: 52 ff., 111-145, 159 f., 180 ff., 265 f. *et passim*; Rahmato, 1988), many of the settlement projects proved ecologically unviable (Wood and Ståhl, 1990: 18, 38). The forced resettlement reached its peak in the wake of the 1984–85 famine and came to a virtual halt in 1989, mainly because the government lacked the economic, administrative and logistic capacity to continue the policy: it was simply abandoned (Pankhurst, 1992: 76, 266).

At any rate, the Blue Nile basin holds only a quarter of the potentially irrigable land of the country, and its development so far has been very limited. At present Ethiopia cultivates 90,000 hectares of irrigated land (compared to Egypt's 3.2 *million* hectares), most of which is located in its eastern parts (i.e. east of the watershed of the Blue Nile basin). In all, only 4 per cent of all the potentially irrigable land in the country (most of it outside the Blue Nile basin) has been developed (Wood and Ståhl, 1990: 17).

Thus it is not so much what Ethiopian governments – or other riparian governments for that matter – have done with regard to the waters of the Nile, but rather what they *might* be doing, that is the cause of anxiety in Cairo. This potential threat is the basis of a very real fear that dictates much of Egypt's security policy. Egyptian leaders are acutely aware of the potential for conflict stemming from water shortage. Thus in 1979, just after signing the peace treaty with Israel, President Sadat stated: 'The only matter that could take Egypt to war again is water' (Starr, 1991). His veiled threat was directed at the Soviet-supported military junta in Addis Ababa. A decade later, in June 1990, Egypt's Minister for Foreign Affairs (now UN Secretary-General), Mr Boutros Ghali stated: 'The national security of Egypt, which is based on the water of the Nile, is in the hands of other African countries' (Pearce, 1991). Mr Boutros Ghali is famous for stating that 'the next war in our region will be over the waters of the Nile', and in 1990 the Egyptian government publicized reports that Israeli engineers were working in Ethiopia on a new dam project on Lake Tana, the source of the Blue Nile (*ibid.*).

Water Schemes and Political Threats

The predicament of Egypt can thus be very clearly stated. While the Nile is the country's source of life, the major part of its flow and all its sources are under the control of other governments. One country,

Ethiopia, is the source of 86 per cent of the water that flows into Egypt (Collins, 1990: 24).

There are no international agreements regarding the use of the Nile water for the common benefit of all the riparian states. There is not even a functioning international forum for negotiation of and planning for its use. In a situation like this, all national development plans made by one government concerning the use of the Nile will be perceived by another government as a threat to its national interest, and thus as a source of international conflict. Whenever a riparian government contemplates increasing its use of the water flow within its own borders, Egyptian leaders are disposed to perceive this as a threat, because it will decrease the flow into Egypt.

In September 1989 Mr Boutros Ghali described this alarming situation to members of the US Congress. He stated that all the countries along the Nile basin will in the near future require more water for their development. He then added:

> What is worse is that each Nile country expects different benefits from the control and management of water resources.... The other African countries ... have not reached the level of agriculture through irrigation that we have, and therefore are not as interested in the problem of water scarcity. It is the classical difference in attitudes found among upstream and downstream countries which are on the same international river. (quoted in Starr, 1991)

Egypt will be affected by planning in all the other riparian states, and above all by possible future schemes in Ethiopia and the Sudan. The latter country will be affected by water planning in seven of the other states, and in particular by Ethiopian schemes. On the other hand, while it may be possible that a government in the upper White Nile basin would regard water development schemes in a neighbour state as a threat, it is unlikely that it would regard them as a deadly threat – that is, a threat to the very survival of its country and people – which is what Egypt does.

Ethiopia will not be affected by water schemes in any of the other countries, but her own development plans are perceived as a threat to vital Sudanese and Egyptian interests. While Ethiopia is not worried by what other riparian states are doing within their own boundaries, she is undoubtedly worried by what they might want to do with regard to the waters of the Blue Nile *within Ethiopia*. There is a long tradition among Anglo–Egyptian planners of considering Lake Tana and the Ethiopian Nile basin as a potential water store for an increased and regulated flow into Egypt. Correspondingly, there is an equally long tradition among Ethiopian leaders of regarding British and Egyptian ambitions in the region with great suspicion. Statements by Egyptian leaders have not given the Ethiopians reason to abandon their tradition of thought in this respect.

Given this tradition of conflicting perceptions regarding the utilization of the flow originating in the Ethiopian highlands, the water that comes from southern Sudan – although it is only 14 per cent of the total flow of the Nile – is of strategic importance to Egypt and the Sudan. Egypt wants more water to irrigate more fields to feed its growing population. To implement her ambitious desert reclamation programme of 6,000 square kilometres of new fields, she needs another 9 cubic kilometres of Nile water annually. To increase the flow of the Nile it is necessary to complete the Jonglei Canal through the vast wetland in southern Sudan, where about half of the flow evaporates in the hot sun. The canal could speed the flow and increase the annual flow by 10 per cent from its present 86 cubic kilometres (Pearce, 1991).

The protracted civil war in the Sudan, however, interrupted the construction work in 1983, and it has never been resumed. In 1960 the Ethiopian government permitted Israeli experts to cross the Sudanese border and establish links with the guerrillas who were fighting the Khartoum government (Yaniv, 1987a: 96); these links continued off and on for three decades (*ibid*.: 157, 221 ff.). The Ethiopians, for their part, have claimed that the Sudan (and other, usually unspecified, Arab states) supported the rebels in Eritrea; and that the Sudan, from the early 1980s onwards, sheltered the OLF (Oromo Liberation Front) guerrillas in southwestern Ethiopia. The turn of events in 1991 – with the collapse of the Mengistu regime, the cessation of the war in Eritrea and the split in the rebel movement in the Sudan – have, at least temporarily, led to a détente in Ethio–Sudanic relations.

The regional balance-of-power game notwithstanding, diplomatic relations between the northern Nile states have continued, and none of the three governments has openly admitted support for the opposition in a neighbouring riparian country (in contrast, for example, to Nasser's position on the war in Yemen). There have been threatening words, but hostile action has been limited and covert. It has been a situation in which images of an enemy and ideas of schemes threatening one's own survival have been constructed and negotiated over a long period of time: they are a basic feature of the political culture among leaders in all three countries. Such images provide models of the world and models for political action among political leaders in the region. Expectations and fears relating to the management of the Nile water are essential elements in the construction of strategic models for action. The critical question to be asked, however, concerns the extent to which riparian governments live up to the hostile imaginings that guide the actions of their neighbours.

The Besieged State

No state in the Upper Nile basin has implemented any water management projects that can constitute a threat to any of the two major states downstream, the Sudan and Egypt. The riparian states are not only too poor to finance such projects on their own, they are also conspicuously lacking the political stability that is necessary to attract assistance from donor nations and lending institutions.

With the exception of Egypt and Tanzania, all the states of the Nile basin have been torn by civil wars; Egypt and Tanzania, on the other hand, have both been engaged in costly interstate warfare. In many cases the civil wars have been going on for decades. The Eritrean war of secession, which ended with the collapse of the Mengistu regime in May 1991, lasted thirty years. The civil war in the Sudan has, with some peaceful intervals, lasted some twenty years; it goes back to an even longer history of conflict. Uganda suffered two decades under incompetent and brutal leaders and devastating civil war. The conflicts in Rwanda and Burundi have flared up at intervals since independence.

The countries along the Nile have also received large numbers of refugees from war-torn countries outside the actual Nile basin, for example, from Somalia and Chad. Millions of people have been uprooted and crossed an international border into a neighbouring country. Yet other millions have become 'displaced persons' within the borders of the states in which they are supposed to be citizens or – to put it more appropriately – subjects.

The scale of the civil wars in the Horn of Africa is indicative of the failure of the kind of state nationalism that the military governments of the region have attempted. In their defence of the embattled state the military regimes of the Horn of Africa, like radical military regimes elsewhere in Africa (e.g. Nasser's Egypt, Algeria, Libya, the Congo, Benin, Burkina-Faso and Ghana), have espoused socialism and tried to blend it with nationalism in order to reinforce the foundations of the state; a kind of polity Markakis (1987: 202–76) calls 'garrison socialism'. In the face of increasing opposition that is not allowed to be expressed in constitutional form (i.e. in parliament, press, political parties, trade unions) and therefore takes the form of armed struggle, the military rulers of the Horn have increasingly come to perceive the state as a besieged garrison. An ever-increasing share of government expenditure has been diverted for the defence of this garrison, and correspondingly decreasing resources have been left for economic and social development. The human, economic and ecological costs have been colossal; and in the process two of the three military dictatorships of the Horn have collapsed.

During the 1980s Sudan's military expenditure fluctuated between 3 and 5 per cent of the GDP per annum (SIPRI, 1991: 177), corresponding to between 163 and 239 million dollars per annum, peaking at 271 million in 1989 (*ibid.*: 172; Lindgren, 1990: Table 10). In 1987 her total foreign debt was 101.9 per cent of GNP (*ibid.*: Table 8). The chronic deficit in her balance of trade was worsened by the effects of the Gulf War in 1991. The flow of incomes and remittances from Sudanese workers in the Gulf states, which were an important source of foreign earnings, virtually ceased, and the country lost a source of income that yielded an estimated 700 million dollars per year (*South*, December 1990/January 1991).

In 1970 the Ethiopian army numbered some 35,000, the biggest army in independent Africa south of the Sahara. Haile Selassie, who was a close ally of the USA, was deposed by a military coup in 1974. In the ensuing years the size of the army increased tenfold: for more than fifteen years the military junta maintained an army in the range of 350,000–400,000 men. The military co-operation with the USA was replaced by a close alliance with the Soviet Union. In the period 1974–85 Ethiopia imported Soviet arms at a value of 5.5 billion US dollars and became the world's eighth-largest recipient of Soviet arms (Kramer, 1987) and the imports continued throughout the 1980s. Ethiopia's military expenditure increased markedly after 1987, and by 1990 it constituted more than 10 per cent of GNP. With a GNP of around 110 US dollars *per capita* (World Bank, 1987b) the country is at the bottom of the statistics of the world's poorest nations. Yet in 1989 her government's military expenditure reached 780 million US dollars, among the greatest in Africa (SIPRI, 1991). In spite of massive military expenditure the military situation got increasingly worse for the government. In May 1991 the dictator Mengistu fled the country. The economy of the state was in ruins.

In 1987 Somalia's total foreign debt was 239 per cent of her GNP (Lindgren, 1990). Vast amounts of the country's resources had been spent on the army and internal security. The civil war had killed tens of thousands of people, and made hundreds of thousands into refugees and 'displaced persons'. The aged dictator, Siad Barre, fled the country in January 1991, but the fighting continued and ripped the country apart. There is now a self-proclaimed independent state in the North and a disintegrating South where the war between competing factions has resulted in the virtual disappearance of state power. The Somali state has in effect ceased to exist.

The human cost of defending the 'garrison states' (Markakis, 1987: 264 f.) has been colossal. Second to Afghanistan, the Horn of Africa in 1990 harboured the world's largest refugee population. Ethiopia hosted 360,000 refugees from Somalia and another 385,000 from the Sudan. At the same time more than a million people had fled from Ethiopia into her neighbouring countries; some 700,000 Ethiopian refugees were in camps in Eastern Sudan, and almost as many were in Somalia. Furthermore, on its western border the Sudan harboured some 70,000 refugees from the civil war in Chad and in addition hosted, until 1989, a large Ugandan refugee population in its southern regions. In 1989, 240,000 Ugandans were repatriated from the Sudan (*Refugees* 81, 1990: 10).

After the demise of the Mengistu regime in 1991, the new Ethiopian government, seeking a rapprochement with Khartoum, stopped supporting the South Sudanese nationalists and closed down the refugee camps on the Ethiopian side of the border. The intensification of the war in the 1990s, and the war between factions of Southern Sudanese nationalists, have resulted in the dislocation of hundreds of thousands of people and new waves of refugees across the borders into Kenya, Uganda and Zaire.

On its southern borders Uganda has received large numbers of refugees from the civil war in Rwanda over the years: in 1990 there was an influx of some 10,000 people, and in 1994 there was a new surge of refugees from the ethnic conflict. Finally, Tanzania, which is one of the few post-colonial countries in Africa that has not suffered civil war (but has been at war with Idi Amin's Uganda), has received large numbers of refugees from both Rwanda and Burundi, and some of these refugees have lived in exile for over twenty years

(*Refugees* 81, 1990). In 1994 a new wave of atrocities sent hundreds of thousands of refugees from Rwanda's killing fields into Tanzania and Uganda.

The actual situation, however, is even more serious than any such figures may indicate. The international definition of the concept 'refugee' refers to a person who has crossed an international boundary to escape persecution in the country in which he or she is a citizen or lives permanently. Over the years the Sudan, with a present population of about 26 million, has accepted about a million refugees from other countries. In addition, within the Sudan hundreds of thousands have fled from one part of the country to another because of war, drought, desertification or famine. In the international system these people are not defined as refugees in the strict sense of the term; therefore they are not under the formal protection of the UN High Commissioner of Refugees; they are regarded as a different category of people – as 'displaced persons'. The number of such 'unofficial' refugees (who are thus 'invisible' in the statistics) is estimated to be at least as large as the officially recognized number.

In addition, the 1980s saw a new category of strangers at the door: the environmental refugees. Growing numbers of people are being forced to move because the environment where they live has become so degraded that human existence is no longer possible. In most Third World countries it is difficult to estimate the number of such 'displaced persons' – refugees from civil war, environmental degradation, drought and famine – because they may be difficult to trace; many move to the slums of rapidly growing cities. In the Sudan, for example, which over the years has been a haven for about a million refugees from neighbouring countries, the number of 'displaced persons' or internal refugees is several million, while 'hundreds of thousands of impoverished peasants from the west migrate seasonally to work in the cotton plantations of the Gezira' (Markakis, 1994: 219).

In Somalia the protracted civil war has driven hundreds of thousands of people back and forth across the border to Ethiopia, and created innumerable refugees within its own borders; in the wake of the collapse of the Siad Barre dictatorship in early 1991 there has been widespread famine as the combined result of civil war and drought. The intensified war between competing factions led to the virtual disappearance of the state, and hundreds of thousands gathered in refugee camps in the deserts of Ethiopia and Djibouti.

In Ethiopia ecological stress and drought (which is a natural phenomenon) and frequent periods of hunger and famine (which is a social product) in various parts of the country have resulted in the temporary or permanent dislocation of hundreds of thousands of people: many of them have, over the years, crossed the border to the Sudan; others have moved within Ethiopia (particularly in the war-torn and hunger-stricken northern regions of Tigray and Eritrea). At the time of the collapse of Mengistu's military dictatorship in May 1991, about 8 million people were threatened by famine. The country's economy and civil administration are a shambles; its food production *per capita* has continued to decrease so that food deficiency has become chronic; having wasted most of its resources on military expenditure, Ethiopia has for many years relied on international donations of famine relief food to feed its rapidly growing and impoverished population.

National and International Conflicts

The present conflicts in Northeast Africa have a long history. In the nineteenth century the Abyssinian state consisted of a loose federation of principalities under local warlords in the central and northern highlands. A number of European powers (the most important being France, Great Britain and Italy) competed for influence and territories in the region – after the opening of the Suez Canal, the Red Sea coast was of strategic importance. Abyssinian rulers and warlords could turn the Europeans' competition for influence to their own advantage, and were able to buy modern arms and build up huge armies that became the strongest in the region. At the time of the European scramble for Africa, the warlord of Shoa (who was to emerge as the 'king of kings' or emperor) was engaged in bloody campaigns against kingdoms and chiefdoms to the south of the Blue Nile and the central highlands. The southern half of the present state was conquered during the last two decades of the century. In the emerging ramshackle empire the administration of the conquered territories was granted to warlords loyal to the emperor. The land was confiscated and redistributed to imperial clients, warlords and soldier settlers, while the previous owners were reduced to sharecroppers and corvée labourers under the new masters. The ruler took up the name 'Ethiopia' for the new empire state; it was the Hellenistic name for the land to the south of Egypt (evidently in the same vein as the Italians, who took up the

Hellenistic name 'Eritrea', which in Antiquity referred to the African coastland; Sorensen, 1993: 21 ff.).

After the Second World War Haile Selassie began the modernizing project of turning this ramshackle empire into a contemporary type of nation-state. In this modernizing and homogenizing process the Amharic language, and the Amharic- and Tigrinya-speaking elites enjoyed a privileged position. A language spoken by a quarter of the population, which less than 10 per cent could read or write, became the 'national language', the only language to be allowed in schools, courts and other public contexts. The expansion of the school system produced a small modern elite which, by the 1960s, found its career prospects hampered by the country's sluggish economic and social development. The attempts at linguistic and other forms of hom-ogenization (often perceived as Amharization) were combined with religious and cultural discrimination (e.g. against Muslims) in military and civil service careers; there were also marked biases in the regional distribution of modern public services such as schools, medical services and development projects.

Together these factors contributed to a situation in which much of the opposition against the central government came to be expressed in one of two modes: in modernizing or in regional and ethnic terms. During the last years of imperial rule the 'question of nationalities' was a hotly debated issue among students and the modern elite. The guerrilla war in Eritrea – still comparatively limited – was a catalyst in this debate.

During the rule of the military junta the policy of centralization and homogenization was intensified and combined with – in the words of the government – 'Red Terror' against all opponents. In response, a great number of ethnic and regional movements (some of them with Marxist or liberal universalist 'Pan-Ethiopian' programmes) recruited increasing numbers of young people to wage guerrilla wars against the government. The opposition was mobilized against the government's (1) attempts at Amharization; (2) centralization and political repression; and (3) Stalinist agricultural policy which im-poverished the peasants and pastoralists. Some of these movements were struggling for the establishment of separate nation-states of their own, while others wanted a radical change in the character of the Ethiopian state.

In May 1991 these forces conquered the besieged state. One of them, the well-organized and militarily powerful Leninist guerrilla movement TPLF (Tigray People's Liberation Front), assumed state power. During its first four years the new government has evidently dropped its Leninist views on economic policy and revised the former regime's policy on vital issues. Most importantly, Eritrea became *de facto* an independent state (and, following a referendum, a *de jure* state in 1993). Furthermore, some of the political movements and factions that fought Mengistu are outlining what may be a more federal constitution for Ethiopia: first, the country has been divided into regional administrative areas with boundaries that correspond to presumed 'ethnic' or 'national' groups and boundaries; second, a certain measure of decentralization grants these regions the right to choose which language they want to use as their first language in schools and administration, and it is also permitted to develop written languages and write and print in the many vernaculars; third, the junta's pseudo-socialist agricultural and economic policy has been abandoned. The most controversial issue, however, is the question of if, and under what conditions, a region may have the right of secession.

The history of conflict in the Sudan goes back to the nineteenth century. Sudan is the largest country in Africa, and there are great ecological, economic and cultural differences between different regions. The North is mainly Arab-speaking and Muslim. In the South there is great cultural diversity, with peoples who speak a variety of Nilo-Saharan languages and are either Christian or belong to indigenous religions. Before the British made the Sudan their colony, state power had been limited to the northern parts of the territory. In the 1860s Egypt controlled large parts of the Red Sea coast (including part of the region that was later to become the Italian colony Eritrea). After the opening of the Suez Canal, Great Britain forced Egypt to give up her ambitions for regional hegemony. For a short period (1885–92) northern Sudan was united in an independent state under a religious and political leader, the Mahdi. This was a period of rapid territorial expansion involving, among other things, military campaigns into the Abyssinian highlands and the challenging of the imperial expansion. In 1892 the Mahdist troops were defeated by a British army; the region from Egypt to the East African lakes came under British rule.

Slave traders and adventurers from Egypt and Nubia began to penetrate and exploit the Sudan and the Abyssinian marches early in the nineteenth century. In many areas the supply of slaves was exhausted by continuous raiding; therefore the traders expanded further south. Markakis writes:

> In the 1850s, traders of many races, including Europeans, moved into the southern Sudan to meet the needs of the northern market. They installed themselves with bands of armed retainers in fortified camps called zeriba, and proceeded 'to fuse trade with robbery'.... Relying on firepower and the tribal rivalries of Nilotic society, they established a robber baron regime; the first intimation the inhabitants of that region had of alien rule. The area around each zeriba was subdued and its inhabitants were forced to provide ivory, food, porters and auxiliaries to raid other tribes for slaves, ivory and cattle. The traders discovered that only cattle could induce the Nilotes to trade, and they robbed one group in order to trade with another. They formed a predatory ruling class which presided over the bloody chaos that ensued as the native tribes were set against each other in a mindless, self-destructive struggle that lasted until the end of the century. The agony of it was inscribed in the collective memory of the people. It was the time, as the Dinka remember it, 'when the world was spoiled.' Associated with Arab greed and symbolised by the figure of the Jallaba trader, it laid a rich store of fear and hatred of northerners that has bedevilled their relations with the South to the present day. (Markakis, 1987: 29)

The British colonial power put an end to this reign of terror, but could do little about some of its local effects: it proved difficult to put an end to the legacy of cattle raids, feuds and tribal conflicts when the old, regional systems of production and exchange had been destroyed. Very little was done to modernize the South: a few elementary schools and clinics were run by missionary societies. Consequently, at the time of independence there were few southerners with higher education, and the people of the South were never involved in the northerners' movement for independence. In the postcolonial state members of the emerging but numerically small southern elite perceived themselves as belonging to a semi-colonial periphery. The gigantic Jonglei Canal project, which will mainly benefit the North, has been seen as indicative of Arab colonialism. The North has dominated the new independent state politically, economically and culturally. The privileged position of the Arab language, the state's association to the Arab League, and repeated attempts to make Islamic law (Sharia) the law of the non-Muslim South have all contributed to the region's opposition against Northern rule. The present struggle of independence thus relates to a very long tradition of resistance.

The history of internal conflict in both countries has corresponded to regional and global conflicts. The Second World War began in effect in 1935, with Mussolini's attack on Ethiopia and the ensuing occupation of the country. In 1941 the British army, consisting of East African troops, defeated the Italian forces, reinstated the Ethiopian emperor and took over the administration of the former Italian colonies in Eritrea and Somaliland and, importantly, of the Ogaden region. In the following decade Britain was the dominant power in the region, being in direct control not only of its own colonies but also of the former Italian ones, and having close contacts with the reinstated emperor of Ethiopia.

The postwar era saw the deconstruction of the colonial empires. In 1952, following a referendum in Eritrea and a United Nations resolution, the British left the former Italian colony to be united with Ethiopia in an uneasy federation; a decade later Eritrea was made into an Ethiopian province. In 1954 the British responded to Ethiopia's demand and handed over the Ogaden to the emperor. Two years later, in 1956, the Sudan became an independent state, and in 1960 the united colonies of British and Italian Somaliland (the latter had been under British administration since 1941) became the independent new state of Somalia. Finally, in 1977, the last European colony in the region was granted independence when France gave up its enclave colony Djibouti at the outlet of the Red Sea.

The years following the Second World War were not only a period of relative European decline and abandonment of classical colonialism, but also the beginning of the Cold War era. In the colonial era Northeast Africa's strategic importance was due to its position in relation to the Suez Canal and the outlet of the Red Sea on the major trade route between Europe and her colonial dependencies in India and the Far East. In the Cold War era its strategic importance was likewise related to the Suez Canal, but now because the Red Sea and Indian Ocean was an artery of oil transport to the world's major industrial powers. The Soviet Union had a strategically advantageous position immediately to the north of the oil-producing countries of the Middle East, and the West sought allies and bases not only in the politically volatile Middle East, but also on its southern flank along the coast of the Indian Ocean.

Immediately after the Second World War Britain was the dominant power both in the Middle East and around the Indian Ocean. Her power, however, was crumbling. During the decade of decolonization the emerging superpowers of the Cold War were increasingly competing for influence both in Northeast Africa and in the wider region. In the

1950s the United States began to take over Britain's role as the major power in Northeast Africa, while the Soviet Union increased its influence in Egypt and among some of the states in the Middle East. Most governments in the region tried to turn the superpower competition to their own advantage: they attempted to increase the power of their states through large-scale import of arms and vast expenditure on internal security. Many of these states, such as Libya, Egypt, Israel, Iraq and Iran, competed for regional influence. For the past thirty years they have been involved in the civil wars in the Northeast African states as suppliers of arms and other forms of support to either a government or its opponents.

Northeast Africa became an arena of Cold War and regional competition. During most of the post-colonial period there have been armed conflicts. Throughout this period Ethiopia has had the largest army in the region, and imported arms and military expertise on a large scale. In 1970 the country had the largest army in independent Africa south of the Sahara. In the 1960s and until the overthrow of the emperor in 1974, the USA was the main supplier of arms to the imperial armed forces, and also provided military advisers. In return the USA obtained a communications base at Asmara in Eritrea. West Germany provided equipment and advisers for the imperial police force.

In 1960 Israel established close links with Ethiopia. The emperor's reasons for this were his escalating conflict with Somalia over the Ogaden, the intensification of the revolt in Eritrea, and Egypt's intervention in the war in Yemen, across the Red Sea. The emperor needed arms and advisers as well as development projects. Israel could provide both. Prime Minister Ben-Gurion's regional strategy involved (discreet and unofficial but nevertheless substantial) military and economic co-operation with Turkey, Iran and Ethiopia (Yaniv, 1987a: 94–7 *et passim*):

> Economic relations were expanded. Israeli experts established a variety of plants in Eritrea and in Ethiopia proper. Sea links between Eilat and Massawa were expanded. Israeli experts established a national university in Addis Ababa. Israeli military personnel trained Ethiopian soldiers to fight counter-insurgency warfare in Eritrea and more conventional warfare in the Ogaden. Israel set up observation posts on the Ethiopian Red Sea coast to monitor Arab and Soviet shipping through the Bab-el-Mandeb Straits and in the Red Sea. Last, but not least, the Ethiopian government permitted Israeli experts to cross the border to the Sudan and establish links with the Christian guerillas who were fighting the central Sudanese government. (Yaniv, 1987a: 96)

The relations with Israel were severed immediately after the fall of the emperor, but they were resumed as soon as 1978 by the military junta that succeeded him; Yaniv (1987a: 222) maintains that by that time Foreign Minister Moshe Dayan and the Israelis in general (and probably also the Mengistu regime) regarded the Eritrean Liberation Movement (he does not state whether he refers to the ELF or the EPLF) as already part of the Arab League.

The Sudanese government, on the other hand, received large amounts of arms from the USA, especially after President Numeiry's massacre of communists and trade unionists in 1971. The Soviet Union and its East European allies exported vast amounts of arms to Egypt during President Nasser's government; later, in the 1970s and 1980s, Libya became a major buyer of Soviet arms. In the early 1970s the Soviet Union emerged as an important exporter of arms to the states on the Horn of Africa, first to the Somali government and, from 1977, to the military junta in Ethiopia. Within a few years the junta increased its armed forces tenfold, intensified its military campaigns against the Eritrean rebels and proclaimed a campaign of 'Red Terror' against its political opponents in the cities. While its countries are the poorest of the poor, the Horn has become one of Africa's most heavily armed and militarized regions.

Patterns of Conflict

In many African countries population growth is on a collision course with water resources. By the end of the century six of the nine states in the Nile basin will face a situation of acute water stress. Half the land under irrigation schemes in Africa is in Egypt and the Sudan. In the latter country about half the land is under rainfed cultivation, while in Egypt all cropland is irrigated. In both countries expectations relating to economic and social development depend on the use of the Nile water. To Egypt the Nile is literally the source of life. The predicament of Egyptian leaders is that governments in the upstream states have the ultimate control of this source. Many riparian governments have great expectations with regard to water development, and they all mistrust the schemes of others. Egyptian leaders fear that upstream governments may divert the flow to urgently needed development projects in their own countries, and thus turn the tap right off at the source, or at least decrease its flow. Despite years of Egyptian efforts, the riparian states have not been able to reach enough consensus to establish an efficient protocol for a water-sharing plan.

During the colonial era, when Great Britain controlled a large part of the Nile basin, it was possible to develop comprehensive plans and treat the whole of the Nile basin as one hydrological system. After independence, however, the new nationalist governments asserted their right to develop the water resources within their own countries as they saw fit – a line of thought particularly threatening to Egypt, at the end of the river. Even more significant, however, was the fact that Ethiopia, the source of 85 per cent of the total flow, was never more than a silent partner to the plans and expectations of Anglo–Egyptian engineers. When the Ethiopians did decide to speak up, however, it was with a studied sense of timing to make their point terrifyingly clear to the Egyptian leaders. On two occasions in 1956, on the morning of Sudan's independence and at the height of the Suez crisis some months later, the Ethiopians bluntly asserted their right to utilize the water resources of the Nile for the benefit of their own people, irrespective of the needs of other riparian countries. Egyptian leaders, on the other hand, have repeatedly stated that they are prepared to go to war over the use of these resources.

All the self-assured and bellicose rhetoric notwithstanding, not one among the eight riparian states to the south of Egypt has implemented any water schemes that could threaten water development in another country (Egypt's High Dam is the only scheme with far-reaching consequences for a neighbouring country). One reason for this is that all these countries are extremely poor, and none of them (with the exception of the Sudan) has been able to get assistance from donor nations or lending institutions for any major water projects. The most important reason, however, is political: all the nine riparian states have been ravaged by civil wars or engaged in interstate warfare.

The roots of the conflicts are to be found in the colonial history of the region, and in the pre-colonial past. In the Sudan the British acquiesced to the northern elite's demands for independence, and disregarded the southerners' demands for secession or federal status. Disappointed by the rejection of its demands, the South exploded in 1955, on the eve of independence. Repression was severe, and Britain's departure left the Sudan in the throes of civil war. A few years earlier the British, following a UN resolution, had handed over the former Italian colony Eritrea to be united in a federation with Ethiopia. When the federation was dissolved and Eritrea became an ordinary Ethi-

opian province in 1960, the opposition took to the battlefield and the
thirty-year-long war of secession began.

The conflict between Ethiopia and Somalia over the Ogaden relates
to the history of British, Italian and Ethiopian aspirations in the area.
The Ogaden is the name of a Somali tribe and its territory. After the
war the region was under British administration, but it was handed
over to Ethiopia in two stages in 1948 and 1954. Since the independence of Somalia in 1960, the status and affiliation of the region have
been a source of conflict between Ethiopia and Somalia. The devastating war that broke out in 1977 precipitated Ethiopia's strategic break
with the West, and her alliance with the Soviet bloc.

The civil wars are thus the legacy of colonialism, but their
continuation is indicative of the impasse of state nationalism in the
region. In the Sudan and Ethiopia (as in Somalia) successive governments have attempted a policy of modernization and nation-building
based on both 'state-capitalist' and 'state-socialist' strategies, but in
neither case have they been able to attain any measure of sustainable
economic growth. The role of the state in the redistribution of
resources has been decisive; therefore, access to it has been essential.
The narrow social base of the ruling nationalist cliques (e.g. of Haile
Selassie and Mengistu; of Numeiry and Bashir; of Siad Barre; of Amin
and Obote) and the privileged position of a certain region of the
country with regard to investments in development and infrastructure,
and of one particular language and culture – Arabic and Islam in the
Sudan, Amharic and Orthodox Christianity in Ethiopia – have
exacerbated tensions and proved catalytic in the mobilization of
disadvantaged groups on the basis of regional and ethnic affiliation.
In defending the state against its political opponents, the nationalist
elites have increasingly relied on repression. As a result of the militar-
ization of the political process, the military have claimed control of
the state. In their struggle for survival the military rulers have spent
enormous sums on armaments and arms imports and, in the process,
ruined the economy of their countries. Manoeuvring in dire straits,
they have on more than one occasion proved capable of a political
volte-face. Such a change usually involved a change of foreign patrons
as well, and left these weak and impoverished states hopelessly caught
in the competing designs of foreign powers in the Horn (Markakis,
1987: 234 ff.).

The civil wars and the strategic schemes and interventions by foreign
powers have a long and interrelated history. The modernizing project

pursued by the nationalist elites has exacerbated the unequal regional and sociocultural distribution of development resources, of welfare and of power and privileges. The civil wars are social conflicts which concern the character of the state: the issue of political centralism, federalism or separatism is at the heart of all these conflicts. Interventions by foreign powers are motivated by regional strategic concerns. Water management and hydropolitics enter as a vital aspect of the conflicts *within* riparian states as well as into the conflicts *between* them and, importantly, constitute a factor of strategic importance in the regional conflict pattern.

In the volatile political process of the region, with perpetual changes in the pattern of alliance and conflict among the competing nationalist elites, with volte-face changes in political ideologies and strategies from *laissez-faire* to Stalinism or vice versa, with switches in the alliances to the Cold War blocs and to regional powers, there is nevertheless one vital factor that has not changed: the appreciation of the strategic importance of the waters of the Nile.

Since the last century the Egyptians and the British have regarded the Nile as a comprehensive hydrological system. Hence they have argued that the control of the water must be subject to comprehensive planning and management. During the colonial era, when most of the Nile basin was under Anglo–Egyptian administration, this perspective was politically viable. In the post-colonial era it was not: the upriver states regarded the Egyptian plans with mistrust and asserted their right to control the flow, irrespective of any prior agreements made by the British and the Egyptians. The political situation had changed, but Egypt's dependence on the Nile remained unchanged.

Since 1948 the conflict with Israel has been the dominant strategic concern of Arab nationalist regimes. For a long time Egypt was a leading force in that conflict. Israel's strategy in Northeast Africa was based on her enduring alliance with Ethiopia, which made possible her continuous support for the rebels in southern Sudan. The war in the South has kept the Sudan in a state of siege, ruined the economy and effectively blocked the completion of the Jonglei Canal (Israel pursued this policy even at the time when the Sudan was a reliable client of the USA). Israel and Ethiopia thus had a hold on Egypt's lifeline.

Egypt, for her part, has been unable to do anything to avert the threat. She can only state that Israel's strategy has not decreased the present level in the flow of the Nile. Egypt may also find it reassuring that Ethiopia has proved unable to engage in any major projects that would decrease the flow. The protracted war in Eritrea, the escalating war in Tigray and the North, the organized struggle by Oromo nationalists and the conflicts with Somalia kept the military government in a state of siege: all resources were allocated to the defence of the state, and this ruined the country. In 1991 Addis Ababa was taken by the opposition forces. The new rulers granted independence to Eritrea but severed their links with the secessionist movements in southern Sudan, which became engaged in a war between competing factions. The soldiers in Khartoum, who have increasingly allied themselves with religious groups, shifted their allegiance from Saddam Hussein's Iraq to Iran. The Cold War has ended. While the importance of the impoverished, famine-stricken arid lands in the Horn of Africa has decreased in the global strategies of northern powers, they are still important in the strategies of regional powers. In the aftermath of the Gulf War there are new strategic designs on the region. It still remains to be seen if the post-Cold-War era will bring peace to the countries along the Nile.

Water and the Arab–Israeli Conflict

Helena Lindholm

In the conflict-ridden Middle Eastern region, water exacerbates already tense interstate relations.[1] Warnings have been given long since by hydropolitical experts and politicians that the next war in the Middle East will be over water. In 1990 the Hashemite king of Jordan, King Hussein, joined the list of statesmen and experts issuing statements making water a potential reason for the outbreak of war. The fact is that water has been an issue in armed violence and war in the Middle East several times, and continues to be an issue of intense conflict. At the same time, in the mid-1990s, it has become almost a cliché to declare that the next war fought on Middle Eastern territory will be a water war, emphasizing the need for careful analysis and the risk that scholars will otherwise become warmongers, through making oversimplified connections between issues of conflict and the actual potential for the outbreak of war. There are also sincere attempts to solve the disputes over water distribution, emphasized not least in the Israeli–Jordanian peace accords in October 1994, as well as in the continued negotiations between the Israelis and Palestinians since the signing of the Declaration of Principles (DOP) in September 1993.

To Israel, relations with her closest neighbours, Jordan, Syria and Lebanon, are to a certain extent marked by the issue of water. In the relations between Israel and the West Bank and Gaza (occupied by Israel in 1967), water is a highly important matter. The Israeli need for water for the country's highly advanced agricultural sector and the joint dependency of Israel and the West Bank on the River Jordan and groundwater aquifers in the highlands of the West Bank are crucial

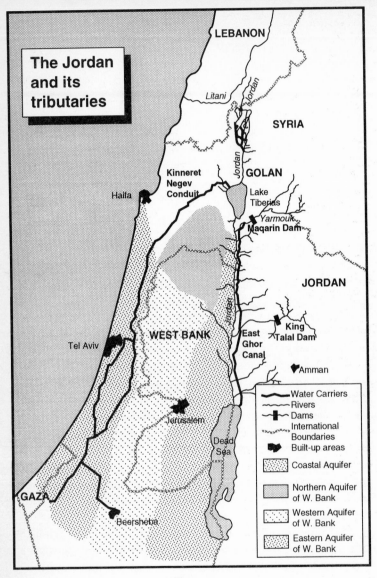

The Jordan and its tributaries

Map 2.1

factors in the Israeli occupation, and are now core issues in attempts to resolve the Palestinian–Israeli conflict, and negotiations on the future status of the West Bank.

Growing populations exert further pressure on natural resources, at the same time as the utilization of water has already reached its limit. Israel, the West Bank, Gaza and Jordan are among those regions that have hit a 'water barrier' (Starr, 1991: 17), implying that these countries have reached the limit of how much water can be utilized. All those regions find themselves below the 'water stress level' (the term coined by Malin Falkenmark, 1990) of 500 cubic metres per person per year. Today, Israel exploits all her reliable runoff waters; all sewage discharges to the Mediterranean are being returned to the land, and approximately 30 per cent of the urban waste is being reutilized in agriculture. Yet there is a gap of 200–300 million cubic metres (m.c.m.) a year (Clarke, 1991).

This essay will deal with the water politics and water security of Israel and the occupied West Bank and Gaza Strip, as well as referring to Israeli relations with Jordan, Syria and Lebanon. To what extent is water a security issue in the relations between the above-mentioned states and regions? Questions of development concerning Israel as well as the West Bank and Gaza will be further addressed.

In the late 1980s and early 1990s, the water shortage of Israel and her surrounding neighbours became acute. Israel and her neighbours experienced an extraordinarily dry summer in 1990, followed by an exceptionally dry winter in 1990/91 – the driest in seventy years. In Israel, water supplies to farmers were reduced by 20 per cent in January 1991, and the country expected a national water emergency. In the winter of 1991–2, there was a considerable increase in rainfall as well as snowfall. This large amount of rainfall did not, however, remedy the acute situation, and will do little for the situation in the long run.

Taking the population growth into consideration, Elisha Kally estimated in the winter of 1991–2 that the expected water shortage for Israel, Jordan, the West Bank and Gaza respectively will be as shown in Table 2.1 by 2010. Lowi's picture of water supply and demand, based on Thomas Naff's research, is indicated in Table 2.2. From these figures, it can be seen that the acute water shortage faces Middle Eastern states with unprecedented problems; problems that can be resolved only through regional cooperation.

Table 2.1   Expected Water Shortage 2010

Israel	Jordan	West Bank
375 m.c.m.	175 m.c.m.	135 m.c.m.

Source: Kally, 1991/92, p. 11.

A Hydropolitical Security Complex

The Israeli water supply is linked to the Jordan River basin, which in turn connects Jordan, Syria, Lebanon, Israel and the West Bank, so that this could be considered a *security complex*. According to Buzan (1991: 190), a security complex is a group of states whose security concerns are linked in such a way that the national security of each state 'cannot realistically be considered apart from one another'. In fact, in our case we could perceive 'regional security complexes' defined and delimited by shared river basins, that is, a *hydropolitical security complex* (see Schulz in this volume, Chapter 3).

All the above mentioned states – as well as the West Bank – are to some extent dependent on the Jordan River system for their water requirements. According to Anderson, the Jordan River basin, including the upper Jordan and the Yarmouk, provides 60 per cent of Israel's water and 75 per cent of Jordan's. At the same time, only 3 per cent of the Jordan basin area – that is, upper Jordan – is situated within the borders of pre-1967 Israel (Anderson, 1988: 7). The Jordan basin is a small river system providing 1,400 m.c.m. annually (Frey and Naff, quoted in Wolf and Ross, 1992: 920); it is the smallest river in the Middle Eastern region, and runs through hotly debated territories. The Jordan River basin system begins in three headwater rivers. One source is the Hasbani River, which originates in Syria and has part of its outflow in Lebanon, making Lebanon part of the river system. Lebanon may also be considered part of the security complex, since the Lebanese Litani River is frequently included in discussions on regional distribution. The Dan and the Banyias begin in the Golan Heights – occupied by Israel in 1967 and annexed in 1981 – and flow into the Jordan River in northern Israel. In the case of the River Jordan, Syria and Lebanon are thus upstream countries related to both

Table 2.2 Water Supply and Demand, Present and Future (m.c.m.)

	Israel	Jordan	West Bank
WATER SUPPLY			
1987–1991			
under normal conditions	1,950	900	650
under drought conditions	1,600	700–750	450–550
WATER DEMAND			
1987–1991	2,100*	800	125†
2020	2,800	1,800	530

Notes: * Including settlements in the occupied territories and the Golan Heights.
  † The Arab population of the West Bank.
Source: Lowi, 1992: 34, from Naff/Associates for Middle East Research Database.

Israel and Jordan, whereas Israel is an upper riparian to Jordan. With the Israeli occupation and annexation of the Golan Heights, however, Israel also controls support flows to the Jordan. The upper Jordan River is then stored in the Sea of Galilee. The Yarmouk River, which rises in Syria and borders Jordan, Syria and the Golan Heights (and thus also Israel), flows into the Jordan from the east. In the case of the Yarmouk, both Syria and Jordan are upstream countries to Israel. The Jordan River basin system thus connects four states – Syria, Lebanon, Israel and Jordan – and the West Bank. The lack of agreement between Israel, Syria and Jordan on how to distribute the resources of the Jordan has turned this small river into a regional trouble spot. From the perspective of international law, neither upstream countries (claiming to be the source of international river flows) nor downstream countries' historical use of surface or groundwater entail absolute sovereignty over shared waters.

Overexploitation of water is a common feature in the hydropolitics of the region. Jordan is overexploiting her non-renewable underground reservoirs by 15 per cent a year (*Middle East International*, 22 February 1991), while Israel is utilizing her resources at 15–20 per cent beyond their replenishment rate (Starr, 1991). Israel's coastal aquifer is overpumped to such an extent that sea-water intrusion has become a serious problem. The Jordan is constantly overused, exhausting the

Dead Sea. In addition, Jordan's water is becoming increasingly saline, partly as a result of overexploitation, and only certain salt-resistant crops can currently be grown on the riverbanks. This overutilization further heightens tensions in the Middle East.

The hydropolitical security complex defined and described in this essay is thus identified as including those states and regions which are to some extent dependent on the same water (river basins and ground-water aquifers): Israel, Jordan, Syria, Lebanon, the West Bank and the Gaza Strip. This implies that the essay is not restricted to an analysis of the *Jordan River basin*. Instead, I have also included the Israeli and West Bank joint dependency on the *groundwater aquifers* in the West Bank, the alarming situation in Gaza, and the Litani River basin. Rather than using the Jordan River system as the sole point of departure for the delimitation of the security complex, the starting point and foundation of the complex is *Israel and her water politics*. Pairs of water relations will be set up throughout, and Israel will serve as the starting point, since Israel is the one entity with water relations with all the remaining units in the complex. I will begin with a description of Israel's water politics. Then I will move on to an inquiry into her relations with the surrounding Arab states, and thus the Arab–Israeli conflict from the perspective of water, and highlight the Palestinian–Israeli conflict in the last section.

Israel's Water Politics

Ever since the early days of Zionism, scarcity of water has been of great concern to Zionist planners and, later, to Israeli politicians. The presence of water was actually a factor in the discussions about defining the territory of the state of Israel.

Chaim Weizmann (in 1948 the first President of Israel) exclaimed at the Paris Peace Conference in 1919 that the boundaries of Palestine were to include 'the headwaters of the Jordan River, the lower Litani in today's Lebanon, and the lower Yarmouk in today's Jordan'. It was also considered important to control the very sources of the water flows, thus emphasizing Mount Hermon and the drainage of the Jordan (Weisgal, 1977, quoted in Nijim, 1990; Jaber, 1989; Rose, 1986). As early as 1916, the World Zionist Organization (WZO) spoke of having the Jordan River system included in Palestine and the Litani River delimiting the northern border (Nijim, 1990: 317). In 1919, Weizmann wrote a letter to British Prime Minister Lloyd George, stating that 'the whole economic future of Palestine depends on its water for irrigation and electric power. This water must come largely from the foothills of the Jordan and the waters of the Litani' (letter of 29 December 1919; see Jaber, 1989: 67). The British, in essence, agreed with the Zionists on the delimitation of the state of Israel. David Ben-Gurion stated:

> It is necessary that the water sources, upon which the future of the Land depends, should not be outside the borders of the future Jewish homeland ... For this reason we have always demanded that the Land of Israel include the southern banks of the Litani River, the headwaters of the Jordan, and the Hauran Region from the El Aujua spring south of Damascus. All the rivers run from east to west or from north to south. This explains the importance of the Upper Galilee and the Hauran for the entire country. The most important rivers of the Land of Israel are the Jordan and the Yarmouk. The Land needs this water. Moreover [it needs] the development of industry on water power for the generation of electricity. (David Ben-Gurion, 1973, *Zichronot* (Memoirs), vol. I: 164, quoted in Cohen, 1986: 122)

The Kuneitra River in Syria and the upper Yarmouk valley were also discussed (Frischwasser-Ra'anan, 1955, quoted in Nijim, 1990).

Thus, from the very beginning lack of water was of grave concern to Zionism, and it has been a crucial factor in the definition of Israel. Israel's annual renewable water supply amounts to 1,800 m.c.m. (Environmental Protection Service, 1988, quoted in Wolf and Aronson, 1992: 925). Some 60 per cent is groundwater and 40 per cent surface water (Wolf and Ross, 1992). Today, Israel receives water from the following sources: river flows (the upper Jordan and the Yarmouk), groundwater (from the coastal plains as well as the aquifers in the mountains of the West Bank), flood flow and waste water. Israel's largest body of surface water is the upper Jordan by the Sea of Galilee.

Development and Israeli hydropolitics

Israeli hydropolitics is related to her development strategy and the advanced agricultural sector. Modernization and state-building based on vast flows of immigration has in itself proved problematic in a region where water is scarce. Rising population figures, partly as a result of the large-scale Russian immigration during the late 1980s and early 1990s, exert further pressure on existing water resources.

One of the foundation-stones of the state of Israel, as well as

Table 2.3 Agricultural Consumption of Water in Israel, 1987/88

	m.c.m.	%
Urban localities	59	5
Moshavot*	58	5
Moshavim*	392	33
Kibbutzim*	484	41
Institutions/farms	24	2
Non-Jewish villages	27	2
Other	135	11
Total	1,179	99

Note: * Moshavot and Moshavim are both small co-operative farms combined with private means of ownership. Kibbutzim are larger, exclusively collective farms.
Source: Israel's Central Bureau of Statistics, 1989: 448.

Israeli development strategy, was the kibbutz movement, consisting of collective agricultural entities. Agricultural policies aimed at self-reliance in food production and the development of Israel has to a large extent been based on large-scale, high-technology agriculture. Agricultural production was encouraged through a system of government support – subsidies and guaranteed producer prices. Israel, however, has also ventured into high-tech industrial development, and has a highly advanced industrial sector. Water is a crucial ingredient in both aspects of Israeli development politics.

In 1987–8 the use of water was distributed as follows: 447 m.c.m. were used in the domestic sphere; 123 m.c.m. went to the industrial sector, whereas agriculture alone consumed 1,179 m.c.m., according to Israel's Central Bureau of Statistics (1989: 448). In 1990, agriculture consumed 1,250 m.c.m. of Israel's water (*Jerusalem Post International*, 23 March 1991). In 1992, 479 m.c.m. were used for household consumption, 107 m.c.m went into industrial use and 941 m.c.m. were consumed by the agricultural sector, implying a 218 m.c.m. reduction in agricultural use between 1990 and 1992 (Israel's Central Bureau of Statistics, 1993). Agriculture thus drained 67 per cent of the total water consumption in 1987–8 (Bureau of Statistics, 1989); reduced to 62 per cent in 1992 (Bureau of Statistics, 1993). Israel's agriculture is water-intensive, with an extensive irrigation system. During later years, however, Israel has succeeded in bringing down her agricultural water consumption, a process which was initiated in 1986.

Agricultural consumption, in turn, was divided into the different localities in 1987–8 which are shown in Table 2.3. The kibbutzim and the moshavim are thus by far the biggest consumers of water in Israel. In fact, the kibbutzim comprise the *single largest user* of water. In 1985–6, 50 per cent of the total cultivated area of Israel was irrigated, implying a 30 per cent growth in irrigated crops since 1965–6 (Israel's Central Bureau of Statistics, 1989: 388). The proverbial villain is thus *irrigated crop production on the kibbutzim*. The overall objective of guaranteeing food supplies has, moreover, entailed extensive water subsidies to the kibbutzim since 1948, implying that kibbutzim and moshavim have not been paying the real costs of water. Incentives for saving water were thus for many years minimal or nonexistent. The policy of subsidies has, however, changed during the last ten years and the price of water has increased. Despite the problems, Israel has succeeded in considerably reducing the amount of water used in agricultural production, while simultaneously increasing agricultural output. In fact she has one of the most water-efficient agricultural systems in the world.

Agricultural production in general and the kibbutzim in particular have been subject to much criticism when Israel's far-reaching economic crisis during the 1980s has been discussed. Critics blame the lenient and excessive lending policy (which was established in order to encourage agricultural production and self-sufficiency in food) for attracting too many people to the agricultural sector, leading to the overmanning, overproduction and inefficiency of Israel's agriculture. A vicious circle has been created where the kibbutzim have been pushed towards single-crop production – such as cotton – by the economic crisis. Cotton, however, is a highly water-intensive crop, and an unsustainable situation is being produced: the water crisis simultaneously pushes the farmers to bring cotton cultivation to a halt.

The consumption of Palestinian villages represented only 2 per cent of Israel's water consumption in 1987–8 (see Table 2.3; Israel's Central Bureau of Statistics, 1989: 448). At the same time, the Palestinian population of Israel amounted to $1.03 million, 19 per cent of the total population of 5.46 million (Israel's Central Bureau of Statistics, 1994: 42). The distribution of water thus 'has a major impact on the geography of unequal economic development along ethnic lines of cleavage' (Ghazi, 1990: 331) and is one of the factors which indicate the ethnic power structure in Israel.

Advanced irrigation and water technology have thus been substantial elements of the Israeli development projects. The water system in its totality is integrated in the National Water Carrier Project, 'the most ambitious development project undertaken in pre-1967 Israel' (Davis *et al.*, 1980: 14). It is a network of canals, reservoirs and pipelines, drawing water from the upper Jordan system and distributing it throughout the country. The Carrier Project is the main supplier of water in Israel, since it combines all regional water flows and projects into one single system, bringing water from the Sea of Galilee to the Negev Desert. All water resources are controlled by the state water company, Mekorot, and administered by the Israeli Water Commission, which in turn is subject to the authority of the Ministry of Agriculture. Mekorot is part of the Water Commission Administration, as is Tahal, the Water Planning for Israel Company. Application of water laws is in the hands of water authorities.

Water technology

Because of the scarcity of water, Israel has developed some of the most advanced water technologies in the world. One of these innovative technologies is cloud seeding and weather modification, which, however, has had little impact on the overall problems (Davis *et al.*, 1980: 23). In fact, the Israeli experiments with the weather affected Jordan and Syria negatively, since the cloud seeding attracted clouds above them, (Nijim, 1990: 320) and does little, if anything, to improve the Israeli water situation. Reuger (1993: 90, Note 113, quoting Dr Gablinger of Tahal, August 1979), however, claims that cloud seeding has in fact had a positive impact and increased rainfall by 10–14 per cent.

Desalination is another means by which Israel's overall water situation could be improved. The first step in this project was a desalination plant in Eilat. By the late 1970s, 50 per cent of Eilat's water consumption needs was met by desalination (*Israeli Economist*, January–February 1977: 6, quoted in Davis *et al.*, 1980: 23). In 1980 the programme was to continue with yet another plant in Eilat and one by the Mediterranean shore. However, these measures can only partially meet Israel's increasing needs. Furthermore, the investments involved are tremendous, rendering the project economically unattractive. Desalination is highly energy intensive, and in Israel there has been a discussion on obtaining desalinated water as a by-product of nuclear energy generation. Initial costs have, however, been hard to overcome, and the unit costs for use of desalinated water have made it a poor alternative. By the late 1980s, therefore, the project had come to a halt. Nevertheless, Hillel Shuval (1992) discusses multinational desalination plants as a possible solution to the current water scarcity in the Middle East. These plants would be situated on the coastline between Israel and Gaza and at Aqaba and Eilat, in the area where the borders of Israel and Jordan meet (see further p. 73 below). According to Shuval, a Gaza desalination plant could also provide the West Bank with water (Shuval, 1992: 141). Although it is expensive, and thus an alternative which may not be economically feasible, Shuval states:

> desalination, while expensive, might well be the most attractive solution, particularly for Israel and the Palestinians (in Gaza). It would not involve water supply sources from across multiple international borders and long exposed pipelines. It will be the simplest politically since it would require the least degree of multi-national agreement. (Shuval, 1992: 141)

Furthermore, Israel has developed water-saving technologies, in order not to waste water in irrigation. Underground storage is one way to save water. The most effective measure is converting from sprinkler to drip irrigation, watering plants at the root. Drip irrigation causes less evaporation than sprinkler irrigation, lessening the risk of salinization. However, drip irrigation is expensive, and the conversion was not initiated until the 1980s. Israel also struggles to enhance public awareness of the need for water saving through TV broadcasts, information in schools, and so on.

Perhaps the most successful Israeli water-saving measure has been the development of waste water recycling for irrigation. In 1986, 35 per cent of Israeli municipal waste water was reused for agricultural and industrial purposes. Water recycling has been declared a national policy, and so waste water is nationalized. The goal is to reuse 80 per cent of waste water in the year 2000. Israeli reuse of water is the highest in the world, and water recycling has proved the most effective and economical alternative to fresh water (Shuval, 1987: 186 ff.).

Environmental aspects

Irrigation has far-reaching ecological repercussions, as it leads to an accumulation of salt in the soil. Evaporation near the soil surface increases the salinity, reducing crop yields. Excessive irrigation is thus *unsustainable* in the long run, and may prove counterproductive in terms of development. According to Postel, the only solution to this devastating problem is to shift 'water away from agriculture' (Postel, 1989: 23).

Another environmental impact relevant to Israel is the over-exploitation of local aquifers, resulting in a fall in water tables and the drying up of water sources. Through the Yarkon–Negev Canal and the National Water Carrier Project, the north and south of Israel are connected in terms of water. Overexploitation of groundwater reservoirs in the south will thus inevitably lead to salinization through sea water penetration from the northwest front to the southeast. Sea water penetrates sand and gravel along the coast, eventually infiltrating the groundwater reservoirs. Furthermore, overexploitation leads to a reduction of pressure against the penetration of saline water from surrounding static saline water belts, causing salinization of the fresh water. The salinity of these static water belts is in principle higher than the salinity of sea water. This salinization process is irreversible, and could spread to large parts of the Israeli water system.

Related to salinization is the question of who controls the West Bank aquifers. Excessive drilling on the West Bank may cause serious salinization of the Israeli water system. A Palestinian state on the West Bank is thus considered a serious threat to the water security of Israel, and excessive drillings may 'constitute a *casus belli* for Israel, because, in contrast to the situation elsewhere, no substitutes can be offered to Israel in this matter' (Amir Shapira in *Al Hamishmar*, 25 June 1978, quoted by Davis *et al.*, 1980: 17). This is one of the reasons why control over the West Bank aquifers remained one of the most difficult issues to resolve in the negotiations on the implementation of the Declaration of Principles. Simultaneously, Israeli drillings from the Western or Yarqon–Taninim aquifer affect West Bank water quality in the same way (see the section below on the West Bank).

There is thus an urgent necessity for Israel to draw water consumption to some extent away from irrigated agriculture; because of both the general shortage of water and the ecological aspects of the current consumption pattern. This may threaten some traditional agricultural methods. At the same time, it should be remembered – as Hillel Shuval emphasizes – that Israel is unlikely to abandon its agricultural development strategy:

It is important to understand the deep ideological commitment of Israel to preserve its agricultural base as an essential part of its heritage and national goal of 'the return to the soil' in its ancient homeland. (Shuval, 1993: 67)

In the same way, it is unlikely that the Palestinians will forsake their agricultural economy, which is deeply rooted in Arab traditions (*ibid.*). The land and the soil are inherent parts of Palestinian nationalist ideology as well. The ideology of being self-sufficient in terms of food supply is an important ingredient in both Zionism and Palestinian nationalism, connected as they are to the 'land'. Water is seen as the 'lifeblood' of the nation, given nationalism's organic and primordial view of the 'nation'. In addition, given the low level of development of Palestinian industries, a future Palestinian development strategy will most probably have to be built on agriculture.

Since Israel is currently exploiting all water resources within its boundaries to their maximum, she has no alternative sources. In addition, the current – albeit diminishing – inflow of Jewish immigrants from the former Soviet Union increases the heavy burden on water resources. In addition, Israel has long looked beyond her borders in order to satisfy her water needs, which brings us to the question of water as an aspect of the Arab–Israeli conflict.

Wars and Water

Hydropolitics and Israeli–Syrian relations

Immediately after the 1948–9 war, Israel initiated the National Water Carrier Project, which implied the construction of a massive water pipeline from the upper Jordan River to the Negev desert. In northern Israel, the National Water Project was linked to development and settlement plans in the Huleh swamps, reclaimed by Israel in 1951. Parts of the Huleh area were situated in the demilitarized zone consisting of the areas in northern Israel (or parts of Palestine that were to fall to the Jewish state according to the UN partition plan of 1947) from which the Syrian army was evacuated in 1949. According to the Syrian view, Israel was not allowed to foster any major changes in these areas. Tensions between the two countries exacerbated as Israel kept insisting on her right to engage in agriculture in the entire Huleh area (Yaniv, 1987b: 163). As early as 1950, settlements were established in the demilitarized zone. In 1953, plans to divert Jordan River waters from north of the Sea of Galilee in the demilitarized zone on the Syrian border were initiated. Israel also had plans for an irrigation canal through the demilitarized zones, something that would separate the demilitarized zones from Syria (Nijim, 1990: 319).

It was this dissension over water between Israel, Syria and Jordan that led to the American Johnston United Water Plan of 1953. The American special envoy Eric Johnston set up a plan – based on the American Tennessee Valley Authority – which aimed at an 'equitable distribution' of the resources of the Jordan and Yarmouk Rivers, and at reaching a co-operative formula for the countries involved.[2] The Johnston Plan was the first attempt at drawing up a development plan for all of the Jordan River basin. Israel, Jordan and Lebanon approved of it, but Syria did not, which in turn hindered Jordan and Lebanon from endorsing it. Neither did the Arab League come out in favour of the American proposal. Although the Johnston plan was never fully implemented, owing to political disagreements, the proposed allocation has served as a guideline for the affected states and, in fact, many of the principles stipulated in the plan have been followed by Israel as well as the Arab states (Anderson, 1988: 10).

Israel stood firm in implementing the National Water Carrier Project in the Huleh area, but was forced to make changes in her original plans and thus moved the project further away from the Syrian border. The Syrians were now unable to disturb the Israeli plan, but began to deploy military forces along the Syrian–Israeli border. A series of skirmishes occurred. Israel failed to deter the Syrians from small-scale military activities – although Syria did not engage in large-scale operations. The National Carrier Project was the main reason for Syrian hostilities and tensions between the two parties.

Meanwhile, Israel told the USA that she would carry on with the Johnston Plan, although it was still unsigned. In the meantime, a Jordanian application was made for a World Bank loan to fund an irrigation project connected to the building of a dam – the Maqarein Dam by the Yarmouk River. Israel feared that this would undermine the Johnston Plan, and the USA attempted to help both Israel and Jordan while still sticking to the Johnston Plan. Syrian fears were escalated by a feeling of being left out of the water arrangements. Thus in 1959 Syria managed to get the issue on to the agenda of the Arab League Summit. The Summit decided to divert the waters of the Jordan River in order to obstruct the Israeli project, but not until 1961 were decisions taken actually to carry the diversion plans out, and not until 1964 was Syria given the green light. According to Yaniv, this indicates a reluctance on the part of Egyptian President Gamal

Abd al-Nasir (Nasser) – then head of the Arab League – actually to implement the project (Yaniv, 1987b: 105). The scheme was intended to divert the Hasbani, the Dan and the Banyias to the Yarmouk River.

Although the diversion plan was to be carried out within Syrian territory, and even though the Arab League had rejected a military option, to Israel the diversion scheme was a *casus belli*, since it would deprive her of her main supply. As early as 1959 Yigal Allon – commentator on strategic and political affairs – advocated that '[a]ny Syrian attempt to thwart Israeli development projects in the Huleh area and/ or concerning the utilization of the water of the Jordan River' should be considered a reason for war (quoted in Yaniv, 1987a: 82). Shimon Peres, then Deputy Defence Minister, reckoned in 1962 that one of the issues that could bring about yet another Arab–Israeli war was 'if Israel seizes waters that are not its own – according to its neighbours' (*Ma'arachot* 146, 1962, quoted in Yaniv, 1987a: 86). Israel's Prime Minister at the time, Levy Eshkol, also declared that water could be regarded as a *casus belli*, since 'the water is like the blood in our veins' (Kally, 1991/92: 6). *Thus from early in Israeli political history, water was closely connected to the issue of state security.* Furthermore, the Israeli economy would suffer great losses if the National Carrier Project was halted.

In the initial phase, however, Israel restricted herself to the strategy of 'flexible response' and tried to obstruct Syrian operations. Prime Minister Eshkol issued statements confirming that Israel would not exceed her 'fair share of water', mixed with warnings that she would not tolerate actions which inflicted injury on her. As the Syrians escalated their military activities, 'Israel was forced ... to fall back on massive retaliation' (Yaniv, 1987a: 106), and bombed the Syrian diversion installations two months before the outbreak of the 1967 war. A gradual escalation of deployments and skirmishes took place, and eventually even the air force was utilized. Syria had threatened large-scale war, and could not back down from her hardline position without losing face and prestige – even though she was left without armed support from the Arab League. Syria further utilized the Palestinian guerrilla organization al-Fatah, which carried out subwar activities in Israel, often aimed at National Carrier Project installations. Water infrastructure thus frequently becomes a military target. Eventually, however, Syria halted the diversion project.

So throughout the 1950s and 1960s Syrian–Israeli relations were marked by armed confrontations which, in practice, led to war. Water was *one* of the main reasons for the frosty relations and armed conflict between the two countries. It should be emphasized that when these events occurred, there was no Arab acceptance of the state of Israel in the region. Although Israel has never received official recognition by the Arab League, it is a fact today that several Arab states have established diplomatic relations on various levels with Israel. The mere fact that armed violence has historically taken place on the issue of water is not, therefore, an indication that this pattern may repeat itself in the future. In fact, for whatever reasons, the mid-1990s point towards more interstate co-operation between Israel and the Arab states, rather than conflict.

With her occupation of the Golan Heights in 1967, Israel gained complete control over the Sea of Galilee – a precious wellspring of water. Furthermore, Israel captured the Banyias, a fresh-water stream that rises in the Golan Heights. Israel claimed sovereignty over the Golan, and the right to pursue claims on the Yarmouk for irrigation purposes (Nijim, 1990: 319). In 1981 the Golan Heights were formally annexed and integrated into Israel. The main reason for the Israeli annexation of the Golan is related to security, but it could be argued that water requirements are part of the motives for Israeli rule in the area. Through the control of the Golan, Israel further guards against any diversions of the upper Jordan. In 1995 the future status of the Golan Heights is uncertain, Syria and Israel being involved in negotiations, however slow the progress, and Israel's Labour-led government having indicated its willingness to withdraw.

There were also Israeli suspicions that Jordan overdiverted the Yarmouk River, which may have contributed to the hostile sentiments of the time (Wolf and Ross, 1992: 940). The contention between Israel and Syria, to a large extent sparked by competition over water, preceded the June War of 1967, and it may thus be argued that water was, if not the main issue, then one of the driving forces behind that war.

Hydropolitics and Israel–Jordan–Syria

Also in the period before 1967, Israel was dependent on water originating in the rainfall of the West Bank. It was drawn by drilling inside Israel proper, but from the very same aquifer system that contained the West Bank water reserves (see section below on the West Bank). Yehuda Litani, correspondent of *Ha'aretz*, indicates that between 1948 and 1967, there was an 'incorrect application' of drilling in the West Bank. According to a memorandum submitted by the water commission, this 'incorrect application' could lead to a salinization of the water resources in the state of Israel. Litani states: *'It is possible that this is the true reason, so far unknown, for the eruption of the Six Day War.'* (in *Ha'aretz*, 27 November 1978, quoted in Davis *et al.*, 1980: 4; emphasis added by Davis).

The argument put forward by Litani, therefore, is that Israel's dependency on the West Bank waters together with Jordanian and Palestinian 'incorrect drilling applications' which seriously affected Israeli aquifers, were one of the *main reasons* behind the war of 1967, and thus behind the annexation of the West Bank from the state of Jordan.

Altering the sovereignty of the West Bank enhanced interstate disputes over the Johnston Plan and on the issue of to whom the Yarmouk water quotas belonged, and whether Israel's water quotas were being maintained. The issue boiled down to the question: who had the ultimate sovereignty over the West Bank and the River Jordan? Jordan and Syria argued that the quotas in the Johnston Plan were linked to 'specific destinations', that is, related to state sovereignty; while Israel maintained that it was she who now administered the western Jordan valley, and that by virtue of the occupation and the Jewish settlements, Israel had a right to pursue claims on the Yarmouk and the West Bank waters, and the right to higher water quotas because she now administered the Golan and the West Bank (Nijim, 1990: 321). Israel has also claimed rights to the West Bank aquifers on the basis of her historic use ('prior use' – see Elmusa, 1993) of these aquifers (see pp. 78 ff. for a further elaboration of Israel's historic use of the West Bank aquifers).

On the foundation of such arguments – the equalization of occupation with state sovereignty, as well as the 'historic use' argument – Israel has claimed a right to be a party in, for example, the Jordanian water project of the Maqarein Dam as well as the irrigation plans for the Ghor (Nijim, 1990). Jordan faces a chronic water shortage, and the Maqarein Dam Plan on the Yarmouk was initiated in 1974–5 to enhance the availability of water for irrigation in the Jordan Valley. The Maqarein Dam was initially planned in 1953. At that time Jordan and Syria agreed to share the Yarmouk, but Israel protested. Since Jordan is an upstream riparian to Israel on the Yarmouk, and since the dam would impinge upon Israeli accessibility to the Yarmouk waters, Jordan was forced to try to reach an agreement with Israel in order to implement the project. This, however, proved easier said than done, since Israel continued to claim control over the Yarmouk. Moreover, the Maqarein Plan was heavily dependent on aid, in particular from USAID, and some of the donors – the foremost of whom was the World Bank – argued that Israel should be consulted as a party in the project (*The Middle East*, February 1981). Both the Johnston Plan and the Maqarein Plan were initiated by the USA to promulgate more peaceful relations in the region (Lowi, 1992: 47).

Moreover, Jordan had to consult Syria about the implementation of the Maqarein Plan, since part of the dam would be built on Syrian territory. At this time, Syria also proved negative towards the project. The failure to reach an agreement between Jordan and Syria brought the project to a standstill in the late 1980s (Taubenblatt, 1988: 49).

The Maqarein Plan was perceived as a threat against Jewish settlement plans in the Jordan valley. According to Reuger (1993: 78), Israel agreed to the main ideas of the Maqarein Dam, but felt that it would be too large. Also, the construction of the East Ghor main canal in the Jordan valley – completed in 1964 and part of the Jordan–Syrian joint programme of the Great Yarmouk – which was intended to increase the water available for irrigation, was perceived as a menace by the Israelis. In 1969, the East Ghor canal was subject to air assault by Israel, as a retaliation against PLO raids.

Israel further feared that Jordan and Syria would draw more water from the Yarmouk, leaving less for her. She made claims to a larger allocation from the River Yarmouk for use in both Israel and the West Bank. To Jordan, the East Ghor Canal and the Maqarein Dam were part of agricultural development plans in the Jordan valley, where the project has resulted in the irrigation of 175,000 dunams out of 181,500. (The dunam is an old square measurement used during the era of the Ottoman Empire. One dunam is equal to approximately 927 square metres.) Between 1959 and 1965, agricultural production in the area doubled (Reuger, 1993: 77).

Jordanian plans were also a danger to Israeli industries using bromine and potassium plants. These industries depended on Dead Sea minerals, but with Jordanian and Israeli exploitation of the River Jordan, the level of the Dead Sea has decreased, adversely affecting the industrial complex. As a consequence of both Israeli and Jordanian development projects, the 'lower Jordan River has become a drainage ditch with very little water flowing into the Dead Sea' (Reuger, 1993: 79), threatening the very existence of the Sea. In the late 1970s, the Israelis planned to construct a canal between the Dead Sea and the Mediterranean (the Med–Dead Canal) in order to 'salvage' the Dead Sea – a plan which is still envisioned, although it would be immensely costly. According to *Jordan Times* (21 November 1993), there are also plans for a canal from the Dead Sea to the Red Sea (the Red–Dead Canal). The Med–Dead Canal would bring water for hydroelectric power, utilizing the drop between the Mediterranean and the Dead Sea. The power would then be transmitted back to the Mediterranean and used for desalination in Ashdod, providing an additional water supply. The canal would include an enlargement of the Dead Sea, in order to provide a greater evaporation surface (Ploss and Rubinstein, 1992: 21).

The canal project heightened Jordan's fears that pumping water from the Mediterranean to the Dead Sea would damage Jordanian agriculture, which is irrigated with water from the East Ghor Canal. So Jordanian and Israeli interests conflicted, highlighting their joint dependency on the same water resources.

Increasing the size of the Dead Sea would naturally also imply far-reaching ecological consequences. It may also threaten Bedouin populations in the area, as well as affecting the tourist industry. So far, the project has proved too expensive and too difficult.

King Hussein's hostile statements against Israel in 1990 were related to a Jordanian application to the World Bank for financial support for the Wahda Dam on the upper Yarmouk River. The dam would be of the utmost importance to the water supply in the Jordan valley and for municipal and industrial use in the urban areas of Amman, which suffer severely from chronic water shortage. The policy of the World Bank, however, is not to grant such funding unless all riparians to a water project approve the plan. Israel feared that the Wahda project would affect her ability to cope with increasing water needs, and thus refused to approve it; while Syria agreed (Starr, 1991: 23 f.). Jordan's water shortage is becoming ever more acute, and Israeli reluctance to grant approval to the project thus served to frustrate the Jordanians. To meet growing demands related to her increasing population, Jordan relies on solutions such as deeper drilling for groundwater sources and expensive measures such as drip irrigation. Technological development could help Jordan out of her extremely difficult situation, but the costs are greater than the country could afford at present (*ibid*.: 27).

Jordan has a water allowance of 870 m.c.m., 75 per cent of which is surface water, mostly from the Yarmouk (Taubenblatt, 1988: 49, Note 9). The annual *per capita* consumption of 205 c.m. is one of the lowest in the world. Projected consumption for 2005 is 1,120 m.c.m. – an unrealistic water use in view of current supplies (Beschorner, 1992: 16). A constant overexploitation of groundwater implies a decline in water tables. Jordan's water situation is threatened not only by a rising population and irrigated agriculture, but by Israeli and Syrian use of the Jordan and the Yarmouk respectively. To Jordan, Syrian plans for the diversion of up to 40 per cent of the River Yarmouk imply a reduced amount of water for irrigation and a risk of rising salinity in lower Yarmouk and lower Jordan. Jordan and Syria both accuse each other of stealing water. In an attempt to compensate for the loss of water from the Yarmouk, Jordan signed an agreement with Iraq for supplies from the Euphrates (Falkenmark, 1989b: 350; Starr and Stoll, 1988: 145). According to Kally, there were previously plans to sell Lebanese and Syrian water to Jordan. This water would have been transported from the sources of the River Jordan through the Golan Heights (Kally, 1991/92: 23). With the state of affairs following the 1967 war and the Israeli occupation and annexation of the Golan Heights, these plans have not been implemented.

With an annual population growth rate of 3.8 per cent, Jordan's water scarcity is reaching alarming levels. The influx of Palestinian refugees from the Gulf in the aftermath of the Gulf War has put Jordan's water situation under further stress. As in Israel, water for irrigated agriculture has been heavily subsidized, despite criticism from the World Bank and other international agencies and serious water shortages. Also as in the Israeli case, the Jordanian government seems to fear the farmers' lobby, which has brought accusations of mismanagement of the country's water situation. Water for irrigation is simply too cheap. As a consequence, a large portion of Jordan's irrigated agriculture is still directed towards water-intensive crops such as citrus fruit and banana trees.

In negotiations between Israel and Jordan since the Madrid conference, water proved to be one of the most difficult issues to resolve. In the peace agreement signed in October 1994, the issue of water took up a large proportion of the text. Among other things, decision was reached on the distribution of the Yarmouk and it was agreed that Israel would divert water from the Upper Jordan to Jordan during the summer months. Both countries' entitlement to the River Jordan was agreed upon. The parties also agreed on joint projects to increase water supply. In the mid-1990s, the water conflict between Isreal and Jordan was in fact – at least for the time being – resolved.

Hydropolitics and Israel–Lebanon–Syria

Lebanon has plentiful water resources, perhaps sufficient also for sharing with neighbouring countries:

> A national water shortage engineering and management system could turn Lebanon into a lucrative Middle East water haven, were there the vision and stability to realize it. Instead, the country is crippled by severe water short-ages in Beirut, seawater intrusion in the coastal aquifer, farm lands neglected by lack of irrigation water, anµd pipelines and aquifers severely damaged by civil war. (Starr, 1991: 28)

Lebanon's water situation was thus induced by its traumatic civil war between 1975 and 1990, and the collapse of the Lebanese state system.

As we have seen, the Zionist movement mentioned the inclusion of the Litani River in the territory of the Jewish homeland as early as 1919. In the late 1970s, with the water crisis becoming patently obvious, it was mooted that water resources might be sought outside Israel's current borders. According to Nijim (1990: 320), Israel's Water Com-missioner between 1969 and 1977, Menahem Cantor, considered the Litani River an option for increasing access to water. The 'Lebanese Option' implied the diversion of the River Litani to Israel (*Middle East International*, 22 February 1991).

Various sources put forward the hypothesis that Israeli involvement in Lebanon is stimulated by concerns over water. It should be noted that most of these sources – at least, of those that I have been able to find – are Arab, and the assumption that Israel's presence in South Lebanon is determined by water needs could also be political. Data and information presented by Thomas Naff and John Kolars, however, could be considered reliable. What remains a fact is that the so-called security zone in southern Lebanon established by Israel following the Lebanon war of 1978, and expanded after the war of 1982, includes the lower Litani as well as the Hasbani and the Wazzani. The hypothesis put forward by, for example, Jaber (1989) and Nijim (1990) is that the Israeli invasions of 1978 and 1982 were motivated not only by military security interests and an urge to defeat the PLO and put an end to PLO operations against northern Israel, but also by water security needs.

In 1984 the government of Lebanon submitted a protest to the UN concerning Israel's water politics in southern Lebanon, accusing Israel of carrying out excavations between the Litani River and the Israeli border with the intention of diverting water from the Litani. Similar experimental diversion schemes were to occur with the Hasbani and Wazzani rivers (Jaber, 1989: 63 f.). Israeli sources, however, firmly denied any plans to divert the Litani, although discussions had taken place in Israel on the possibility of obtaining water from the river.

Furthermore, an FAO report stated in the early 1970s that Israel had installed underground pumps along the Lebanese border in order to draw water from the south of Lebanon. After establishing the security zone in 1978, 'Israel prohibited Lebanese farmers of the occupied villages from digging wells in the area without explicit orders from the IDF' (Butterfield and Madi, quoted in Jaber, 1989: 66, Note 12). Water researchers John Kolars and Thomas Naff establish that Israel is, in fact, diverting water from both Litani and Hasbani. From the Hasbani River, she is diverting approximately 100 m.c.m. a year. The diversion of Litani waters is still, according to Naff, insignificant (about the same amount as is taken from the Hasbani), but it nevertheless exists. Tamimi states that 'this river [the Litani] adds at least 800 m.c.m. annually to the Israeli water resources or about 50% of this vital resource' (Tamimi, 1991/92: 23) – a figure which, in the light of Thomas Naff's research, does not appear to be accurate. According to Naff, the Litani is more interesting than the Hasbani for future Israeli needs, because of its 'quality and quantity'. He states that although there is 'no doubt' of Israel's needs for finding new water sources, and Israel is already using Lebanese water springs, this does not prove that the invasions of 1978 and 1982 were 'primarily motivated' by a wish to control the Litani. Naff's conclusion, however, is that Israel will *not* withdraw from southern Lebanon, because of water needs (Naff, 1991). In addition, there is no evidence that Israel is diverting additional water from the Litani.

The Israeli project could thus be perceived as a *threat* against Lebanese water security and the water available for agriculture in Lebanon (Jaber, 1989: 67). Even such a cautious observer as Anderson states: 'the Litani represents the only additional surface supply of high-quality water within reach of Israel, and further disputes seem inevitable' (Anderson, 1988: 17). Viewed from a different perspective, the rich Litani River, situated near Israel's border, may also provide a source of co-operation and water sharing. Water from the Litani could be sold to Israel, Jordan and the Palestinians on a strictly commercial basis.

According to Shuval, the Lebanese use the Litani primarily for power production. Furthermore, large amounts of water from the Litani simply flow into the sea (Shuval, 1992: 139). In light of the emerging co-operative tendencies in the Middle East, this perspective appears more likely than another war over the Litani in the near future.

Water allocation is also an issue in Lebanon's intricate ethno-religious group relations. The lack of irrigation in the south of Lebanon has been a reason for Shi'ite grievances. Discussions on the diversion of the Litani water to Beirut was, according to *The Middle East*, one of the underlying reasons for the establishment of the Amal movement (*The Middle East*, February 1991).

Israel and the Palestinians: Occupation and Water

The June War of 1967 and the ensuing Israeli occupation of the West Bank and the Golan Heights ensured fresh-water resources for Israel – not only from the Golan Heights and from full control over the Sea of Galilee, but also by obtaining control over the groundwater resources of the West Bank and greater access to the River Jordan. There are three groundwater aquifers – together making up the mountain aquifer – on the West Bank: one in the north; one in the east, flowing towards the Jordan River; and one in the west, flowing towards the Mediterranean. The western aquifer is called the Yarqon-Taninim aquifer in Israel; before 1967 it was already shared by Israel and the Palestinians. Utilization of this aquifer was initiated by Jewish settlers in the 1930s, and it is still primarily tapped from wells situated within the pre-1967 boundaries of Israel. The northeastern aquifer, called the Schem-Gilboa aquifer by the Israelis, was also used by Israel before 1967, since the water from this aquifer, like that from the western one, flows naturally into the Israeli territory. Israel's claims on both the western and the northeastern aquifers are thus to a large extent based on her historic use of them (for a critical account of Israeli claims based on the argument of prior use, see Elmusa, 1993). With the occupation, Israel gained control over the eastern and northern aquifers too. The most substantial part of the mountain aquifer is thus located in the West Bank, although the western aquifer is partly situated in Israel. As Anderson states:

> The West Bank has become critical as a source of water for Israel, and it could be argued that this consideration *outweighs other political and strategic factors.* (Anderson, 1988: 8; emphasis added)

According to Anderson, water would thus be the main reason behind the continued Israeli occupation of the West Bank.

It should be emphasized that from an international law perspective, there is no obvious or 'objective' 'owner' of the western aquifer, since its water is used by Israel and the Palestinians, and both parties must be considered legitimate. The ultimate question boils down to who owns the rain that falls in this region? An equitable distribution of the mountain aquifer needs to be reached.

West Bank waters, Israeli hydropolitics and the Palestinians

Israeli exploitation of the West Bank water seriously affects the availability of water to its Palestinian inhabitants. There is competition between the state of Israel and the Palestinians there, as well as between Jewish settlers and Palestinians. At the same time, harsh restrictions on Palestinian water use constitute a serious impediment to the development of Palestinian agriculture.

All water resources in the West Bank are today controlled by Israel. Between 1967 and 1982, the West Bank waters were controlled and managed by military rule. In 1982, however, the responsibility was transferred to Mekorot, with the purpose of integrating the West Bank's water with the overall water network in Israel. The new move was ordered by the then Minister of Defence Ariel Sharon (Schiff and Ya'ari, 1990: 97). Thus it was no longer the Civil Administration – which had ruled the occupied territories since 1981 – that controlled water allocation in the West Bank.

Today, the West Bank aquifer supplies 25–40 per cent of Israel's water (Starr, 1991: 24). Estimates differ widely, but the lower figure appears to be the most reliable. Falkenmark mentions 'possibly as much as one fourth' (Falkenmark, 1989b: 350). Lowi states that 'more than one-quarter of the state's sustainable annual water yield, origi-nates in the rainfall over the western slopes of the West Bank', and that about 40 per cent of the 'groundwater upon which Israel is dependent' stems from the joint Israeli–West Bank aquifer system (Lowi, 1992: 40).

Twenty-five per cent of Israel's yearly consumption amounts to about 475 m.c.m., which should be compared to the full potential of the West Bank aquifers: 600–800 m.c.m. (again, figures differ widely among different authors; see below). Shuval's figures assert that the potential of the West Bank aquifers amounts to 632 m.c.m. yearly

(Shuval, 1993: 46). Palestinian consumption in the West Bank amounts to 110 m.c.m. (*ibid.*). Tamimi argues that combined Arab and Israeli consumption amounts to 645–55 m.c.m., the Palestinian share of which was estimated at 110–20 m.c.m. (Tamimi, 1991/92: 7 f.).

According to these figures, then, approximately 82 per cent of the water resources of the West Bank is utilized by Israel proper or the Jewish settlements in the territory. The Palestinian inhabitants are thus restricted to (at the most) 18–20 per cent of the estimated potential of the area (JMCC, 1989: 3).

West Bank water resources are rather limited, but would – according to, for example, Heller (1983); Abed (1990); Heller and Nusseibeh (1991) – be sufficient to supply the Palestinian population.

Abed argues that the water resources of the West Bank are 'potentially more than adequate to meet the needs of the present and future population well into the next century' (*The Middle East*, August 1989). Water is the one resource which is abundant in the West Bank, and is 'the only West Bank/Gaza resource upon which Israel is dependent' (Heller, 1983: 129). On the other hand, Anderson notes that the actual amount of water in the West Bank is subject to discussion and confusion. Israel perceives the West Bank to be self-sufficient in water; in contrast, Jordan considers that *Israel* possesses abundant water resources within the pre-1967 borders (Anderson, 1988: 9). Elisha Kally writes:

> Each of these four areas: the Gaza Strip, Israel, the West Bank, and Jordan, *has sufficient water supplies from local sources to satisfy the present non-agricultural needs*. In terms of the future (meaning here the first two decades of the next century), this will still hold true for Jordan and Israel, *but not for the Gaza Strip and West Bank. The local and natural water sources in these two areas will not be able to satisfy their municipal demand.* None of these areas has enough water at the present time to satisfy the agricultural demands. (Kally, 1991/92: 8; original emphasis)

Kally does not distinguish between the needs of Jewish settlers and those of Palestinians. Adding up these needs plus future water demands for all sectors (municipal, agricultural and industrial), he estimates (*ibid.*: 11) that the West Bank water shortage will amount to 135 m.c.m. in 2010.

According to Heller and Nusseibeh (1991: 109), however, the overall water balance of the West Bank, including rainfall, amounts to 836 m.c.m., 'which is far in excess of present utilization rates by Palestinians, and still in excess of present utilization rates of West Bank waters by Palestinians and Israelis combined'. This leaves the West Bank with a positive balance of 200 m.c.m. (Heller and Nusseibeh, 1991: 109). The two authors further claim that there are still unexploited water reservoirs in the region. The crux of the matter is that tapping these resources would require extensive investment. Shuval states that there is an annual 60 m.c.m. of unutilized water in the eastern aquifer (Shuval, 1993: 47).

In contrast to the above-quoted statement by Heller and Nusseibeh, Shuval (1992a: 58f.), for example, claims that the Palestinians in both the West Bank and Gaza are in a position of 'water stress'. So whether the West Bank water supplies are sufficient to support its population or not is a debated issue. Perhaps it could be stated that whereas the current Palestinian population could be self-sufficient in water, it is the *joint dependency that causes stress*. In addition, a potential Palestinian state-formation with an influx of Palestinian refugees from neighbouring Arab countries would cause serious water supply difficulties.

Palestinian water usage is subject to harsh restrictions imposed by the Israeli government. Military Order 158 (1967) effectively controls the development and utilization of the sub-surface waters (Rowley, 1990: 39). The law establishes that:

> No person is allowed to establish or own or administer a water institution (any construction that is used to extract either surface or subterranean water resources or a processing plant) without a new official permit. It is permissible to deny an applicant a permit, revoke or amend a licence, without giving any explanation. The appropriate authorities may search and confiscate any water resources for which no permit exists, even if the owner has not been convicted. (Military Order 158, 19 November 1967, Amendment to Water Law 31, 1953, quoted in JMMC, 1993: 22)

So it is the area military commander who decides whether or not licences for owning or drilling for water are to be granted. Israeli sources claim that forty-six permissions have been granted to the Palestinian population, both by 'residents themselves and by the Civil Administration'. Only eight of these were for agricultural purposes, the remaining were for domestic use (Israel Information Service, 1991a). In addition, as Tamimi maintains, Palestinian wells may not exceed a depth of 140 metres, while Jewish wells may be deeper than 800 metres. This is one of the reasons why Palestinian wells have in many cases run dry (Tamimi, 1991/92: 6). Quiring states:

> This lack of water resource development, together with the confiscation of wells on 'absentee property', means that there are fewer wells providing less water for Palestinian agriculture in the Jordan Valley today than were avail-

able on the eve of the 1967 war. (*Middle East International*, September 1978, quoted by Davis *et al.*, 1980: 19)

Under the Absentee Property Law of 1950, 'all 1948 Palestinian Arab displaced persons and refugees' are declared absentees, which implies that they are 'alienated from all rights to Israeli citizenship, to their lands, and to their properties in Israel' (Davis, 1987: 17). Property and land of absentees could thus be confiscated by the state of Israel by virtue of law. Consequently, not only have draconian restrictions been imposed on drilling in the West Bank, but existing wells have been confiscated under the Absentee Property Law. In addition, restrictions are placed on the amount of water Palestinians are allowed to pump from each well. Availability of water is further subject to other means of repression by Israeli authorities. Cuts in water supplies is one of several economic sanctions utilized in order to curb the *intifada*. Official reasons for such cuts are often a failure in paying bills to Mekorot. In the dry summer months, West Bank towns and villages are frequently cut out of the water system for days or even weeks at a time.

What is more, Palestinians compete for the use of water not only with the state of Israel, but also with the Jewish settlers. Today, there are approximately 97,500 settlers in the West Bank, 3,500 in Gaza (Peace Now, quoted in *New Outlook*, January/February 1993: 24) and 120,000 in East Jerusalem (JMCC, *Weekly Report*, 17–23 March 1991: 8). In 1987, the settlers constituted about 10 per cent of the total population of the West Bank and contributed 35 per cent of GDP. The total amount of water consumed *in* the West Bank is 152–75 m.c.m (see above). Israeli sources reveal that total West Bank consumption amounted to 152 m.c.m. in 1988/89, and that 90 per cent – 137 m.c.m. of the total – was consumed by Palestinians (Israel Information Service, 1991a). Figures revealed by Lowi (drawing on Kolars, 1990) show that the Jewish settlements are allocated 40–50 m.c.m. (Lowi, 1992: 42), which implies that 22–33 per cent of the water consumed *in* the West Bank is used by the settlements. According to Saleh (1990), the water consumption of the Jewish settlers represented 52 per cent of the total consumption in the West Bank (Saleh, 1990: 337). Again, figures differ widely from author to author. What remains beyond doubt, however, is that there is a highly unequal distribution of water, to the disadvantage of the Palestinians.

In 1986, Jewish settlers exceeded their water quotas by 36.4 per cent (Schiff and Ya'ari, 1990: 97). Ninety-five per cent of the water consumed by the settlements is directed towards irrigation (Kahan,

1987: 113). Jewish settlers are not subordinated to Military Order 158 (or any other military rule), but are free to drill wells without permission. In addition, Tamimi claims that the Palestinians pay twice as much as Jewish settlers for the same amount of water (Tamimi, 1991/92: 7). The water consumption of Jewish settlers is subsidized by the government, which implies price differentials for Palestinians and settlers (see also Elmusa, 1993: 63; Lowi, 1992: 41). Mekorot has thus worked to develop water sources primarily for the Jewish settlers.

Israeli fears of Palestinian drilling constitute quite a different problem from the Palestinian perspective. Deep drilling on behalf of the Jewish settlers seriously affects Palestinian wells and springs, which to an increasing extent have become saline or even dried up. The intensified establishment of Jewish settlements during the former Likud-led government (which lost power to a Labour-led coalition in June 1992) further aggravates the West Bank water stress. The fact is that Israel could not do without the West Bank water – a fact which has produced inextricably entangled relations of joint dependency on the same water resources.

The unbalanced 'ethnic power structure' which works to the detriment of the Palestinians and the unequal distribution of water adds to the grievances experienced by the Palestinians. Control over the West Bank waters is perceived as an indispensable necessity, and eventual Palestinian statehood is perceived as a threat to Israel's water security.

Palestinian development hampered

Palestinian lack of water is thus a result of the military occupation, which has characterized all facets of life in the West Bank and Gaza since 1967. Furthermore, Palestinian agriculture has been made dependent on the water allocation system established by the military occupation. Although most of the water consumed by West Bank and Gaza Palestinians is for domestic use, lack of water is a serious constraint on the development of Palestinian agriculture. In the period 1983–5, agriculture represented 25.4 per cent of the total GDP of the West Bank – a reduction from 37.4 per cent in 1968–70 (Kahan, 1987: 14). Palestinian agriculture in the West Bank is dependent on rain, which falls seldom and irregularly, and production is related to the rainfall, so that yields vary dramatically. The low profitability of rainfed agriculture means that any development is reliant on the development of irrigation. As we have seen, however, Palestinian use of water for irrigation is severely restricted by Israeli authorities so as not to affect Israeli pumping needs.

Following the occupation of 1967 (under the Labour government), Israel's development strategy was directed towards integrating the economies of the occupied territories closely with the Israeli economy. Improvement of water utilization and increasing irrigation would stimulate the agricultural development of the West Bank. As a result, there was a slight increase in the area of irrigated land, while cultivation of non-irrigated field crops decreased. In 1986, most of the irrigated land of the West Bank was utilized for field crops and vegetables. A large portion (30 per cent of the total) was set aside for fruit trees. Thirty-two per cent of the irrigated dunams were watered by traditional systems, although major changes have been made. Traditional irrigation systems have to a large extent been replaced by modern capital-intensive methods. Yield per dunam did progress up to 1975–6, but thereafter the overall trend has been one of decreasing yields. This is partly due to problems of irrigation and a lack of water (Kahan, 1987: 17, 33 ff.). The soil conditions and topography of the West Bank actually make it unsuitable for irrigation (Heller, 1983: 130). According to Kahan (1987: 129), only 6 per cent of the land was irrigated in 1985. Constraints are also related to low efficiency in the carrying of water to farms and the use of traditional systems of irrigation. Waste is also the result of inadequate management of springs and wells. Moreover, water rights are often based on the number of pumping hours allocated to each farm, which encourages farmers to overirrigate (*ibid.*: 89 ff.). Palestinian agriculture is also obstructed through the dumping of Israeli produce and the restrictions on export of Palestinian produce, as well as by repressive Israeli measures such as curfews and other collective punishments; but also by internal Palestinian structures and a rural economy based on patron–client relations.

The potential Palestinian demand for irrigation water in 1986 was 345 m.c.m., according to Kahan (1987: 164). Kally's (1991/92: 10) figure is more moderate: he states that the expected demand for irrigation in the West Bank is 180 m.c.m. The technology needed for the installation of irrigation systems capable of reducing evaporation, and thus the risk of salinization, is capital-intensive – an impediment to the development of such techniques. Installation of irrigation systems would also imply that tapping would be pursued on the western subterranean aquifer, thus affecting the water available to Israel and further enhancing salinity (Heller, 1983: 89). In any political settlement of the Israeli–Palestinian conflict, therefore, a bilateral agreement on water utilization is an absolute necessity, as is joint management.

Naturally, in estimates of future demands the influx of Palestinians from surrounding Arab states and other parts of the world must be included.

Lack of water in Gaza

There is an alarming water shortage in Gaza. Water is extremely scarce, and the little there is suffers from pollution. This emergency situation makes Gaza perhaps one of the most critical spots in the Middle East. Gaza camp residents consume approximately 44 litres of water a day, less than the minimum emergency ratio specified by the World Health Organization (*Jordan Times*, 21 November 1993).

The Gaza Strip is one of the most densely populated areas in the world. The population was approximately 700,000 in 1991. It is estimated that the population will reach 1.48 million by 2010 (Heiberg and Øvensen, 1993: 74). These mounting population figures will put heavy pressure upon already scarce resources. The water scarcity in Gaza does not affect only agriculture: water for drinking and domestic consumption is also at risk. Shuval writes:

> Gaza already faces a severe and immediate water crisis with much of its drinking water hardly fit for human consumption. Gaza cannot survive without the immediate importation of good quality water from desalination or an external source such as the Nile–*El Arish* pipeline. (Shuval, 1993: 65 f.)

In Gaza, water shortage and poor water quality have thus reached such alarming levels that the *drinking* water is exposed to acute dangers. Water – or rather, the lack of it – is thus one of the reasons why life in Gaza is difficult. Combined with lack of land, lack of development, lack of sewage, lack of public services, lack of employment, poverty and the ever-present occupation structures, this has served to aggravate the socioeconomic grievances of the Palestinians. The autonomy for Gaza (and Jericho) that was implemented in May 1994 has not yet (autumn 1995) seemed to alleviate the water situation in Gaza, although donor countries are to invest in the water sector.

The only source of water in the Gaza Strip is groundwater in sandstone aquifers, and the only surface water is collected in wadis. Sixty m.c.m. of renewable water a year is available, while Gazans use 95 m.c.m. every year through overpumping (Wolf and Ross, 1992: 925). Lack of fresh water was the major constraint on the development of Gaza's agriculture in the pre-1967 period (Kahan, 1987: 12). Overexploitation results in a loss of water exceeding the natural replenishment rate, as well as sea water intrusion. The groundwater level is being reduced by 15–20 centimetres a year. Gaza's location by the sea makes its limited fresh water resources extremely vulnerable to overpumping. Once the delicate balance between fresh water and sea water has been damaged, it is difficult to restore. Sea water has already extended 1.5 kilometres into the sweetwater aquifer (*ibid.*: 24). Palestinians claim that the salinization of Gaza's water is due to Israeli pumping of groundwater close to the boundaries. On the other hand, Israeli hydrologists assert that the salinization of water in Gaza is due to overpumping by the Palestinian population during the period prior to 1967 (Shuval, 1993: 65). After the 1967 war, there was inadequate control of the permits for water drilling, resulting in too many new boreholes: 'Farmers drilled and used as much water as they wanted' (Kahan, 1987: 25). In the mid-1970s, however, harsh restrictions were imposed upon permits for digging new wells, limiting the amount of water available to Gazan peasants and farmers. In addition, the use of pesticides and fertilizers and the insufficient sewerage services have led to serious contamination, affecting health conditions.

Deterioration of water has a detrimental effect on agriculture. In the period 1983–5, agriculture amounted to 15.9 per cent of Gaza's total GDP, a decrease from 28.8 per cent in 1968–70 (Kahan, 1987: 14). Furthermore, Gaza's agriculture is based to a large extent upon citrus fruit, with a high demand for water. The irrigated area of the Gaza Strip amounted in 1987 to 50 per cent of the total cultivated area, which equals 108,500 dunams (*ibid.*: 26). Potential water demand for irrigation is estimated at 130 m.c.m. (Kally, quoted in Kahan, 1987: 90).

Jewish settlements in Gaza are mostly located along the southern coast, near the aquifer, and the agriculture of the settlements is 87 per cent directed towards citrus fruit. Sixty per cent of the total cultivated land on the settlements is irrigated (Kahan, 1987: 110). Israeli sources claim that Jewish settlers' consumption amounts to 3 per cent of the total consumption in Gaza, and that the Jewish settlers use sophisticated drilling methods, enabling them to use water that would otherwise flow into the sea (Israel Information Service, 1991a). Gaza settlers receive most of their water from the Israeli National Water Carrier.

Gaza's precarious situation could perhaps be improved by utilizing Nile water transported by pipelines; this, however, would impinge upon Egypt's water situation, which is already precarious, and would make the Palestinians dependent on Egyptian goodwill. There are also plans for a desalination plant in Gaza (Shuval, 1993: 66), and for increased conservation of rainwater to alleviate the situation (Shawwa, 1993: 31 ff.).

As for the Nile (see Hultin, Chapter 1 in this volume), there was in fact a proposal to sell water from the Nile to Israel in relation to the Camp David accords of 1978/79. The project was not implemented due to internal resistance in Egypt and Ethiopia. While Kally (1991/92: 22) seems still to consider a project to sell water from Egypt to Israel, which could also supply Gaza and parts of the West Bank with a certain amount of water, a viable option, Tamimi (1991/ 92: 22) is more sceptical, in view of the Egyptian water situation. Shuval mentions the importation of water from Egypt to Gaza and the Negev as a possible way of overcoming the current water stress, as part of a 'Regional Water for Peace Plan' in the Middle East (Shuval, 1992: 139; 1993).

Concluding Comments: Water as an Imperative for Regional Cooperation?

In analyses of the Palestinian–Israeli and Arab–Israeli conflicts, water is a frequently forgotten topic, although during the last few years it has been increasingly acknowledged. Yet as I have tried to show throughout this essay, it is a matter of tremendous importance, although I do not by any means wish to argue that water is the only determining factor behind the conflicts between Israel and the Palestinians or Israel and the Arab states. One cannot study Israeli water politics without discussing her security politics and her relations with the neighbouring states and with the Palestinians. Likewise, one cannot analyse the overall conflicts without addressing the issue of water.

Frustration over unequal distribution of water exacerbates Palestinian grievances. The denial of access to the water resources of the West Bank, and the very lack of it in Gaza, threaten the economic development of the West Bank and Gaza, and human well-being. In this sense, the water needs of Israel are a threat to the Palestinians. In addition, the scarcity of water in the region is in itself to be considered a threat to states and peoples. Israeli dependency on water located outside her pre-1967 borders is a tremendously important aspect of state security. The current water stress in the region and the increasing salinization of fresh water create an *ecological* threat to regional security of an as yet unknown kind.

At the same time, joint Israeli, Palestinian, Jordanian and Syrian dependency on the Jordan River basin, as well as Israeli and Palestinian dependency on West Bank aquifers, render peaceful and co-operative relations even more indispensable.

In view of population increases not only through birth rates but also through large-scale immigration to Israel, Jordan and, potentially, the West Bank, water will remain scarce. There are basically two ways of alleviating water scarcity: either to increase supply, which could be done through technical developments such as desalination or regional import schemes; or to decrease demand. Both approaches are needed if the water situation is to be improved. Kally (1991/92: 32) argues that the problem of water in the West Bank and Gaza can be resolved only through importation – a project which must be worked out in a regional co-operation scheme.

Shuval argues that a regional water importation scheme should be implemented. This scheme could include the following: a pipeline could be built from the Nile which could thus provide Gaza, as well as the Israeli Negev desert, with water; another pipeline could be built from the Litani River to be stored in the Sea of Galilee to supply the West Bank, the Galilee region in northern Israel and Jordan with additional water; and finally, a smaller variant of the proposed Turkish Peace Pipeline (see Schulz, Chapter 3 in this volume) could contribute water to Syria, Jordan and the West Bank (Shuval, 1992: 139 ff.; 1993: 66 ff.). Importation of water through pipelines crossing several state borders is, however, problematic in several ways. First, it would be an immensely costly project. Second, all states involved, if only through having a pipeline crossing their territory, would have to give their approval. Third, in a situation characterized by political conflict and uncertainty, there is a risk of water supply being cut off in the event of potential hostilities, or of pipelines and infrastructure being targets for military violence by militant groups. Shuval's solution to this predicament would be for Turkey to supply Syria with additional water, replacing the supplies currently drawn from the Yarmouk, in turn leaving scope for Jordanian and Palestinian use of the Yarmouk (Shuval, 1993: 73). The Turkish pipelines would not cross that many international borders.

Furthermore, if Jordan received additional water from the proposed Unity Dam on the Yarmouk, or other sources, she could help to alleviate the Palestinian situation through building the Western Ghor Canal so that it runs partly on the western side of the Jordan River (Shuval, 1993: 64). With the Jordanian–Israeli agreement, this proposal may become a reality.

Turkey (see Chapter 3), one of the few Middle Eastern countries which possesses an abundance of water, is also involved in other discussions on the alarming water situation in the Middle East. Turkish private firms have also been involved in negotiations with the Israeli Water Commission for eventual water transport in huge floating polyurethane bags from water-wealthy Turkey to the far poorer Israel. These discussions have been subject to much criticism from Arab states. Recently, there have been reports that bags capable of containing up to 3.5 m.c.m. will soon be in production by a Canadian company. Such an advance may help to alleviate the region's water scarcity in a manner which would be cheaper than desalination (*The Middle East*, May 1994: 13). There are also proposals that water from the Litani River could be used by Israel, Jordan and the Palestinians (Lesch, 1992: 133).

The Middle East peace conference, initiated by the USA following the Gulf War, which began in Madrid in October 1991, also dealt with water issues. The forum for this was the multilateral part of the conference which discussed several issues of a regional character, among them the matter of water. Invited participants were Israel, the Jordanian–Palestinian delegation, Syria, Lebanon, Egypt, the Gulf states, the North African Arab states, the USA, the OSS, the EC, Canada and Japan. Syria and Lebanon refused to participate in the multilaterals. At the multilateral discussions on water in Vienna in 1992, Israel, Jordan and the Palestinians agreed to co-operate on hydrological data, previously withheld from the Palestinians. The third session on water was held in Geneva in 1993, and there was some progress. Desalination projects were discussed, and there were seminars on regional water co-operation (Israel Information Service, 7 June 1993). Another session took place in Oman in April 1994; here again progress was noted. The parties agreed, for example, on the establishment of a Palestinian Water Authority to distribute and manage water resources in Gaza and Jericho. Also in the bilateral discussions, water has been an unavoidable issue. The Declaration of Principles (DOP) signed between Israel and the PLO on 13 September 1993 includes a commitment to co-operation in the field of water, including a Water Development Programme, which is to work out the principles of management and water rights, as well as 'equitable utilisation'. The DOP also included a commitment to the establishment of a Palestinian Water Administration Authority (Declaration of Principles on Interim Self-government Arrangements, in *Journal of Palestine Studies*, vol. XXIII [89], no. 1, Autumn 1993: 115–21).

In order to enhance the security of the region and to obtain a satisfactory guarantee of resources for development, it is of paramount importance that the current anarchic water relations are transformed and elevated into a 'mature regional security complex' (Buzan, 1991), and that joint institutions for management be set up, a process perhaps to be initiated by the multilaterals, the DOP and the Jordanian–Israeli peace agreement. On co-operation on the Jordan River, Israel, Syria, Jordan and the Palestinians would be the relevant parties involved in such a management institution; on co-operation on West Bank aquifers, the Palestinians and Israel would be the concerned actors. It should be emphasized, however, that in the case of the Jordan River basin there is precious little water to share; this has a negative impact upon the actors' willingness to cooperate. The interests and needs at stake are vital for all parties. Importation of water from other countries in the region might thus be a necessary condition for overcoming the water crisis – a scenario which, due to political constraints and conflicts, may not be a realistic one. Israel has developed a master-plan for regional water management and sharing in the case of peace, written by the chief water engineer of Tahal for the Jaffee Center of Strategic Studies at Tel Aviv University. The report, however, is classified (Lesch, 1992: 148, Note 38).

There is growing insight that there is no way out of the water trap, and the current situation of a zero-sum game, except co-operation. What is clear is that regional co-operation on water utilization and management is of paramount necessity in order to enhance the security of every region involved – including the West Bank and Gaza. The vulnerable predicament of each region can be overcome only through co-operation. The transnational character of ecological issues (the flow of rivers does not take state borders into consideration) creates an opportunity for alliances built on environmental concerns. The Middle East is, however, perhaps on its way to implementing regional water co-operation schemes through overall agreements relating also to other issues of conflict, and close to the point where such schemes are inevitable from the perspective of security for states and peoples.

Notes

1. It should be emphasized that many of the figures and assessments given throughout this essay are accounts of parties in a conflict and not altogether objective and reliable descriptions. Figures differ widely between various sources, so I have tried to present different accounts and figures, or the figures most frequently used in the literature.

2. The Johnston Plan suggested the following division of waters. From the Yarmouk River, 377 m.c.m. were to be allocated to Jordan, while 25 m.c.m. were to be allotted to Israel and 90 m.c.m. to Syria; from the Jordan River 100 m.c.m. were to be apportioned to Jordan (water from the Sea of Galilee was also included in this amount), and 22 m.c.m. were to go to Syria, while the remaining flows of the Jordan were to be allotted to Israel. The share of the Jordan that was to be allocated to Israel was never specified, but was estimated at 361 m.c.m. In addition, Jordan was to receive 243 m.c.m. from wadis and wells, Syria was to be given access to 20 m.c.m. from the Banyias, and Lebanon was to be allocated 35 m.c.m. from the Hasbani (Taubenblatt, 1988: 45). See Lowi (1992:47 ff.) for a critique of the Johnston Plan from the perspective of conflict resolution. Israel also argued that the Litani River should be included in the plan; this, however, was rejected by Johnston as well as the Arab states on the grounds that the Litani was entirely within Lebanon's borders. The main concern for Israel was not to be stopped from diverting water to the Negev (Reuger, 1993: 60), and she tried to obtain US support for such a diversion scheme, though at the same time not violating the Johnston Plan's distribution quotas (*ibid.*: 72) Reuger further notes that the plan is ambiguous and that all the parties concerned, including the USA, have different figures for the actual allocations (*ibid.*: 79)

3

Turkey, Syria and Iraq:
A Hydropolitical Security Complex

Michael Schulz

This chapter[1] deals with the emerging water problems and their security implications for the Middle East, in particular the predicament of Turkey, Syria and Iraq. Shortage of water has further heightened the already existing tension between many of the states in the region. Malin Falkenmark points out the importance of water:

> The central importance of water to life processes prompts the plausible hypothesis that socioeconomic development would be particularly difficult to achieve in countries where dry and hot climate does not allow easy access to water neither for plants nor for humans. (Falkenmark, 1990: 7)

An examination of the relations between Turkey, Syria and Iraq in the context of their dependence on the Euphrates and Tigris waters will be pursued. Theoretically, these aspects can be defined as a hydropolitical security complex. The concept of a regional security complex is elaborated by Buzan (1991). Hydropolitics must be seen as one dimension of ecopolitics. Ecopolitics is becoming, rather rapidly, a major concern for most states in the Middle East.

> The severity of Middle Eastern water problems will unavoidably increase substantially during the remainder of this century. (*MEED*, January 1991: 10, quoting from the Middle East Research Institute at the University of Pennsylvania in the 1984 publication Water in the Middle East.)

Lester Brown points out the necessity of including the ecological dimension in economic development planning:

> The deterioration of the earth's biological systems is not a peripheral issue of concern only to environmentalists. The global economy depends on these biological systems. Anything that threatens their viability threatens the global

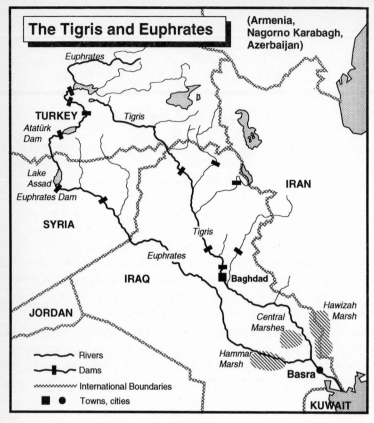

Map 3.1

economy. Any deterioration in these systems represents a deterioration in the human prospect. (Brown, 1977: 7)

The shortage of water has made ecopolitics – or rather, hydropolitics – a major issue for states like Turkey, Syria and Iraq. At the same time the water issue links these states' national security. National security must therefore include the ecological dimension. In turn, this makes it necessary to introduce a broader conception of issue-orientated security analysis. My intention is to elaborate and test this perspective on one case, contributing yet another dimension to the concept of 'regional security complex' (Buzan, 1991; Buzan and Rizvi, 1986).

The rainfall in the Middle East varies from 250 to 400 millimetres per annum, but in Maghreb, and some parts of Lebanon, Iran and Turkey, the annual rainfall amounts to as much as 1,000 mm. Agriculture demands at least 400 mm per annum. For Turkey – and to a much larger extent for Syria and Iraq – dependence on the Euphrates and Tigris is high. The Euphrates and Tigris are two rivers that have constituted a lifeline for human beings in the Middle East since 3500 BC, when the Sumerians established the first civilization around them. Ever since the 1950s there has been a dramatic increase in water requirements due to population growth and advanced development planning. Turkey, Syria and Iraq all have rapidly growing populations and are at the same time pursuing development strategies that are heavily dependent on water. All three states are using water from the same sources, which may create a situation of 'overuse', implying scarcity of water, if the problem of management co-operation is not solved.

Today, therefore, water is a concern for national security in most Middle Eastern states. Turkey is the state which controls the headwaters of the Euphrates and the Tigris. Still, parts of Anatolia province, in southeast Turkey, are suffering from a general shortage of water. The downstream states of Syria and Iraq are even more dependent on the river water as an alternative to insufficient rainfall. Although shortage of water is not an imminent problem, it could become a dire emergency in the very near future.

The real problems the three states are currently facing are the problems of *management, apportionment* and *development planning,* which have led to disagreements between them. The risk of future water shortage therefore constitutes one of the most strategically important security issues for the above-mentioned states. The fact that Turkey has a Ministry of Energy, Iraq has a Minister of Irrigation and Syria a Minister for the Euphrates Dam proves the high governmental priority given to the Euphrates–Tigris basin.

The joint dependency on the river waters clearly indicates that the national security of all the states is linked. The security perception must therefore be based on the region as a level of analysis. The traditional definition of national security is thus questioned. In the future, economic, environmental and ecological dimensions must also be included in the understanding of national security. As Michael Renner points out:

> An estimated 40 percent of the world's population depends for drinking water, irrigation, or hydropower on the 214 major river systems shared by

two or more countries; 12 of these waterways are shared by five or more nations. (Renner, 1989: 37)

The Middle East is an area of heated political tension with ethnic, religious and national implications due to the region's state- and nation-building processes. New dimensions of the already often complex conflict pattern must be further elaborated. The looming ecological crisis in the region has for too long been neglected in social science (see Starr and Stoll, eds, 1988; Starr, 1991; Rabo, 1986; Falkenmark, 1989b; Kolars, 1986). The water dimension will have tremendous future implications for the regional security, and could thereby change the whole shape and structure of the Middle Eastern region.

> A Central Intelligence Agency risk assessment paper for the United States government has estimated that in at least ten places in the world war could erupt over dwindling shared water resources. The majority of those potential crisis spots are in the Middle East; it was no accident that when, in 1992, the Pentagon undertook a drastic review of possible future conflicts that might call for American intervention, one of the first contingencies studied was a war between Syria and Turkey. (Bulloch and Darwish, 1993: 16)

To enable us to find some of the reasons for the water disputes between Turkey, Syria and Iraq, the following questions will be examined:

- What are the causes of tension over water between Turkey, Syria and Iraq?
- How are Turkey, Syria and Iraq respectively using their water from the Euphrates and Tigris?
- Have there been any attempts to solve the disputes and to find co-operative options that would serve as an impetus for Turkey, Syria and Iraq to share the water supplies?
- How could Turkey, Syria and Iraq solve their water problems in the future, and what options are there for new co-operative structures and institutions to deal with water disputes?

In order to answer these questions, I will follow certain analytical steps. The first step is to define and delimit the hydropolitical security complex as one complex, or set of complexes, in the Middle Eastern region. The second is to make an inventory of those states and other actors, mainly ethno-religious groups, involved in the complex, and relate them, in an analytical hierarchy, to other complexes. The third is to analyse the various sources of change that can result in co-operation on water in the future.

Water Shortage in the Middle East

The water shortage in Israel, Syria and Jordan and their dependency on water from the Jordan River is a factor which is to be added to the already complex Palestinian–Israeli security complex (see Lindholm's contribution, Chapter 2 in this volume). Morocco, Tunisia, Algeria, Egypt and the states in the Arabian Peninsula are heading for an enormous crisis, since groundwater levels and supplies are rapidly reaching the perilous zone (Starr, 1991: 17).

There is also a close relationship between growing population rates and the need for more investments and regulations to enhance the water supply in the region. Egypt, for example, is in desperate need of water and is at the same time expecting an estimated population of 75 million by the year 2000. The future costs of water supply will be tremendous, and compared to other regions in the world the median cost *per capita* is already the highest in the Middle East. Joyce Starr (1991) refers to a World Bank Report estimating that the median cost *per capita* was 300 US dollars in 1985. At the same time, the current situation and the future prospect of costs and supply possibilities do not allow any further increase in the use of water (Starr, 1991).

Turkey's energy demands, for instance, are rising dramatically, as is her population, which is estimated to have grown from 21 million in 1950 to 45 million in 1980 (Kolars, 1986: 54). In 1990 Turkey had a population of 56.5 million; with annual average growth rates of 2.2 per cent, this is set to exceed 70 million by the year 2000 (Beschorner, 1992: 29). Furthermore, the populations of Syria and Iraq are growing rapidly, implying increased water requirements. With this estimated future population growth, the three states, especially Syria and Iraq, will soon reach the critical level of water scarcity. This will further complicate the problems of management.

Rivers like the Euphrates, the Tigris, the Nile, and the Jordan are all shared by several states; at the same time, most of these states are heavily dependent on the river waters. It is, however, easier for an upstream state, since the possibility of controlling the supply for irri-gation is not dependent on the goodwill of other states. Turkey is the headwater state to the Euphrates and Tigris, and is therefore able to control the output. Turkey is also the most water-rich state in the region, with the exception of perhaps Lebanon and Iran, and at the same time, ironically, an oil-poor state. Still, the water shortage in other regions requires closer co-operation between the states involved. From the perspective of a security complex one could express it as follows:

> On this basis, security complexes can be treated as objects for policy in the sense *that problems can only be resolved within the context of the relevant complex as a whole.* (Buzan, 1991: 225, emphasis added)

Unfortunately, since World War II the disputes over water in the region have escalated. The step to war over water is close. Syria and Iraq were very close to full-scale war in 1975 because of a disagreement over the use of the Euphrates water. Disputes between Turkey, Syria and Iraq were quite common during the 1980s, especially after the Turkish presentation of the Güneydogu Anadolu Projesi (GAP) project at the end of the 1970s. Its centrepiece, the Atatürk Dam, was initiated in 1983 when construction began. Still, it is not the water scarcity in itself which creates the tense situation among the states but, rather, the complex underlying webs of other conflict patterns. Political distrust and disagreement are impediments to solving the problems of water management. The water issue could therefore be seen as yet another catalyst to an already combustible security situation.

> In an already overheated atmosphere of political hostility, insufficient water to satisfy burgeoning human, developmental and security needs among all nations of the Middle East heightens the ambient tensions. (*MEED*, January 1991: 10)

The Euphrates–Tigris Hydropolitical Security Complex

The Euphrates and the Tigris are the two largest rivers in the Middle East (excluding the Nile); the Euphrates is the longest (2,700 kilometres) in the whole region of West Asia. Both rivers rush down from the Anatolian highland regions and on the lower mountains they curl down to the Mesopotamian plain, where their colours change from black due to soil erosion to a more brownish shade. From a satellite, the map in the Mesopotamian desert plain in Syria looks yellow where the river banks are surrounded by a green belt which turns completely yellow further south in the Iraqi desert. Finally, both rivers unite to form the Shatt al Arab River, which flows into the Persian/Arabian Gulf. (It should be noted that the Gulf is perceived as Persian from the Iranian perspective and Arabic from an 'Arab' viewpoint. I simply call it the Persian/Arabian Gulf, at the risk of insulting both parties.) In periods of flooding, massive water amounts and sediment around the rivers cause problems for all states, in particular for Iraq.

The concept of hydropolitical security complex should contribute to the understanding and analysis of how water scarcity is affecting the security situation for Turkey, Syria and Iraq, and what underlying conflicts can be identified. The analysis, of course, has to be done from the perspective of water.

According to Barry Buzan's definition of the regional security complex – 'a group of states whose primary security concerns link together sufficiently closely that their national securities cannot realistically be considered apart from one another' (Buzan, 1991: 190) – it could be argued that various security issues among states link their national security concerns. The Middle East could also be seen as a regional security complex full of other sets of security complexes, or subcomplexes, which all have their own security issue that connect the states in inextricably entangled relations. The Palestinian issue is a security concern for many states in the region and thereby forms, in an analytical way, the Palestinian-Israeli security complex (Schulz, 1989).

From the perspective of this book, the Euphrates and Tigris form the security issue for the three 'user' states, and are thereby in focus from a security perspective. The hydropolitical security complex is thus defined as including those states that are geographically part 'owners' and technically 'users' of the rivers and further, as a consequence, consider the rivers as a major national security issue. In this way Turkey, Syria and Iraq compose a security complex or, rather, form *the Euphrates and Tigris hydropolitical security complex*.

Each of the above-mentioned states is linked to other security complexes in the Middle Eastern region with other security issues; this in turn creates new analytical complexes. The vertical horizontal relations to other complexes will be further elaborated, although the horizontal level is the most important. Vertical relations imply those security issues that can be related to a higher structural level, such as superpower rivalry (in this case indirectly), whereas horizontal relations are security issues related to the same structural level, such as the Palestinian–Israeli conflict. The Kuwait–Iraq war must also be included as part of the analysis. This implies that the great powers can, as indicated above, be implicitly related to the hydropolitical security complex. Territorial disputes between states like Iraq and Kuwait, or Iraq and Iran, have been and are common in the Middle East. Iraq, for instance, has always been considered a threat to some states in the Arabian Peninsula. Roberson writes:

> The attitude of the GCC states towards Iraq was long-standing in that Baghdad had inherited Ottoman policies towards the Gulf. This is the background to the territorial disputes involving Iraq with Kuwait, Iran and Saudi Arabia. (Roberson, 1986: 164–5)

The formation of the complexes is constantly changing, and the security issues also alter over time; this in turn can transform the sets of complexes in the Middle Eastern region. Roberson explains the constantly changing complex formation as follows:

> Because these states [in the Middle East] are new, the pattern of their relationships is in an early stage of development. A prominent feature of the developing Middle East state system is a constant pattern of realignment which has thus far prevented the rise of a hegemonic power. This feature underlines the supreme difficulty in establishing regional security, a feature within which the Arab statesmen move and breathe. (Roberson, 1986: 160–61)

The constant pattern of realignment between Middle Eastern states further enhances insecurity in the relations between Turkey, Syria and Iraq and in the region as a whole. In order to outline the structure of the hydropolitical security complex, let us first make an inventory of the above-mentioned states as related to the Euphrates and Tigris basin.

The hydropolitics of Turkey

To a great extent, the water needs of Turkey must be seen from a development perspective. To modernize and industrialize as well as increase output from agriculture, Turkish energy demands have drastically increased since the 1950s. The state Hydraulic Works was created in 1953 in order to – among other tasks – construct dams for hydroelectricity generation.

As we saw above, Turkey is the state, with the exceptions of Lebanon and perhaps Iran, with the best water situation of all the countries in the Middle East. Yet some parts of Turkey are suffering from water shortage, not least the metropolitan areas of Istanbul,

Ankara and Izmir, and along the Aegean and the Mediterranean coasts as a result of tourist development. Water shortage is, however, also mainly a consequence of the priority given by Ankara to supplying eastern parts of the country as well as industrial complexes in the southeast with water from the various dams situated in the southeast. The local population, therefore, gains a much lower amount of water from these dams. The Euphrates and the Tigris are the two most important rivers which make it possible to irrigate the agricultural areas of Anatolia to produce electricity and drinking water. The poorly industrialized and underdeveloped nature of the southeastern parts of Turkey, with sparse employment possibilities, has long been a reason for emigration to Western Europe. The Turkish government has tried to realize several development plans and, in this way, to create a more even development among the various parts of Turkey. The southeast is therefore in focus for this planning. Both the Tigris and the Euphrates have been under consideration by development planners for diverting water to these areas also, but it is mainly on the Euphrates that these projects have been realized hitherto. The first scheme was the Keban Dam, finished in 1973 (Starr and Stoll, 1988: 12).

The GAP project, initiated in 1983 and intended to be completed by the year 2006, including the massive Atatürk Dam, is designed to stop the periodic flooding of areas next to the rivers, to create electricity and an opportunity to irrigate dry cultivated areas. *The Middle East* (October 1989: 20) mentions the year 2001, whereas *Time* (5 February 1990: 32) estimates the year of completion at 2005. The exact date is, naturally, difficult to pin down, since the plans and prospects are changing all the time owing to technical and financial obstacles. The whole project includes thirteen smaller projects, seven on the Euphrates and six on the Tigris, and involves an area of 74,000 square kilometres with 4.5 million inhabitants. The area which will be irrigated is 1.6 million hectares which will double Turkey's production of cotton, oil and feedplants, as well as rice. The final project will result in 80 dams, 66 hydroelectric power plants and 68 irrigation systems bringing water to the 1.6 million hectares of land. Most of the funding of the GAP project is provided from Turkish sources. The World Bank's refusal to give financial support is based on the fact that there is no agreement on water rights between the riparian states (Beschorner, 1992: 31–2; *The Middle East*, 11 March 1990; October 1989: 20; Kolars, 1986: 53–67).

The hydropolitics of Syria

Although rivers like the Asi (Orontes is its Turkish name while Asi is its Arabic name) and the Yarmouk are used by Syria, she is mainly dependent on the Euphrates and, to a much smaller extent, on the Tigris. Syria is using the water mainly for domestic consumption, irrigation and industrial purposes. The Euphrates, however, has not been adequately utilized in a region known to have a highly fertile soil. As early as 1947 the first scientific study of the exploitation potential of the river was presented. In 1956 Syria planned the Al-Ghab valley project, which also involved drying swamps and opening new areas for cultivation, including a new dam on the Asi River. In 1966 the USSR and Syria agreed that the USSR would provide Syria with equipment and technical assistance. Still, by 1961 Syria had started to plan several large-scale projects on the Euphrates. The General Administration for the Development of the Euphrates Basin was set up in 1968. Syria also created a Ministry for the Euphrates Dam. The Tabqa Dam, completed in 1973, became one of the first important sources of power production and irrigation. The water around the dam is forming an artificial lake called the Assad Lake (Tabqa Lake) with a storage capacity of 11.9 billion cubic metres of water (Bari, 1977: 234–5; Maoz and Yaniv, 1986: 95–6).

The population rise in Syria, 3.4 per cent per annum, is one of the highest in the world, and may in the future create serious problems related to the supply of fresh water. Power cuts and water shortages in the cities are regular occurrences. In the winter of 1988–9 the rainfall was 40 per cent (*Middle East Review*, 1990: 161–2) below average. This seriously damaged the wheat crop as well as the water level of the Euphrates, leading to a reduced electricity output. The cotton harvest was also badly affected by the 1987–8 summer drought, and fell from 126,000 tonnes in 1986–7 to 96,489 tonnes (*ibid.*).

More power station construction and expansion programmes have been launched in recent years; among the first was the Euphrates Dam (completed in 1978), financially assisted by the Soviet Union. The dam project was also part of the drainage improvements to the Euphrates valley. It was, however, disturbed by the appearance of chalks and by the saltiness of the Euphrates water (Maoz and Yaniv, 1986: 48). In 1988, at least nine major power station schemes were under way (*Middle East Review*, 1989: 156). Although Syria has invested huge amounts of money in developing the irrigation system for the agriculture sector, it is still at a disappointingly low level. In 1986 only 11 per cent (*ibid.*: 157) of the cultivated land in Syria was artificially irrigated by Euphrates water.

However, the latest developments in Syria have transformed the income structure from agricultural production, mainly cotton, towards expansion of the more profitable oil sector.

The hydropolitics of Iraq

Iraq is the last downstream state where the Tigris and Euphrates rivers finally unite and flow out into the Persian/Arabian Gulf. Iraq is strongly dependent on the goodwill of Turkey and Syria to let enough water flow through the Euphrates to the Iraqi side. The river is used for both irrigation and desalination. At the same time, Iraq is trying to prevent and control the floods in order to prevent recurrent large-scale destruction. The first barrage was built in 1955–6, making it possible to divert the water to the Habbaniya Lake. However, in addition to the Euphrates, the Tigris, because of its greater volume, is the river which is mostly used for controlling the floods. The Samara barrage on the Tigris, which was also built in 1955–6, together with the Euphrates barrage, protected Iraq from flood catastrophe (Bari, 1977: 232–3).

Iraq has also developed advanced irrigation systems for its agricultural sector. Today, she is using sophisticated techniques to irrigate the agricultural areas around the two rivers. It is estimated that 50 per cent of Iraq's agricultural area is irrigated. Iraq is the only state – apart, perhaps, from Israel – in the Middle East which is considered to be self-sufficient in agriculture, based on irrigation. The high output from irrigated farming depends on huge investments in new technology (Starr and Stoll, 1988: 12; Springborg, 1986: 33–52).

Having outlined the fundamentals of the hydropolitics of each of the states included in the Euphrates–Tigris hydropolitical security complex, we shall now delve into the role of water in the relations between the affected states.

Main Conflicts of the Euphrates–Tigris Hydropolitical Security Complex

How, then, did disputes over water arise between the states? What kind of problems have caused these disputes? The following three

sections give a chronological description of incidents that have caused
tension between the states, and the kinds of problems that have arisen
during the years.

Several conflict formations dealing with water could be identified.
Carl Widstrand has identified and divided conflicts over water under
the following five headings, which could also be seen as five research
areas (Widstrand, 1980):

- conflicts between upstream and downstream states;
- conflicts between governments and farmers;
- conflicts between farmers;
- conflicts between donors;
- ecological conflicts.

It is – as will be shown – necessary to include two more points:

- conflicts between the state and ethno-religious groups;
- inter and intra conflicts between ethno-religious groups.

The nature of the upstream–downstream dilemma (mentioned in the
first point above) has already been explained, but the remaining points
need to be elaborated. On the second point Widstrand states: 'In
most cases, government agricultural or planning policy does not coincide with the individual farmer's perception of reality, nor his wishes'
(Widstrand, 1980: 135). This also implies that the various socioeconomic
differences between farmers makes them potentially more or less
willing to support the government's development plans for irrigation
installation, depending on the relative situation and how the government plans affect various groups of farmers, and so on. This can
automatically give rise to conflicts between donors who impose demands on how the project should be carried out. Very often the
various donors have a connection to a state, which in turn again
implies an underlying conflict between donor states.

Ecological factors are seldom taken into account when project costs
are considered; this is often a result of state needs to realize prestigious projects quickly. The interesting thing is that the conflicts in the
case of the Euphrates and Tigris also include ethno-religious implications rather than merely socioeconomic structures. This is a dimension which must be added to Widstrand conflict formations, and will
therefore be further analysed. For pedagogical purposes, let us first

make an inventory of the state actors' relations, and thereafter continue with the ethno-religious dimension of the hydropolitical security complex.

Turkish–Syrian relations

There is no real evidence or indication of a crisis which could have escalated to an open state of war between Syria and Turkey, yet there have been several occasions when Syria has protested against Turkey's dam-building projects, and vice versa. The first controversy, however, was not over the Euphrates or the Tigris, but over the Asi (Orontes) River, which flows through Syria in a generally northern direction, then enters the province of Hatay and bears southwest towards the Mediterranean. The Asi Dam was started by Syria in 1956 in order to dry up the Al-Ghab valley swamps and open new areas for cultivation with irrigation water from the dam. Turkey reacted critically, since she was afraid that the Syrian dam project would imply a loss of water for Turkish farmers. After some years the Turks started to plan their own Asi Dam, and thereby try to solve their water problem. Turkey also hoped that when the Asi River problem was solved, this would open talks between Turkey and the UAR (United Arab Republic) and thereby settle the Euphrates water problems, which would include the Tigris as well. The United Arab Republic, a confederation between Syria and Egypt in the years 1958–62, rejected the Turkish demands.

In the 1960s, both states started to put forward several large-scale, prestigious development plans for the Euphrates and Tigris. In 1974 Turkey completed the first step in a larger irrigation and power project when the Keban Dam was finished. Moreover, Turkey had plans to build yet another three dams on the Euphrates. In 1973 Syria had completed its first dam on the Euphrates, which is similarly used for irrigation and power production. The intensification of the utilization of the river waters implied a decrease in the flow. The third state, Iraq, became the party which was most worried about this reduction in the availability of water. Tripartite talks took place on the issue in the early 1960s, and in 1966 Turkey promised to supply both Syria and Iraq with 300 cubic metres per second of the waters. But in 1974, when Turkey began to fill the Keban Lake in order to use the dam, both Syria and Iraq complained. Syria and Iraq needed water to fill up their respective lakes at Tabqa and Habaniyya for the purpose of irrigation. Turkey had to settle the conflict by increasing the river's water flow back to normal. At this time Syria, in contrast to the UAR period, advocated a tripartite conference in order to decide the apportionment of the Euphrates water.

In the early 1980s Turkey's second major dam on the Euphrates, the Karakaya, was to be augmented by another dam project. Once again, the Syrians raised their voices (Maoz and Yaniv, 1986: 95–7). Yet another cause of tension was the filling in January 1990 of the Atatürk Dam, which is a part of the greater Turkish GAP project. The GAP project has in itself caused a lot of concern in Syria, which feared a drop in the water flow and demanded extra supplies.

Turkish–Iraqi relations

Turkish–Iraqi water relations are centred around the Euphrates. Iraq's major concern has always been the risk that Turkey, as well as Syria, could strangle the flow of Euphrates water. Turkish–Iraqi relations were strained in the period when Turkey started to fill the Keban Dam and Syria simultaneously filled the Al Tabqa Dam (Starr, 1991: 1–2).

The Turkish Atatürk Dam project, initiated in 1983, became the next important cause of tension. Relations became increasingly hostile as Turkey started to fill the reservoirs in 1989 and culminated with the drastic fill-up of the dam in January 1990. This caused a 75 per cent drop in water supply for a whole month. Even Syria became worried about the sudden drop in water availability. It should also be noted that Turkish–Iraqi relations have been less frosty than Syrian–Iraqi relations, mainly because of Turkey's dependence on oil from Iraq (*Time*, 29 January 1990: 25).

Turkish and Iraqi policies on the issue of Kurdish separatism have often coincided. For instance, when Turkish raids on the Kurdish separatist movements were taking place in northern Iraq, it coincided with Iraq's policies to curb the Iraqi Kurds. In 1987, however, when Iraq was excluded from the Turkish–Syrian economic protocol – in particular from the discussion on the division of the Euphrates waters – a tense situation was created between Turkey and Iraq (Beschorner, 1992: 38).

Syrian–Iraqi relations

As mentioned above, Iraq has always feared that Turkish and Syrian dam projects could cause a huge drop in the amount of water passing through the Euphrates. The filling of the Turkish and Syrian dams at the beginning of the 1970s became a serious crisis between Syria and Iraq. In 1974 the effect of the filling reduced the flow of the Euphrates to approximately 25 per cent of the normal flow. Several severe threats were put forward from both sides. Iraq complained that over three million Iraqi farmers were suffering because of the reduced water flow, and even threatened to bomb the Al Tabqa Dam. A Syrian soldier on the Iraqi side was caught placing explosives in the holy city of Kerbala, which further heightened the tension. In 1975, after two years of drought, Syria and Iraq nearly came to a full-scale war when Syria and Turkey blocked the water flood and the level of the Euphrates was continuously lowered to a considerable extent. Large amounts of crops were lost in Iraq because of the water shortage. Syria denied that she was the cause of reduced water and claimed her rights by saying: 'The Syrian Euphrates Project is Syria's future' (*An-Nahar*, 17 May 1975, quoted in Starr, 1983: 127). Both Syria and Iraq placed troops along their frontiers, and the direct war risk could be reduced only with the help of mediation from Saudi Arabia, although the dispute was never settled (Kienle, 1990: 97–100; Maoz and Yaniv, 1986: 132; Starr, 1991: 12–15; and Farouk-Sluglett and Sluglett, 1990: 198).

As early as the 1940s Syria was engaged in military violence over water rights – this time with Israel. It thus seems as though Syria is one of the states in the Middle East for which water is such a concern that she does not shrink from the use of arms. Thus, conflict over water has been an issue leading to the brink of armed conflict between Syria and Turkey. Consequently, water is an issue which is closely connected to military security.

The disputes over the flow of the Euphrates have continued, and the Atatürk Dam also causes strained relations between Syria and Iraq, although it is a Turkish project. In 1984, for instance, Iraq accused Syria of withholding up to 60 per cent of Iraq's share of the Euphrates. Syria denied all these accusations (Kolars, 1986: 66).

Subcomplexes

Although water is causing management problems, these issues could probably be settled rather easily, since there is enough water for all three states. Domestic as well as external political problems, however, are causing almost inherently infectious and intertwined relations between Turkey, Syria and Iraq. Within the larger hydropolitical security complex, patterns of subcomplexes can be identified. In fact, these patterns are what make water problems so difficult to resolve.

One of the most difficult analytical problems with the Middle Eastern states is that they cannot be considered as homogeneous nation-states but, rather, as multi-ethno/religious, or multinational states. The Middle Eastern region is characterized by a variety of state-building projects, each state containing several different ethnic or ethno-religious groups. Due to direct or indirect Great Power influence in creating 'new' states within the region, these groups extend over one or, in most cases, several territorial borders. After the defeat of the Ottoman Empire the Great Powers divided the Middle East into new 'nation-states'. The old Ottoman districts of Mosul, Baghdad and Basra became the new state of Iraq. Parts of the maimed former Greater Syria became Jordan, Palestine and Lebanon, and the remaining parts became the state of Syria. The rest of the Ottoman Empire became what today is Turkey, a part of the old Empire which was 'liberated' by Kemal Atatürk. Turkey (Turkish majority dominating the Kurdish minority), Syria (with a dominant religious Alawi minority) and Iraq (a Sunni Arab minority dominating Shi'ite Arabs and Sunni Kurds) are some examples of modern states where different ethno-religious groups strive to strengthen and expand their own interests in relation to the dominant ruling elite. Still, the power relations among the various ethno-religious groups within each of the above-mentioned states is even far more complicated than this. First, there are more ethno-religious groups involved in each state. Second, there is an even more complex web between the states in the Middle East. This in turn creates a situation where the security concerns of the various states are inextricably linked.

The regional security complex is normally conceived of as an inter-state system defined 'in terms of the patterns of amity and enmity substantially confined within some geographical area' (Buzan, 1991: 190). Owing to the fact that ethnic groups, especially in the Third World and the Middle East, extend over one, or in most cases several, territorial borders, the patterns of amity and enmity are shaped by interethnic as well as interstate relations (Schulz, 1989: 119; Jørgensen, 1991: 112). These interethnic relations also shape some of the dimensions inside the Euphrates and Tigris hydropolitical security complex. It must also be pointed out that, for instance, the Kurdish issue in itself could form a security complex in which Turkey, Syria, Iraq, Iran and the USSR would be included. In the context of this essay, however, the interethnic relations must be related to and focused upon the water perspective. Only in this way is it possible to highlight the difficult and important conflict patterns dealing with disputes over water. John Kolars writes:

> First, it must be recognized that the provinces where the Euphrates project is taking place are those with significant linguistic and religious minorities not fully integrated into the Turkish milieu. Martial law, skirmishes with dissidents, and sometimes a less than cooperative local population inevitably slow the processes of development. (Kolars, 1986: 64)

Although Kolars identifies the problems in realizing the Euphrates projects, he underestimates the fact that various minorities often do not identify with the Turkish government and their economic planning, and that Ankara often neglects the minorities' demands and need. However, the need to include the various levels, from the micro-level to the macro-levels, and also to differentiate between the ethno-religious groups, will illustrate some of the problems which are stressed in the hydropolitical security complex.

The Ethno-religious Dimension of Hydropolitical Security Issues

The Kurdish question is one of the issues that connect the three states as well as the former Soviet Union and Iran. The Kurds are divided between these states, and constitute a national security concern for each of the states in this security complex. In what follows I will restrict myself to the Kurds in Turkey, Syria and Iraq (unless other sources are mentioned this section is based on the Minority Rights Group Report No. 23, 1985, 'The Kurds', by David McDowall).

Many of the Kurds in Turkey, Iraq and Syria reside in the Euphrates and Tigris basin, and would supposedly benefit from irrigation schemes and enhanced agricultural production. The Kaban Dam, for instance, must also have brought some benefits to the Kurds, although most of the hydroelectricity is transferred to western Anatolia, which is less densely populated by Kurds. The Atatürk Dam is projected to create three million job opportunities by the year 2000. The whole Southeast Anatolia Project (GAP) is part of Ankara's official strategy to fight Kurdish poverty. Thus the $14 billion GAP (*The Middle East*, October

1989: 20) is the largest scheme in Turkish history. Possibly more than one million Kurds moved westwards in the period 1950–80. Many left Turkey and became guestworkers in, for example, West Germany. It is assumed that economic progress has solved some of the under-development problems in parts of Anatolia where Kurds are situated. The GAP project, according to Ankara, will contribute towards a more interdependent relation between the Kurdish community and the rest of Turkey.

Still, the national aspirations of the Kurds in Turkey must not be neglected, since Turkey has never countenanced any Kurdish separatist tendencies. Turkey has never accepted the idea of a future Kurdistan and has worked against such political movements since its establish-ment in 1923. Turkish policy does not even recognize the existence of the Kurds – the Kurdish minority are labelled 'mountain-Turks'. In April 1991 Turkey's President Ozal removed the ban on speaking the Kurdish language (in non-official places only). In practical terms this changed little, since Kurdish has always been spoken in Kurdish areas. The constant repression of Kurds in Turkey, especially in the eastern and southern parts of Anatolia, has only increased Kurdish resistance and demands on Ankara. Terrorist acts have also been committed by, for instance, the Kurdish Workers' Party (PKK) against Turkey's damming of the Euphrates. Indications are that Damascus is using the PKK for these purposes, further heightening the tension between Turkey and Syria (*The Middle East*, October 1989: 19; Starr, 1991: 31).

Syria's involvement thus highlights the way in which states utilize and manipulate ethnic groups to promote their own interests. Syria has long experience in manipulating the grievances of ethnic commu-nities. In the 1960s she utilized Palestinian al-Fatah, stationed in Lebanon, which committed terrorist acts against Israel's National Water Carrier Project. Turkey has often asked Baghdad and Damascus to curb infiltration by Kurdish separatist PKK guerrillas. More than 2,000 people (*The Middle East*, March 1990: 7), including civilians and Turkish soldiers, have been killed since 1984. The PKK launches its attacks from areas near Iran, Iraq and Syria. The appearance of a hitherto unknown group called the Kurdish–Arab Front Against Turkey, which has threatened to destroy the Atatürk Dam, has also strained Turko–Arab relations. This group has stated: 'We are ready to blow it up. Dear Arab brothers, let's unite our efforts to destroy it as soon as possible.' (*The Middle East*, March 1990: 43).

Both Damascus and Baghdad are to some extent exploiting the

Arab population to deflect attention from their own situation. Syria and Iraq have a long-standing ideological dispute, and are at the same time preoccupied with internal problems, among others their own respective Kurdish populations.

Other ethnic groups like the Assyrians, Armenians, Yezidies and other smaller groups are all located in the Euphrates–Tigris areas. With the continuation of repression from the states involved in their attempts to stop any nationalist aspirations from these ethnic groups, there is a risk that the dams in Turkey, Syria and Iraq will be targets for terrorist attacks. Turkey considers the Euphrates and Tigris of vital importance, and is well aware of its security implications for Syria and Iraq. A hypothesis is thus that one of the reasons for the Turkish refusal to recognize the existence of Kurds and Armenians is the fact that both the Euphrates and the Tigris rise and pass through Turkish Kurdistan and Armenia.

The mass flight of the Kurds to Turkey and Iran, escaping from Saddam Hussein's persecution in the aftermath of the Iraq–Kuwait war, has further accentuated the ethnic dimension of future water problems. What will happen if Kurdish national rights are in focus for the international community and the UN? Will the Kurds be even more determined in their demands for a Kurdistan? A Kurdish uprising, *Serhildan*, is feared by all states in the hydropolitical complex. What will Turkey, Syria and Iraq do then to secure the flow of water? The future is certainly hard to predict.

The Marsh Arabs in southern Iraq, living in Iraq's ancient marshlands, certainly do experience the effects of the Iraqi government's continuing effort to drain the marshland. The so-called 'River Project' was conceived as a land improvement project in the 1950s. Iraq began to carry out the project in the 1970s in order to desalinate the Euphrates water. The 565-kilometre Saddam River, between the Tigris and the Euphrates, which starts near Baghdad and ends close to Basra in the south, is designed to reclaim polluted land by washing it with surplus irrigation water.

The regime of Saddam Hussein has, however, clearly shown that the intention behind the complex Tigris and Euphrates diversion scheme was not only to improve the agricultural sector. Large areas of agricultural land in the Amara region have been flooded deliberately. At the same time the marshes in the south are being drained. The flood weapon is thereby double-edged; Iraqi opposition groups portray it as a new tactic in the Baghdad regime's effort to subdue the south.

The huge diversion scheme has not only caused eco-genocide, whereby 57 per cent of the 15, 000 square kilometres of marshland has been turned into dry land, but also a genocide of the Marsh Arabs who have been living in these areas for nearly 5,000 years. The drying marshes make the Marsh Arabs an easy target for Saddam Hussein's forces. The reaction from the Marsh Arabs has been to declare a 'hydro-*jihad*'. It must also be remembered that it was in the marshes that Iraq first tried chemical warfare in 1984 (*The Middle East*, June 1994: 34; *The Middle East*, May 1994: 11–12; *The Middle East International*, 4 March 1994: 13; Bulloch and Darwish, 1993: 136–40).

Alawi-Baath versus Sunni-Baath

The problems between Syria and Iraq can also be tracked down to the political controversy and rivalry among the two Baath regimes in Damascus and Baghdad. In practice the two regimes are, in contrast to the ideological ideal, stratified and organized in an ethno-religious hierarchy whereby ethno-religious groups other than those that serve as the power base are marginalized. Loyalty is thus given to the ethno-religious group rather than to the Baath Party – something which has serious ramifications. As a consequence, domestic security policy implies a strong security apparatus around the regime due to lack of trust towards other ethno-religious groups. But external relations can also create hostile attitudes, because many ethno-religious groups also live in neighbouring states.

The Baath first came to power in Iraq in 1963, when they overthrew the Qassem regime and stayed in power for eleven months until the Aref regime was installed. In 1966 the Baath came into power in Syria, and in 1968 it came back into power in Iraq . The rivalry between the regimes has continued ever since. Both parties claim to be the leading ideological force in pan-Arabism, and are therefore contenders for the role of leading 'regional power'. As Kienle explains it:

> The dispute over Arab legitimacy was partly addressed to the Ba'thi audience in order to underpin claims to Ba'thi legitimacy. As in the later periods, though, it was certainly also addressed to non-Ba'thi audiences, inside and outside the two countries, whose support enhanced the general inner-state as well as regional position of the regimes, if not their chances of short-term survival. However, as Syria and Iraq had chosen the same method of drumming up and retaining support, they necessarily had outbid each other. Clearly also the Ba'thi competitor, commensurate with the higher degree of

Arab legitimacy with which it was credited among a wider public, had to be accused more virulently than other Arab regimes. (Kienle, 1990: 55)

The ideological dispute rooted in regional power struggles cannot be seen as the only explanation for the hostile attitudes between Baghdad and Damascus. As Kienle says, the need for legitimacy is also an important factor. The Syrian regime is very much an Alawi one and the Iraqi is a Sunni one; both are 'minority' regimes in their respective states. The Alawi sect is a branch of Shia Islam, something which certainly eased Syrian–Iranian ties during the Iraq–Iran war as well as ties with the Shia minority inside Iraq. Iraq's support for the Islamic Sunni majority in Syria during the 1970s and early 1980s disturbed Damascus. This has further contributed to the hostile attitude of Baghdad's Sunni regime towards Syria, and vice versa. Neither Syria nor Iraq is a homogeneous nation-state, which makes it rather difficult for 'minority regimes' to gain support from other ethno-religious groups inside each territory. Samir al-Khalil writes of Iraq:

> A distinction must be maintained between an Iraqi national 'character' and Iraqi nationalism. Iraqi nationalism understood as a sense of identity with a territorial entity known as Iraq does not exist. (Khalil, 1989: 120)

The regimes in Damascus and Baghdad, therefore, have difficulty in using Arab legitimization to win internal support. On the other hand, it is useful when it comes to attracting external support from other states in the Middle East. In the dispute over the Euphrates waters in the early 1970s the regimes tried to discredit each other as non-'pan-Arabists' and 'imperialists'. The Sixth Regional Congress of the Syrian Baath Party (in Damascus, 1975) stressed the Iraqi regime's lack of Arab legitimacy. The Alger agreement of 1975 between Iran and Iraq was put forward as treason against Arab interests. The following resolutions were adopted at the congress:

- To condemn the suspicious rightist regime in Iraq for colluding with Iran and signing the Iraqi–Iranian March agreement, which confirms its complete link with imperialism and colonialism, [and for] its persistence in liquidating the revolution in Arabistan and its betrayal of the Arab nation's questions.
- To condemn [Iraq] signing the Turkish–Iraqi agreement on the installation of oil pipelines to Iskenderun harbour.
- To condemn [Iraq's] unnational stand ... regarding ... the Palestine question.

- To condemn [Iraq's] methods of suppression and terror against our Arab people in Iraq. (Kienle, 1990: 102, from *al Baath*, 21 April 1975)

Furthermore, Damascus referred to the regime in Baghdad as the 'Takriti regime' or the 'tribal Takriti regime' in order to undermine its Arab legitimacy. Takriti is the home village of Iraq's President Saddam Hussein. Many of the regime members are relatives of his from Takriti. The accusations and replies from Baghdad against Syria's water policy were nevertheless softened and Radio Baghdad:

> ... referred to the Syrian regime's hostile attitude to Iraq, an attitude which is manifested in its cutting off the Euphrates river water, an action which is jeopardizing the livelihood of the Iraqi peasants who rely on this water. (quotation from Radio Baghdad, 27 March 1975, in Kienle, 1990: 103)

Iraq also tried to 'prove' Arab legitimacy in several statements and speeches. The Iraqi Baath's Regional Commander, Naim Haddad, said in a speech on Radio Baghdad (4 April 1975):

> Today US imperialism is pushing certain regimes, particularly the Syrian regime, to cut off water from our masses.... But we will be victorious as we have been before. The masses of our Arab people in Syria will discover this criminal design, which is neither new to us nor unexpected. The same Syrian regime adopted a negative policy when the revolution in Iraq nationalized the monopolist oil companies and even requested an increase in revenue from the oil flow. (Kienle, 1990: 103–4)

This distrust and rivalry between the two Baath regimes has persisted until today, and could perhaps be one explanation for Syria's participation in the coalition against Iraq during the Kuwait–Iraq war in 1990–91 as well as its support for Iran in the Gulf War. Thus, ideological conflict and ethno-religious differences are some of the factors which explain the difficulties in achieving agreements on the management of the Euphrates and Tigris waters.[2]

Complexes Related Horizontally

Turkey, Iraq and Syria can all be connected to other sets of security complexes. They can also, as was pointed out above, be 'members' of a security complex with a completely different security issue in focus. I will discuss some of the most important security issues which can be related to the Euphrates-Tigris complex on the horizontal level. The security issues related to the hydropolitical security complex on this level are connected to and intertwined with the underlying sub-complexes in the Euphrates–Tigris complex.

The Palestinian–Israeli issue

The Arab–Israeli or Palestinian–Israeli conflict can be related to the Euphrates–Tigris complex in two different ways: first through direct involvement in water issues; second through the internal political struggles in Turkey, Syria and Iraq (what might be called destabiliz-ation policy). Israel is one of the most efficient users of water in the world, but has nevertheless reached the barriers of consumption. The need to find new methods has resulted in trade negotiations with Turkish firms over water (Starr, 1991: 27). Israel is interested in buying water from water-rich Turkey; the water would be transported by floating reservoirs from the Turkish dam to the port of Haifa. The investment is expected to be $250 million, including transportation (*The Middle East*, May 1990: 38). The negotiations have further strained the fragile relations between Turkey and the Arab states, in particular Syria and Iraq, since Turkish water could then be used in Israel – a fact which upsets Iraq as well as Syria.

The other issue (destabilization) is more closely connected to the indirectly related subcomplexes. Israel, for instance, has periodically supported the Kurdish guerrillas with arms for resistance against their respective states. In the early 1960s she provided the Kurds in Iraq with arms and advisers. Israel, however, was not the only supplier; other important suppliers of arms were the USA and Iran. Iran has always been considered by the Baath regime in Baghdad as a potential supplier of arms to the Kurds in Iraq, especially during the Iraq–Iran war (MRG Report No. 23, 1985: 21).

Israel can be expected to provide various 'guerrilla-groups' situated in the Euphrates-Tigris basin, mainly Kurdish, with arms in the future. The continued potential risk of 'terrorist acts' against completed dams as well as dam-building areas provides an impetus for sophisticated security arrangements in Turkey, Syria and Iraq. Among other external actors, the Israeli 'divide and rule' policy is therefore a potential threat to future co-operations on water between Turkey, Syria and Iraq.

Syria and Lebanon, which are also included in the Palestinian–Israeli security complex, are naturally both concerned about Israeli strategic and geopolitical aspirations in southern Lebanon. The Euphrates is by far the most important river in Syria, but in the future other rivers could be increasingly interesting. Lebanon is a water-rich state which could provide Syria with water. Israel has already come under suspicion of having plans to deliver water from the Litani to Israel. Syria's water supply could therefore be lowered if neighbouring states exploit the water without co-operation (for a more elaborated analysis, see Lindholm, Chapter 2 in this volume). A further potential risk of Iraqi involvement in the Palestinian–Israeli conflict is Jordan's intention to build water pipelines from the Euphrates in Iraq. This is Jordan's response to its already alarming scarcity of water; her current precarious predicament is largely a result of harsh competition for water in the Jordan River basin.

The Iraq–Kuwait war

It is difficult to estimate the direct consequences of the Iraq–Kuwait war and its implications for the hydropolitical security complex. Rather, it is the indirect and potential changes that are at stake. Still, Iraq gave high priority to saving its dam facilities, since they placed some of its foreign hostages as human shields at the dam buildings (*MEED*, January 1991: 13). One direct consequence is the hardship and problems for Iraqi peasants caused by the Allied bombing of bridges and irrigation installations, which has led to difficulties in cultivation. Food supplies will therefore also be reduced. Turkey as well as Syria joined the Allied forces, and this could also make it harder for Baghdad, especially with Saddam Hussein still in power, to find new ways to deal with the constant threat of lowered water flow in the Euphrates. After the civil war in Iraq, where Saddam Hussein's army crushed the revolts, the prospect for the future looks dim indeed. Fresh water supplies have been severely limited since the bombing raids. During the war the water situation was exceedingly poor and drinking the polluted water carried a risk of infection and disease. In southern Iraq water was short (April 1991) due to lack of spare parts, chemicals and fuel (for pumps) and the absence of communications. At one point cholera had almost reached epidemic proportions (*Middle East International*, 19 April 1991: 7; 22 February 1991: 7; *The Middle East*, February 1991: 9). Today, however, the Iraqi regime has slowly managed to rebuild most of its irrigation potential, albeit with double motives like the draining of the marshland.

The oil dimension must also be connected to the Kuwait–Iraq war. The oil-rich Mosul district has always been an area of Iraq upon which Turkey has pursued territorial demands. Both Syria and Turkey want to gain influence in this area as a benefit for participating on the side of the Allies. The historical distrust between Turks and Arabs, due to the fall of the Ottoman Empire and the rise of 'new' states in the region, has further cemented the suspicious attitudes between Turkey and the Arab world. Particularly over the disputed Hatay province, which Syria still claims, the strained relations between Turkey and the Arab world are evident (*Middle East International*, 25 January 1991: 23).

The involvement of the superpowers in the Iraq–Kuwait war has indirect implications for the water situation, due to the damage done to water infrastructure in the massive bombings. In addition, the Iraqi regime's strategy of dumping oil in the Arabian/Persian Gulf during the war will further complicate the water situation in these areas due to the negative effects on the desalination installations situated next to the seashore of Saudi Arabia at the Arabian/Persian Gulf.

Consequently, one could say that the Euphrates–Tigris security complex was also, in its implicitly specific way, related to the Iraq–Kuwait war on a vertical level.

Sustainable Development and Ecological Problems

A completely different aspect of the water problems within the three states of Turkey, Syria and Iraq is the ecological and environmental damage due to the establishments of dam projects, irrigation systems and hydropower stations. Several dam-building projects in the Third World are prestigious projects with little concern for ecological effects. Sandra Postel puts like this:

> Most governments continue to expect traditional dam and diversion projects to relieve regional water stresses. Yet the engineering complexities of these projects, along with their threats of ecological disruption, multibillion-dollar price tags, and 20-year lead times leave little hope that they will deliver water in time to avert projected shortages – if, indeed, they are completed at all. (Postel, 1984: 52)

The fact is that all states in the Euphrates–Tigris basin are working hard on building traditional 'projects' and at the same time neglect the problems that arise on the local level or 'micro' level. Farmers and peasants are not always familiar with the new technical equipment and installations, and there is clearly a gap between the states' intentions and the needs on the local level. As a heritage from the Ottoman Empire sectarian stratification still keeps traditional social ties which are shaken apart by 'modernizing' projects. The sect, the tribe, the clan and the family are strongly affected by these Euphrates–Tigris projects, which further strain relations between governments and local populations. Annica Rabo, who has made an anthropological study of villages along the Euphrates in the northeast of Syria makes the following statement: 'the Euphrates Scheme cannot be evaluated today as a successful development project regardless of its technical advances' (Rabo, 1986: 188).

Local peasants and farmers have not benefited from the Euphrates Dams as was expected. Irrigation schemes are not working as intended, and local populations have been forced to accept governments' 'development strategies' without any concern for their demands and wishes. Rabo describes the effects of the Euphrates Scheme in one village:

> While technical problems are now taken better care of, costs are steadily increasing, thus making the continuation of the irrigation and reclamation scheme both slow and uncertain. (*ibid.*: 196)

To facilitate reservoir flooding, local populations are sometimes displaced from areas that will be flooded. In these cases resistance is very strong. Costly projects, which are often far behind schedule, create further ecological backlashes such as water loss from evaporation during the summer months; in wintertime large amounts of sediment are carried by the rivers (especially by the Tigris), and water draining back after irrigation tends to be more saline. All three states are having great problems with salinity. There is a risk that the groundwater reservoirs will be overused by rich landlords who are drilling and pumping up groundwater for irrigation. The poorer peasants suddenly realize that their water amount is lowered and that they therefore risk losing their crop due to lack of irrigation. In their eyes, therefore, the new development projects constitute a threat to their existence, so the socio-economic consequences of these projects automatically lead to political implications for the regimes. One large-scale Turkish project, with the idea of transferring water from the Black Sea to the Euphrates–Tigris basin, was not realized for technological and economic, as well as ecological, reasons, and also because of resistance from the local population (Starr, 1991: 7, 11–12).

No doubt there is a great need to close the gap between the traditional view of development and 'sustainable development', which includes the ecological dimension. Sustainable development also has to be connected to the concept of national security. Co-operation among states to share the costs of a more sustainable development is a necessity for the people in these areas. The insecure political Middle Eastern region, with its unstable regimes, ethno-religious and national antagonisms, has also destabilized the economic strength of its states due to huge investments in the military sector. As Lester Brown points out:

> The new threats to national security are extraordinarily complex. Ecologists understand that the deteriorating relationship between four billion humans and the earth's biological systems cannot continue. But few political leaders have yet to grasp the social significance of this unsustainable situation. (Brown, 1977: 37)

There is clearly a need for co-operation between the states in the Euphrates–Tigris hydropolitical security complex, but what are the chances of such a development?

Sources of Change and Future Co-operation

There have been many disputes in the Euphrates–Tigris basin over the years but, as I will show, there have also been several occasions when the respective state representatives have met and talked about existing problems and future co-operation plans over the Euphrates and Tigris waters.

Ever since 1962, when Syria declared its intention to build its Tabqa Dam, negotiations have taken place between Syria and Iraq. It is interesting to note that these negotiations have continued although the regimes in power altered over the years. One of the very first tripartite meetings concerning water between Turkey, Syria and Iraq was in Baghdad in 1965. Iraq demanded 18 billion cubic metres, Turkey claimed 14 billion and Syria needed 13 billion from the Euphrates (Bari, 1977: 238). The claims were unrealistic, however, since the river does not carry that amount of water; thus the problems of management were exposed. Both Iraq and Syria based their arguments and needs on a World Bank report which was extended by a Soviet report some years later. The tripartite meeting decided that it was better for

Syria and Iraq to have bilateral talks. Thus a series of bilateral meetings took place until the critical years in the first half of the 1970s.

In 1972 a meeting was held between Iraq and Syria implying a turning point on the Euphrates question. This was also the year of the last tripartite meeting. No agreement was reached, however. The Turkish–Iraqi agreement, in 1973, to build an oil pipeline across Turkey to the Mediterranean exacerbated the tension between Syria and Iraq. The already existing oil pipeline across Syria was considered insecure due to Syrian political threats to shut off the oil taps.

The Turkish Dam project (GAP), including the Atatürk Dam, was also subject to talks and meetings during the 1980s, and Turkish President Turgut Özal has pledged that Turkey will 'never use the control of water to coerce or threaten' (*Time*, 5 February 1990: 32). Syria and Iraq were not convinced by this statement. Since 1987, however, Turkey has provided Syria with 500 cubic metres per second of Euphrates water. Syrian complaints concern the deteriorating water quality due to Turkey's utilization of the water in industrial plants and after irrigation, which increases water salinity (*ibid.*).

Turkey is very much aware of the future political and social problems which shortage of water can cause. In connection with the Atatürk project, President Özal introduced the idea of building two water pipelines from Turkey to other parts of the Middle East. Turkey popularized them as 'Peace Pipelines'. To calm down its neighbour states and at the same time to provide other Middle Eastern states with water, Turkey is prepared to take water from the Seyhan and Ceyhan rivers and send it through one 'Western Pipeline' and one 'Gulf Pipeline'. The Western Pipeline would pass to Syria through the cities of Aleppo, Hama, Homs and Damascus, continue to Jordan and its capital, Amman, and finally reach Saudi Arabian cities like Tabuk, Medina, Yanbu, Mecca and Jeddah. The pipeline would transport 3.5 million cubic metres per day. The Gulf Pipeline is supposed to pass through Iraq, Kuwait and Saudi Arabia, to continue to the smaller Gulf states like Bahrain, Qatar and the United Arab Emirates, and finally to reach Oman. This pipeline would transport 2.5 million cubic metres per day. The Gulf Pipeline would also be less costly than the Western Pipeline, because of the lower topography in the area. Technically, financially – with support from IBRD and the Islamic Development Bank – and most of all ecologically, this project is feasible. It would take at least eight to ten years to complete, but still it would be a first step towards a more multilateral co-operation in the Middle

East. (The section above is mainly based on Duna, in Starr and Stoll, 1988.)

Although there are great political obstacles to be overcome, the pipelines could serve as an opportunity to start negotiations over water and the need for better management in the Euphrates–Tigris security complex. In November 1991 Turkey was scheduled as host state for the Middle East Water Summit. This could perhaps have provided a first step in discussions over the pipelines and would have served as an initial attempt to heal the wounds after the Kuwait–Iraq war. The conference announced attendance by twenty–two Middle Eastern and North African ministerial delegates as well as representatives from the USA, the Soviet Union, Europe and Japan. Even Israel was thinking of participating, although Syria threatened not to come if Israel was part of the conference. The Peace Pipeline seems to provide a reason for every state in the region to consider the probable potential benefits (*The Middle East*, August 1991: 29–30).

The Iraq–Kuwait war, the collapse of the USSR and Turkey's new relations with central Asian states, the sudden death of Turkey's President Özal and the Gulf states' distrust of Turkey were among other factors which contributed to the cancellation of the 1991 Water Summit. The latest attempt to discuss water co-operation was made in Muscat, Oman, in April 1994. Over forty states and organizations participated including, for the first time ever, an Israeli delegation in a Gulf state. Syria and Lebanon boycotted the meeting because the Israelis participated in the water talks (*The Middle East*, June 1994: 32–3).

Clearly the political obstacles to be overcome are great, but the Water Summit could provide a new platform for the region's states to negotiate and talk with each other. Several regional economic and political regimes have been established over the years; many of these are under the umbrella of the pan-Arabic ideology. The League of Arab States, the Council for Arab Economic Unity, the Arab Common Market, the Organization of Arab Petroleum Exporting Countries, the Arab Fund for Economic and Social Development and the Arab Monetary Fund are some examples of institutions that are putting forward the idea of realizing a common goal: the unity of the Arab nation (Sayigh, 1982: Ch. 9).

The pan-Arabic ideology has also created a great benefit for many of the states connected to the various regional regimes, but at the same time it has automatically excluded several 'non-Arabic' states and minorities. The economic and political boycott of Israel is the most obvious example, but the refusal to co-operate with Turkey and Iran could also serve as good illustrations.

In the light of the ideological and political decline of the pan-Arabic movement and force, the water issue could become the first to bring all the states together. As early as 1953 the first agreement was made for sharing joint water resources. Israel, Jordan, Syria and Lebanon agreed on how to distribute the water from the Jordan basin. Over the years this agreement, with its principles, has become a blueprint for other states in the region (Andersson, in Starr and Stoll, 1988: 10).

Conclusions

The interesting fact is that in contrast to, for example, the Jordan River basin, there seems to be enough water in the Euphrates–Tigris basin for all actors involved. Existing problems are mainly problems of management, and arise due to political disputes which could be divided into several areas:

- The relations between, on the one hand, central governments in Turkey, Syria and Iraq and on the other, ethno-religious and national groups:
  - regional ambitions among the Baath regimes;
  - Kurdish relations with respective central governments;
  - regional conflicts related to the internal political struggles in the respective states surrounding the Euphrates–Tigris basin.
- Strained Turkish–Arab relations.
- Economic difficulties.
- Rifts in the social formations of local populations due to the implementation of modernizing projects.
- Ecological problems.

The case study of the Euphrates–Tigris hydropolitical security complex indicates the importance of including the water dimension in security studies, particularly in regional security analyses. The development trends at hand clearly show that water shortage could be a reality in the very near future. The water is most probably also of bad quality as a result of overirrigation and salinization. In the Euphrates–Tigris basin it is, however, possible to arrange the water flow in such a way that water could be shared efficiently by all parties, even with an increased population rate. The water also has to be used in such a way that ecological and environmental demands will be satisfied. One can only imagine the kind of accusations that could be raised in the future if one upstream state, like Turkey, were to supply Syria and Iraq with polluted water of poor quality.

Still, one has to be aware of the political obstacles that have always disturbed possibilities of co-operation in the Middle East. The most important conclusion must be that the states in the hydropolitical security complex can best solve their water problems by co-operation on development. Joint dependency on shared river systems decreases the possibilities for implementing national development strategies. Thus, management institutions on a regional level are required in order to safeguard both development and security. In the Euphrates–Tigris security complex Turkey, Syria and Iraq could arrange tripartite meetings for development planning, which could become a model for co-operation between regional institutions on development issues as well as security issues.

I have tried to demonstrate that future peace and co-operative agreements cannot be achieved without solving the water shortage and the management problems. On the other hand, initiatives like the Turkish 'Peace Pipelines' and the 1994 Middle East Water Summit in Oman could develop into arenas where the states in the Euphrates–Tigris hydropolitical complex, and in the Middle Eastern complexes in general, could agree on the use and management of water. However, one important obstacle to overcome is to convince all parties that they must agree to participate in water summits. No state that is dependent on water can be left behind in solving the water problems in the region. In other words, ecological interdependence could be seen as an imperative for regional co-operation. Indeed, it is hard to see what other choice is left for the people of the Middle East.

Notes

1. In most of the sources used in this essay, water has merely been one issue among several other Middle Eastern problems. Very few deal with water problems only. This has created some problems in finding relevant sources. Many articles in various publications discuss the issue, but few academics have actually dug deeper into the matter. One of the most difficult tasks in completing this essay has thus been to find literature dealing with the Euphrates–Tigris

complex. Three very important exceptions are Starr (ed.), 1983; Starr and Stoll (eds), 1988; and Starr, 1991. The author is indebted to many researchers at the Padrigu department, especially Helena Lindholm, but also to Khalid Saleh (at the Department of Political Science, Gothenburg University) for valuable suggestions and criticism. I would also like to thank one of my students, Mats Rahmberg, for providing some relevant articles concerning technical aspects of the Dam projects in Turkey.

2. A more detailed discussion of sectarian solidarity and its connection to regionalism and tribalism is explored in Dam (1980) and Batutu (1981). In Syria and Iraq reliance on regional and tribal ties seems at present to be a precondition for staying in power. According to Dam, regionalism and tribalism do not necessarily give rise to sectarianism. Batutu as well as Dam argues that there is sectarianism in Syria but Dam, in contrast to Batutu, says it does not exist in Iraq. This indicates the difficulty of finding a clear-cut explanation (it certainly goes beyond the scope of this essay) of the roots of the conflict between the two Baath regimes. However, it is important to note the various views.

4

India: The Domestic and
International Politics of Water Scarcity

Elisabeth Corell and Ashok Swain

Introduction

Massive population growth, combined with the post-independence struggle for modernization, has made India vulnerable to the scarcity of fresh-water resources. On an average level, water availability is not a cause for alarm, but regionally and seasonally the shortages are significant. India alone contributes eighteen million people to the planet every year. As the population increases and the sum of available water resources remains constant, the maximum *per capita* demand that a country can support decreases correspondingly. Rapid urbanization also puts pressure on water resources. The expansion of the large cities in India has increased the demand for water and, at the same time, accelerated the contamination of sources. Due to the adoption of the Green Revolution strategy, the irrigation sector now needs more water than before. At the same time the massive use of fertilizers and pesticides in agriculture pollutes the water. Likewise, while industries are in need of more water for their operational requirements, industrial waste contributes to polluting the source and flow of the fresh-water resources.

Unlike its developed counterparts, India lacks the bureaucratic and administrative institutions to deal effectively with problems arising from greater demand for water. This situation is being further complicated and aggravated by political expediency from its policymakers. The scarce water resource is being used as a tool in the hands of political actors in their attempts to gain power. The religious importance of certain water sources for some ethnic groups in this multi-ethnic country has helped the politicians here. Their use of water as an instrument to organize the groups along ethnic lines is, of course, exacerbating already existing differences in society, resulting in more social unrest.

The Indian Setting

The liberal democratic state in India was founded in 1947 in a moment of insurgent idealism, after one of the longest and most ideologically middle-of-the-road national liberation movements in the developing world. The atmosphere of the early post-independence period was one of intense excitement; the economic stagnation and financial timidity of the days of British rule were being replaced by a passion for speedy social progress, which was to be achieved through a combination of the most advanced modern technology and massive popular mobilization.

Due to the pre-independence partition, independent India had lost a sizeable chunk of its most fertile irrigated land in the Indus and Ganges basins to the newly created state of Pakistan, at both the western and eastern ends of its border. The new government under Jawaharlal Nehru, facing a severe food scarcity and massive post-partition migration, almost immediately launched a grand scheme of large-scale surface water development to increase agricultural production. The urgency of the food crisis at that time demanded this response. One year after independence, in 1948, 160 large-scale surface water development projects were being considered, investigated or executed, and two years later, 29 per cent of the First Five-Year Plan (1951–5) budget was allocated for that purpose (Hansen, 1966: 47, 110, 373). After the First Five-Year Plan, the government's actions started to show results when the growth rate in annual food grain production shot up to 3.1 per cent from 0.1 per cent in the pre-independence period (Blyn, 1966: 96).

This initial spectacular success in the agricultural sector inspired the Indian leadership to orientate India's development strategy towards one overriding and widely accepted national goal: 'maximizing self-reliance'. To achieve this objective, India adopted the strategy of 'mixed' economy, paving the way for a dominant public sector which operated the industrial and agricultural infrastructures and laid the ultimate emphasis on heavy industry and maximized food-grain production. The energy requirements of this rapid industrialization doubled government efforts towards large-scale surface water development projects that had initially been taken up for agricultural purposes.

Besides the goal of achieving self-reliance, other reasons might be attributed to India's post-independence priority in building large-scale water development projects. In the first years of independence, the onerous mission of the central leadership was to keep the country united, so at that time the agenda for integration transcended all other concerns. By allocating these centrally planned water development projects which had become the 'symbol of prestige with local pressure groups' (Sen, 1962: 17), the post-independent Indian leadership effectively brought various regions into the national mainstream. The construction of these projects brought political legitimacy to the new leadership in the eyes of the masses by being projected as the harbinger of future development at a time of high expectations. Finally, this strategy mobilized foreign funds to central government, which enhanced its ability to distribute this largesse without incurring political debit by raising resources domestically.

It would be preposterous to surmise that the Indian endeavour to intensify the exploitation of surface water has been an insignificant achievement. The expansion of irrigation facilities has greatly contributed to agricultural production, and since the mid-1970s India has been self-sufficient in food-grain production in spite of its overwhelming population growth. The amelioration of hydro-energy has allowed India to develop an impressive industrial infrastructure very quickly. But at the same time, the price of using river water projects as an important means of achieving economic independence has been very high. The projects' own capital, recurrent, and rehabilitation expenditures have greatly increased the country's foreign debt. The complications do not end there. The construction of these projects has not only damaged the environment at their locations, but the diversion of water at upstream sites has also caused ecological problems as well as antagonism in downstream areas. India's overambitious river water exploitation has affected neighbouring downstream countries, adding another important dimension to the fragile security environment of South Asia.

Before we turn our attention to the Ganges, Ravi–Beas–Sutlej, and Cauvery case studies, it is important to take a look at our motives for choosing them. To concentrate on our main objective, we have avoided theoretical debate by choosing to use Peter Wallensteen's definition of conflict to explore the relationship between scarce water resources and political conflicts. He defines conflict as 'a social situation in which a minimum of two parties strive at the same moment in time to acquire the same set of scarce resources' (Wallensteen, 1988: 120). To give a picture of the various types of conflicts which can arise over water resources we will deal with three types, as illustrated by our case studies.

Typology of Conflicts

State-versus-state conflicts

Since the beginning of the twentieth century, population growth and economic development have led to competition for mineral resources and fossil fuels, exemplified in competition for colonial areas and spheres of influence. Due to recent technological developments reducing the resource usage and massive exploration of new areas of deposits, the scarcity tendency has shifted from non-renewable resources to renewable ones (UNFPA, 1992: 23–5). Fresh water, soil, forests, oceans and air are renewable natural resources because they are ecologically integrated in a feedback loop system which guarantees their replacement or preservation of their quality. This, of course, does not mean that such resources are unlimited.

In the present-day world, it has become unfashionable, uneconomical, and at the same time not strategically prudent to conquer others' territories. However, conflicts over natural renewable resources, mainly fresh water, have grown as demands have increased, and the supply side looks more and more insecure (Ullman, 1983: 139–40). When one state works for development by acquiring or exploiting more than 'its share' of water resources, it affects the interests of other states. The overuse of water by one state can do at least as much harm to the people of neighbouring states as military aggression (Brock, 1991: 408). Subsequent actions by the affected states to protect their interests can eventually breed conflict.

State-versus-group conflicts

Scarcity of water also has the potential to breed a conflict between the state and internal actors. Resource exploitation by the state agency in a particular area or region might be perceived by the local population as exploitation for the benefit of the other regions. Environmental issues may be politically manipulated to activate the regional parties or help to form new environmentally based groups to challenge the actions of the state.

If the affected people belong to an ethnic minority group which perceives itself as being exploited by the majority which rules the state, this might further stretch already existing social dichotomies and contribute to active conflict. Likewise, if water use is perceived as a deliberate imposition on a particular region or people, it might lead to the formation of a new actor in conflict with the state. The historical or religious importance of the exploited resource might aggravate the probability of the ensuing conflict. In the absence of a speedy resolution, these conflicts might lead to struggles for autonomy or secession. Weak state structures due to strong ethnic identities and lack of resources make the developing countries more vulnerable to this phenomenon.

Group-versus-group conflicts

These conflicts are linked to parties within a state with conflicting ideas or incompatibilities. Competition for the use of a scarce water resource can be seen as an incompatibility among the groups in a society. The perceived exploitation or overuse of common water resources by one party might help to organize new parties or to persuade already existing parties to take up this issue with the intention of protecting their interests. The formation of a new party might take place expeditiously as a response to certain acts of the perceived exploiter, or it might develop as a gradual outcome of persisting resentment.

The battle for protecting one's own share of water or acquiring that of others can potentially create conflicting groups in a society. The activation of groups may take place along already existing religious, caste, class, linguistic, regional or other lines, or scarce water resources may themselves bring a 'we – them' dichotomy into the society. If one party – rightly or wrongly – perceives the state as a collaborator with the other, then this group conflict might become a 'state-versus-group' conflict, and subsequently turn into a secessionist movement.

Conflict over the Ganges

The River Ganges, about 2,510 kilometres long, flows through India and Bangladesh. It rises in Gangotri, on the southern slopes of the Himalayan range in India, and moves through Indian territory in a

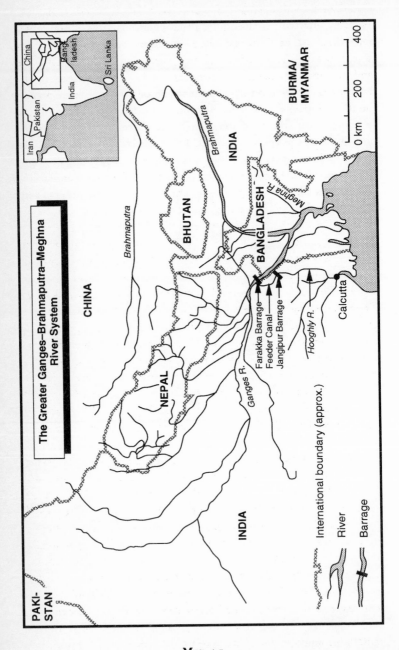

Map 4.1

southeasterly direction to Bangladesh. Before entering Bangladesh, the mainstream of the Ganges bifurcates into two channels: Bhagirathi-Hooghly, which is the name of the Ganges in West Bengal, and Podda, or Padma, as the Ganges is called in Bangladesh. The Padma, the border between India and Bangladesh, flows for about 112 kilometres and then moves towards the southeast to join the Brahmaputra at the heart of Bangladesh, and the combined flow runs south to empty into the Bay of Bengal.

The Ganges: politics of the conflict

The 'state-versus-state' water dispute over the Ganges dates back to 1951, when Bangladesh was the eastern province of the Federation of Pakistan. It originated when India planned to construct a barrage at Farakka, 18 kilometres upstream from the East Pakistan (Bangladesh) border, in order to preserve and maintain the Calcutta port by improving the navigability of the Bhagirathi-Hooghly river system. The government of India's plan included a 38-kilometre canal to take off from the barrage in order to supplement the dry-season waters of the Bhagirathi-Hooghly at the lower point, which would make the current strong enough to flush off the silt and clear the Calcutta port. All the south Asian rivers, including the Ganges, which originated from the Himalayas face a 'dry-season' period from the beginning of January to the end of May every year. The shortage of water starts in January, due to transformation of rainwater into snow in the Himalayan catchment area, and this situation continues for five months. The arrival of summer in May helps to melt the snow, and increases the flow of the rivers.

When she found out about the Farakka proposal, Pakistan wanted to discuss this issue with India. After four unsuccessful meetings, India unilaterally decided to start the construction of the barrage in 1962. The tensions before and after the 1965 Indo–Pak War meant a long interlude to the negotiations. After 1967, several talks were held at a bilateral level, but did not produce anything. India put forward the argument that Pakistan was dragging her heels in the negotiations in order to create misgivings between India and East Pakistan, hoping to push the East Bengalis closer to Pakistan. The Pakistani view was that the Indian strategy aimed at escalating hostilities between East and West wings of Pakistan, by suggesting that the West was not serious about protecting the interest of the Bengalis.

With the independence of Bangladesh in 1971, it was expected that the water-sharing dispute could be resolved, since India had helped Bangladesh in her liberation struggle. The initial enthusiasm between the two neighbours helped set up the Indo–Bangladesh Joint River Commission to develop the waters of the river common to the two countries on a co-operative basis. But as the Bangladeshi leader Sheikh Mujibur Rahman was aware of the emotions involved in the Farakka issue for his own fellow-countrymen, he was reluctant to bring this issue up with India, whose support was very much needed for his survival. So the specific question of sharing the waters of the Ganges was taken up with his Indian counterpart only in May 1974 (Misra, 1978: 42).

The Farakka Barrage and the feeder canal were completed and ready for use at the beginning of 1975. On 21 April 1975, the barrage was commissioned on a trial basis for forty days following a short-term agreement signed by the two countries. Though this agreement was hailed as a breakthrough and 'an outstanding example of mutual understanding and accommodation' by the Indian government (Lok Sabha Debate, 21 April 1975), it was not welcomed in the same spirit by ordinary Indians and Bangladeshis. In the eyes of the Indian opposition, the release of 11,000 cusecs (cubic feet per second) to 16,000 cusecs of water in the dry season is nothing in comparison to the needs of 40,000 cusecs to flush the heavily silted up Hooghly. At the same time, the Bangladeshi opposition did not hesitate to project it as another pro-Indian act by their government, overlooking the salient interests of Bangladesh itself. On 15 August, Bangladeshi President Mujibur Rahman was assassinated by army majors, and some claim that the short-term agreement was one of the reasons for his dispute with the army. After the death of Mujibur, India's Prime Minister, Indira Gandhi, hardened her attitude towards Bangladesh. Mujibur was considered to be closer to India, and India's hope to keep Bangladesh within its fold was shattered by that incident. Indian apprehension intensified when the new leadership in Bangladesh was backed by the Islamic forces of the Middle East. The water of the Ganges provided an easily available tool to the Indian policymakers to teach their Bangladeshi counterparts a lesson and, if possible, to force them to follow their dictates. At the beginning of the next dry season, in January 1976, India unilaterally diverted the water at Farakka without any consultation with Bangladesh. The new rulers of Bangladesh raised this issue in various international fora with a political strategy of their own. Going to international fora like the UN, the Non-Aligned Movement Summit and Islamic Foreign Ministers' Conference with a legitimate complaint like this gave the new military leader much-needed international acceptance. This anti-Indian posture also gave the leadership support at home. However, considering India's clout and stance, the reality of the situation had forced the Bangladeshis to keep negotiations going at bilateral level.

In March 1977, India witnessed a political transformation when the opposition Janata Party took over the reins of the government from the Congress Party. The new government attempted to strengthen India's relations with its neighbours, which would bring them a political victory over their Congress rivals. This occurred when President Ziaur Rahman of Bangladesh was advocating forming an Association for South Asian Regional Co-operation (SAARC), believing that it would help him to keep his country free of Indian domination. In this milieu, both countries came to an agreement to share the Ganges water during the 'dry seasons' extending over a period of five years. They also pledged to work towards a long-term arrangement to augment the dry-season flows of the river. According to this agreement, in November 1977, India was allowed to withdraw 20,500 cusecs and Bangladesh 34,500 cusecs at Farakka during the most acute period.

On 25 March 1978, both countries exchanged alternative proposals for augmenting the dry-season flow. The Bangladeshi plan proposed the building of upriver storage dams in Nepal, and India proposed a scheme to divert water from the Brahmaputra to the Ganges through a link canal across Bangladesh's territory. It was important for Bangladesh to involve Nepal in the project, since it would be more difficult for India to break a trilateral commitment than a bilateral one. Moreover, the storage dams in Nepal would not be a liability in any way, politically or economically, to the Bangladeshi leaders.

On the other hand, India wanted to work to augment the Ganges scheme at bilateral level with Nepal only because of her desire to divert the increased flow to her southern part, which is chronically deficient in water. Moreover, the Ganges–Brahmaputra link has the potential to be an excellent and economic navigable connection between India's northeastern states and the mainland. These considerations did not permit the contesting parties to accept each other's proposal for augmentation (Swain, 1993: 436–7).

When Congress came back to power in India in 1980, critics of the 1977 agreement again became active. The Congress Party in the state of West Bengal was critical of the Janata government's action in 1978.

With the change of government, they started demanding the revocation of the 1978 agreement, which they considered had overlooked the essential interests of their state. Fear of losing popular support also forced the ruling Communist Party to join with Congress. An all-party delegation from West Bengal called on Prime Minister Indira Gandhi on the eve of the new Bangladeshi President General Ershad's visit to New Delhi in October 1982, and demanded that their state be assured a minimum of a 40,000 cusecs flow during the dry seasons (*Far Eastern Economic Review*, 15 October 1982). Despite these pressures, the Indian Prime Minister signed a Memorandum of Understanding with the Bangladeshi President by extending the 1977 agreement, with some changes, for another eighteen months. Indira Gandhi's reason for signing the agreement might have been that she wanted to wait for a more favourable political climate to revive the link-canal proposal rather than totally destroying the relationship.

The MoU signed in 1982 expired after eighteen months, and the inability of both parties to reach an agreement on augmentation deadlocked any negotiable settlement. India's internal politics were instrumental in this regard. The coming general election and Indira Gandhi's assassination in 1984 pushed this agenda further back in the minds of Indian policy makers. India's refusal to renew the arrangement in 1984 and its unilateral siphoning of water at Farakka were perceived in Bangladesh as a pressure tactic aimed to make her agree on the link-canal proposal (Bertocci, 1986: 233).

When Rajiv Gandhi became Prime Minister after the assassination of his mother in November 1984, India's foreign policy took a change of direction. Rajiv Gandhi's vision of playing an active and important role in the world arena brought a change in India's attitude towards its neighbours. This was reflected first in October 1985, when President Ershad and Prime Minister Gandhi reached an understanding on the sharing of river waters. They agreed to sign a fresh MoU which preserved the terms of the previous agreement for a three-year period, and both sides pledged to work to augment the dry-season flow.

Bangladesh suffered catastrophic floods in August and September 1988 – so devastating that three-quarters of the country went under water. President Ershad described the flood as 'a catastrophe of an unprecedented dimension' and 'a man-made curse', and appealed for international assistance (Keesing's Contemporary Archives, 1988: 36288). He refused to accept any assistance from India, whom he did not hesitate to describe as the main culprit. The failure of the government machinery to cope with the disaster was turning public opinion against him. To save his government from public wrath, Ershad used this anti-India card, and India was especially annoyed by Dhaka's return of helicopters sent to help flood victims. Ershad's fresh attempt to internationalize the water management issue by bringing it to the UN, the Commonwealth and the South Asian Association for Regional Co-operation (SAARC) made the relationship deteriorate further (*Far Eastern Economic Review*, 13 October 1988).

The 1985 agreement lapsed in November 1988 without any extension, and soon afterwards India started to withdraw water at Farakka on its own initiative. Continuous domestic political upheavals in both countries, with the burgeoning of Islamic ideals in Bangladesh and rising Hindu fundamentalism in India, have precluded any further arrangement on this issue. The Ganges is considered the holiest river by the Hindus, and in their mythology it is described as the gift of the God to their civilization. The constitutional conversion of Bangladesh from secularism to Islamic ideals in the 1980s has provided grounds for India's Hindu political organizations to project the conflict as a struggle between Hindus and Muslims. In this situation the Indian government has very limited room to negotiate. At the same time, on the Bangladesh side, the power struggle among various groups does not allow the regime to bring any compromise to its stance – this could immediately be termed a 'sell-out' to India. Khalida Zia's government, which came to power in the 1991 election by blaming Mujibur Rahman's consent to the Farakka withdrawal in 1975 on the opposition (led by his daughter), does not want to lose political capital by giving any concessions to India.

The Prime Ministers of both countries met in New Delhi in May 1992 and agreed to make renewed attempts to find a solution to this issue. Though a long time has passed, not even a short-term agreement has been feasible. The availability of water in the dry seasons has reportedly fallen well below the previous acceptable figure, 55,000 cusecs. While the political situation is still volatile in both countries, no one wants to make any compromise with the figures already allocated in past agreements.

The Ganges: incompatibility in the conflict

This case study directly involves two primary actors, India and Bangladesh, struggling for the scarce water resources of the Ganges. It

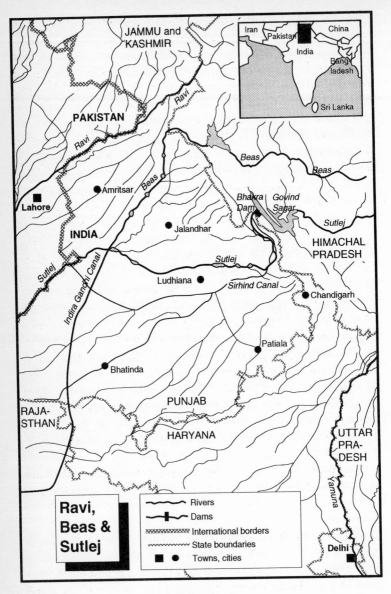

Map 4.2

presents an excellent picture of a bilateral conflict where two state actors have locked horns over water. The dispute over the Ganges revolves around the question of how its water is to be shared for the five dry-season months. During the rest of the year, there is more than sufficient water for India to draw some of it without creating distress for Bangladesh. But in dry seasons, while the average minimum discharge to Farakka is falling below 55,000 cusecs, India asks for 40,000 cusecs while Bangladesh needs all it can get to save its large territory from ecological problems such as loss of agricultural land, forest and fisheries, heavy siltation and river-bank erosion. This conflict has stopped short of use of physical force because the sheer size and strength of one party has acted as an effective deterrent. However, the non-armed character of this conflict should not lead us to underestimate its seriousness when we look at the deterioration which has taken place in Indo–Bangladeshi relations in the past twenty years.

India's invaluable assistance to the Bangladeshi independence struggle in 1971 led to great friendship between two countries in the initial years, but predominantly due to Farakka withdrawals, it was not long before the relationship eroded and was replaced by conflict. As we have said, in past years, the issue of the Ganges water has caused both states to indict each other innumerable times in various international as well as regional and bilateral fora. Bangladesh's animosity towards India has now reached such a pitch that it has prompted a seasoned Bangladesh watcher to remark: 'In many respects, Bangladesh has returned to the position held by Muslim Bengalis in the 1946 election in India, when they voted more strongly in favour of the Pakistan movement than any other group of Muslims in united India' (Baxter, 1989: 442).

Conflict over the Ravi, Beas and Sutlej

The Indus and its five tributaries, Jhelum, Chenab, Ravi, Beas and Sutlej, supply the largest irrigation system in the world. Its annual flow is twice that of the Nile and three times that of the Tigris and Euphrates combined. The 1947 partition line between India and Pakistan cut across the Indus; the upper waters are in India, but they all flow into Pakistan. The Indus Water Treaty of 1960 allocated the waters of the three eastern rivers – Ravi, Beas and the Sutlej – to India, while the waters of the western rivers – Indus, Jhelum and Chenab – were for the use of Pakistan (Choudhury, 1968).

The Sutlej, Ravi and Beas flow eastward, originating in the Himalayas. The Beas, the shortest of the rivers, rises near the Rohtang Pass and flows into the Sutlej at Harika in India. The Ravi rises near Kulu and emerges into the plains near Madhopur in India, flows along the boundary between India and Pakistan for a few kilometres, then enters Pakistan near Lahore. The Sutlej rises near the Manosarovar lake and, turning southwest, enters the Punjab plain near Rupar. It forms the boundary between India and Pakistan for about 160 kilometres, and enters Pakistan near Suleimanki. The Ravi, Beas and the Sutlej together carry about one-fifth of the total runoff of the Indus system.

The Ravi, Beas and Sutlej: politics of the conflict

The Indus Water Treaty brought an agreement over sharing the waters of the Indus and its tributaries between India and Pakistan. But the state-versus-group dispute between the Sikh-dominated Indian province of Punjab and the majority Hindu provinces of Haryana and Rajasthan, with the perceived support of Indian central government over the waters of the Ravi, Beas and Sutlej, has continued to simmer. In 1955 the central government, on the basis of an interstate conference on the Development and Utilization of the Waters of the Rivers Ravi, Beas and Sutlej, allocated the waters between the different states as follows: Rajasthan got 8.00 MAF (million acre feet), Punjab (Punjab and Haryana) 7.2 MAF and Kashmir 0.65 MAF (Jain et al., 1971). For the proper utilization of waters of these rivers a major multipurpose project was conceived: the Beas project. It consists of two units, the Beas Dam at Pong and the Beas–Sutlej link. While the building of the Pong Dam on the Beas was needed primarily to store waters for the Rajasthan canal, the purpose of the Beas–Sutlej link project was to divert certain amounts of water from the Beas to the Sutlej. A dispute over the sharing of the cost of these projects among the states soon emerged. Moreover, Rajasthan demanded that central government should have control over the headworks of these rivers, so that Rajasthan would get her due share.

After the partition of Punjab into Punjab and Haryana in 1966, a conflict surfaced over their respective shares in the water allocated to the undivided province. While Haryana demanded 4.8 MAF out of a total 7.2, Punjab claimed total control of the waters, arguing that the rivers run only through Punjab and all the available canal systems were in the reorganized Punjab. This water issue was used by the Punjabi leaders to build up a separate identity for their own state, which was reorganized on the basis of language. It became more complicated when the Akali Dal, a Sikh party, came to power in Punjab in 1967 after defeating Congress. The new Akali government did not allow Haryana engineers to carry out surveys in its territory. Haryana, on the other hand, basing its claim on 'needs and principle of equity', asserted that Punjab had no legal right in the matter, as the surplus waters had been acquired by central government on payment of compensation to Pakistan.

Having failed to solve the water-sharing issue bilaterally with Punjab, Haryana formally requested central government to allocate the shares in accordance with the provision of Section 78(1) of the Punjab Reorganization Act 1966 (Kumar et al., 1984: 80). The Haryana contention was that it was not a party to the 1955 agreement, hence its interests had to be protected. Before determining the shares to be allocated to Punjab and Haryana, central government appointed a committee of experts to collect facts relating to river flows, areas irrigated and existing utilization. The government also tried to resolve the dispute through the offices of the Planning Commission and the Chairman of the Central Water Commission. Punjab's steadfast refusal to share the water with Haryana could not be tolerated by central government for long. The Anandpur Sahib Resolution in 1973 by the Sikh opposition groups in Punjab, which asked for more power for the state units vis-à-vis the centre, made the New Delhi policymakers suspicious about their real intentions. So when India was under 'emergency rule', central government tried to force its authority to prove that it was really in command of the situation. On 24 March 1976 it issued an executive order regarding the appropriation of river waters, in which 3.5 MAF of water were allocated to Haryana, 0.2 MAF to Delhi and the balance, not exceeding 3.5 MAF at any time, to Punjab. This unilateral act, which was favourable to Haryana, can be easily understood if one analyses India's political configuration at that time. After the Declaration of Emergency in 1975, real power had slipped from the hands of Indira Gandhi to her second son, Sanjay Gandhi, who was ruling the country with the help of his friends. In this unconstitutional set-up, the powerful Chief Minister of Haryana, Bansi Lal, was an important member. While Sanjay Gandhi was not happy with the 'anti-centre policies' of the Sikhs in Punjab, it was not difficult for Bansi Lal to obtain this executive order which, he thought, would bring him political benefits at home.

As expected, the central government's decision invoked protests from the people and the government of Punjab. In a general election in 1977, Indira Gandhi and her Congress Party were defeated. Elections were also held in the provinces, and the Akali Dal came to power in Punjab by routing Congress, disparaging them on the grounds of regional discrimination. To fulfil election pledges, the Akali Dal formally adopted the Anandpur Sahib Resolution at its Ludhiana Conference in 1978 and demanded that water sharing between Punjab, Haryana and Rajasthan be adjudicated by the Supreme Court (Gupta, 1985: 1187). The Akali Dal filed a case in the Court, questioning the constitutionality of the central government's order of 1976, which was challenged by the State of Haryana as well.

The Akali Dal was defeated in the 1980 election and Congress came to power, both in Punjab and at the centre. It was alleged that Congress, while it was out of power, had encouraged a violent Sikh fundamentalist movement in Punjab in the late 1970s to destabilize the Akali government. After losing power, the Akalis tried to win back their original vote-bank, the Punjabi Sikhs, on religious grounds, and the water issue was used liberally to show that the interests of the Sikhs can never be protected by the Hindu-dominated centre. To make matters worse, after their accession to power in Punjab, Congress withdrew the case on water distribution from the Supreme Court. The Congress government in Punjab did not take this decision because they were not aware of the consequences – rather, it was a symbolic gesture of accepting the unchallenged authority of Prime Minister Indira Gandhi. A case against the centre by a state when both are under the same party rule could be misread by others as the loss of authority at the party high command level. However, this action favoured the Akali Party politically, as it was searching for weapons to get back at Congress.

To assuage the anger of the Sikhs, Indira Gandhi tried to negotiate the issue among the states of Punjab, Haryana and Rajasthan, which were all under Congress rule. The executive order of 1976 was replaced by an accord on 31 December 1981, signed by the Chief Ministers of Punjab, Haryana and Rajasthan. According to the agreement, the Ravi–Beas–Sutlej water was calculated at 17.17 MAF as opposed to the earlier 15.85 MAF on the basis of a new report. This 17.17 MAF were allocated between different states as follows: Punjab: 4.22 MAF;

Haryana: 3.50 MAF; Rajasthan: 8.60 MAF; Delhi Water Supply: 0.20 MAF; and Jammu and Kashmir: 0.65 MAF. Even though this accord raised the quota of the state of Punjab from 3.5 to 4.22 MAF, it also made compensations so as not to annoy the state of Haryana. It made it obligatory for Punjab to construct the 6,500 cusecs Sutlej Yamuna Link (SYL) Canal on its territory by 31 December 1983 at the latest, to deliver Haryana's share of the water. Punjab raised various objections, like the rehabilitation of the families whose lands were to be acquired for the canal, but could not stand up to pressures from the centre. Prime Minister Indira Gandhi formally launched the construction of the canal at Karpoori village in Punjab on 8 April 1982, and the very next day the Akali Party started agitating to prevent it. Sant Langwal, leader of the Akali Party, led the *Nahar Roko* (Stop the Canal) movement to block work on the SYL Canal. The issue of water alienated the Sikhs even more from the national mainstream, and inflamed the ongoing violent actions by the Sikh separatists inside and outside Punjab.

After the assassination of Indira Gandhi by her Sikh bodyguards, Rajiv Gandhi tried to bring a peaceful solution to the Punjab crisis – partly due to his realization of the magnitude of the problem and partly to his desire to make India a major player in the international arena, which precluded an unstable domestic arena. In his political immaturity he acceded to the pressures of the Akali Dal and signed an accord with its leader, Sant Longwal, in July 1985. In this accord, it was agreed that the claims of Punjab and Haryana to shares of the water would be referred for adjudication to a judicial tribunal (*The Times of India*, 28 July 1985). The Congress-ruled states, Haryana and Rajasthan, refused to accept it for fear of losing support at home, and raised a legal question regarding the validity of the accord. The massive protest from the two states brought some realization of real politics to Rajiv Gandhi and forced him to back down from the commitment. Even though the 'Rajiv–Longwal Accord' did succeed in dividing the Akali Dal, it failed to assuage Sikh resentments altogether. The centre's decision to appoint the Eradi Tribunal, which did not include riparian principles in its term of reference, to deal with the water dispute created anger among the Sikhs. A major faction of the Akali Dal launched a popular movement against any verdict by the Eradi Tribunal and demanded the scrapping of all water agreements made after 1955 (*Indian Express*, 5 February 1987).

The construction of the 213-kilometre-long SYL Canal failed to

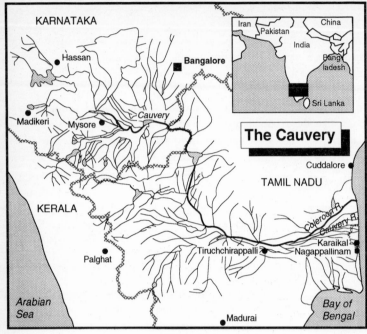

Map 4.3

reach its completion due to opposition in Punjab. In October 1986
the Sikh farmers of the Ropar district of Punjab, where the SYL Canal
begins, forced the workers to abandon work on the project. The
farmers were worried that the construction of the canal would either
take away their fertile land or cause waterlogging (Shiva, 1991: 161).
Various Sikh separatist organizations routinely killed the migrant non-
Sikh labourers, which created problems in finding construction workers.
Since 1993 some sort of peace has returned to Punjab after a long
period of terrorism and violence. The Congress Chief Ministers of
both Punjab and Haryana met regularly in the early 1990s under the
auspices of the Congress-ruled centre to find a solution to this old
dispute, but without success. The fear of alienating the Sikhs again has
staved off the direct intervention of the centre for the time being. The
inaction of central government has exasperated the state of Haryana,
which has applied pressure by occasionally stopping the water supply
to the national capital, New Delhi, from the River Yamuna whose
upstream falls within its territory. This water issue is ticking away like
a time bomb ready to explode again in the near future.

The Ravi, Beas and Sutlej: incompatibility in the conflict

In the present analysis it is not hard to see the contributions of the river water sharing dispute to the ongoing separatist movement in Punjab. This Sikh-dominated province was traditionally using the waters of the rivers Beas, Ravi and Sutlej for its own purposes. While its own demand for water is increasing, it is hard for any Punjabi to accept the decision of central government favouring the demand of the two non-riparian Hindu-dominated provinces, Haryana and Rajasthan, to divert 60 per cent of the water. Sikhs, an ethnic minority group, perceive the act of the centre as a tool of exploitation, politically manipulated by Akali Dal to build a strong group identity, which has led to a state-versus-group conflict.

Recently, the centre has started a political process to assimilate the secessionist Sikhs. However, besides the territorial dispute and bickering over the joint capital of Punjab and Haryana, the city of Chandigarh, the water issue has seriously hampered this process. The Green Revolution in both Punjab and Haryana has led to intensive use of water in these two states, and neither wants to sacrifice her vital interests. Since agriculture is the foundation of their economy, it is difficult for either of them to abandon claims to a scarce resource like water. Rajasthan, mainly a desert state, virtually depends on the waters of these rivers for its survival. This situation has put central government in a delicate situation. Any action it takes to divert the waters of the Ravi–Beas–Sutlej rivers is, rightly or wrongly, interpreted by the Sikhs of Punjab as Hindu India's favour to the two Hindu-dominated states, Rajasthan and Haryana, sacrificing the interests of the Sikhs. The upstream location of Punjab gives the Sikhs hope that autonomy or independence from the Indian union will give them absolute authority to use all the water. The water issue has become inextricably linked to the wider religious and political demands that have led to this confrontation with the centre (Clarke, 1991: 95).

Conflict over Cauvery

The River Cauvery is the fourth-longest river in peninsular southern India. With its origin in the Western Ghats mountains the river flows eastward through the lower part of Karnataka state, through the lower centre of Tamil Nadu state, and develops into a delta at Thanjavur

before entering the Bay of Bengal. Although there are tributaries to
the river in both states, almost 75 per cent of the water is contributed
by Karnataka. A smaller part of the upper river basin stretches into
the state of Kerala. The small union territory of Pondicherry is situated
on the coast, surrounded by Tamil Nadu.

The Cauvery: politics of the conflict

The sharing of the waters of the Cauvery River has been a contentious
issue between Karnataka (Old Mysore) and Tamil Nadu (the Madras
Presidency) for over a century. The origin of the present group-versus-
group dispute can be traced back to the 1892 agreement between the
then Mysore and Madras. Madras claimed that its farmers had rights
over Cauvery waters from centuries of tending the intricate irrigation
system in the Thanjavur delta, and the lower riparian state was given
veto power over all the irrigation works of the upper riparian state.
The area was ruled by representatives of the British colonial power,
who were more interested in the coastal region and the economically
important port at Madras, so Madras was favoured and Mysore's claims
were overlooked. (Ramana, 1992: 37–41).

In 1924 another agreement was signed. Madras agreed to the
construction of Mysore's Krishnarajasagar Dam as well as to Mysore
extending its irrigation to 110,000 acres. The agreement recommended
a revision after fifty years – in 1974 – and also provided for settlement
of disputes regarding the interpretation of the agreement through arbitration or, if the parties agreed, through the central government of
India.

After independence in 1947 the problems started. By 1950 a number
of large dam projects were planned in Tamil Nadu. Mysore (now
Karnataka) objected to Madras (now Tamil Nadu) taking up these
projects. According to Karnataka, the 1924 agreement did not permit
Tamil Nadu to construct new irrigation works on the main river basin.
It was agreed to postpone this discussion until the revision. Apart from
the revision clause in the 1924 agreement, the case of Karnataka was
advanced because the reorganization of the states that followed Indian
independence resulted in the part of the river basin where Cauvery has
its origin being excluded from Tamil Nadu and included in Karnataka.

In 1974 the 1924 agreement expired, and since then efforts have
been made to arrive at an amicable solution, led by central government.
It is a catalogue of failed attempts.

At one point the three states had almost agreed to the setting up of an authority to settle the dispute, but it never materialized. In 1976 the states agreed to look into the sharing of the available waters and set up a committee, which again never materialized. Petitions filed in the Supreme Court of India seeking directions from the union of India to refer the dispute to a tribunal under the Inter-State Water Disputes Act 1956 were withdrawn on 24 July 1975 because of the suspension of fundamental rights during the Emergency (Ramana, 1992: 45).

In 1983 a Tamil Nadu Farmers' Society filed a writ petition, citing the union of India, the government of Karnataka and the government of Tamil Nadu as respondents. The petitioners said they were entitled to the lower riparian rights of the Cauvery River because of cultivating their lands over the years, and also alleged that the inflow into the Cauvery from Karnataka had diminished due to the construction of new dams, projects and reservoirs. The Supreme Court allowed the petition and directed central government to constitute the Cauvery Waters Disputes Tribunal in 1990. The fact that at that time the centre was ruled not by Congress but by the National Front, a coalition of regional parties and the national opposition, under Prime Minister V. P. Singh of Janata Dal, probably explains why such a tribunal could be constituted. As we mentioned above, Janata Dal wanted to show itself as a powerful alternative to the long-ruling Congress Party, so there were some policy changes. Singh was also a strong political ally of the then ruling party in Tamil Nadu, the DMK, and its leader, M. Karunanidhi. In fact, DMK was one of the constituents of the National Front. At the same time, Congress ruled Karnataka, and this factor contributed to the centre taking a pro-Tamil Nadu stand on the water issue.

In June 1991 the Cauvery Waters Disputes Tribunal passed an order on an interim relief sought by Tamil Nadu and Pondicherry, whereby Karnataka was told to release water on a weekly basis from June to May. One month later the governor, the centre's representative in the state of Karnataka, issued an ordinance making the decision or order of any court or tribunal inapplicable unless it was the final decision of the Cauvery Waters Disputes Tribunal, thus 'cancelling' the interim relief.

This seemingly strange act – a representative of the centre challenging the centre – may have an explanation. It served the political interests of Bangarappa, who had become Chief Minister of Karnataka due to the direct intervention of Rajiv Gandhi. But Bangarappa lacked strong support in his own Congress Party, so the death of Rajiv was an unforeseen political disaster for him. With the help of this ordinance, Bangarappa raised the intensity of the conflict and thus united the whole of Karnataka by referring to the interest of the state. It gave him a reprieve from the dissidence within the state and secured his position *vis-à-vis* the central leadership, unable to take any direct action against him which would only have backfired.

Two days later the President of India referred questions to the Supreme Court, and later in 1991 the Supreme Court gave the opinion that the Karnataka ordinance was beyond the legislative competence of the state; the Court also supported the jurisdiction of the tribunal by stating that the tribunal is competent to grant any interim relief to the parties in the dispute when a reference for such a relief is made by central government.

This led to serious consequences. In mid-December 1991, at a procession in Karnataka's capital, Bangalore, violence erupted, which spread and intensified, resulting in arson and eviction of people from their homes, especially Tamils living in slum areas. Then the violence spread to the southeast of Karnataka, to the Cauvery basin and the districts bordering Tamil Nadu. Tamilian farmers were driven away, and their houses were looted and burned. By the end of December the violence had spread to Tamil Nadu, where Kannadiga homes were attacked and Kannadiga landowners driven out. Road traffic between the two states was interrupted, and it is estimated that when the conflict was at its highest intensity about 100,000 people moved from Karnataka to Tamil Nadu (Guhan, 1993: 42).

Since then a number of political initiatives have evolved around the Cauvery issue, without any solution to the problem. In July 1993 the Chief Minister of Tamil Nadu, J. Jayalalitha, went on a fast in protest that the order given by the tribunal two years earlier had yet to be implemented. Water Resources Minister V. C. Shukla, from central government, had personally to persuade her to stop fasting and negotiate between the two states. It was agreed to set up a committee to monitor the flow of the Cauvery waters to Tamil Nadu.

Chief Minister Jayalalitha is clearly using the Cauvery issue as a tool in her political game, and never loses an opportunity to use a problem to mobilize support for her party. Challenging the centre on any regional issue reaps political benefits in Tamil Nadu, and the centre has responded by appointing a Jayalalitha-hostile governor in the state of Tamil Nadu. The deterioration of the relationship between the central Congress leadership and Jayalalitha's AIADMK Party can be at least partly explained by the differences over the Cauvery water sharing. Chief Minister Jayalalitha claims that the food security of her state would be threatened if the Tamil Nadu share of the Cauvery water were reduced.

Another important factor is that Jayalalitha's AIADMK Party was going through rough times as a coalition with the Congress Party failed and suffered heavy attacks from the oppositional party, DMK. Demonstrating a strong commitment to an issue like Cauvery has given Chief Minister Jayalalitha a lot of goodwill. To quote some political commentators: 'Centre-bashing is the surest way to become a cult-figure in Tamil Nadu' (Swamy and Rai, 1993: 15). In fact, Karnataka Chief Minister Veerappa Moily, attacked by dissidents within his own party, seems to have enjoyed the respite given by the fast and the attention it attracted. This time both leaders profited from using the Cauvery issue for political purposes.

The Karnataka government feels disadvantaged by the 1924 agreement. Despite the fact that 75 per cent of the catchment areas of the Cauvery basin lies within its territory, its utilization is small. The total utilization of the Cauvery waters is 671 tmc (thousand million cubic feet), of which Tamil Nadu uses 489 tmc, Karnataka 177 tmc and Kerala 5 tmc (Ramana, 1992: 43).

These are, however, disputed figures. Many investigations of the waters have been made, but because of the sensitivity of the issue it is very hard to find accurate information. An illustration of this is the admission during cross-examination in the Cauvery Water Disputes Tribunal in February 1994 by the head of the Tamil Nadu Technical Cell that information provided to the tribunal by Tamil Nadu regarding the state's cultivable area was incorrect (*Indian Express*, 17 February 1994). Researchers from the two states also use different methods in calculating the water flow; some even argue that the groundwater table should be included.

The stand of the Tamil Nadu government has been that Karnataka's irrigation development was done without the consent of Tamil Nadu, and that it should therefore be declared unauthorized since the 1924 agreement is still valid and Karnataka is withholding water.

Tamil Nadu has had an early lead in Cauvery irrigation, mainly because of the flatland in the river basin where water runs slowly and has created a delta. This environment encouraged early irrigation systems around which historical cultures developed, such as the famous Chola dynasty, which probably regulated the water flow as early as 200

AD. The Tamil identity has strong connections to the rice-growing agricultural culture of the Cauvery River.

The upper riparian state of Karnataka was in a less favourable position, since the water mostly runs faster on slopes through the state. Therefore, less water-consuming crops, like barley, are traditionally grown here. Due to an increasing population – especially in the state's capital, Bangalore, one of the most rapidly expanding cities in India today – better techniques and a growing industry, Karnataka has rapidly begun to develop its irrigation system fed by the Cauvery in the last two decades. This has made the lower riparian state, Tamil Nadu, anxious about consequences for the state's main economic income and employer, the agriculture of the Cauvery delta.

The Cauvery: incompatibility in the conflict

The actors in this dispute, as we have seen, are Kerala state, the union territory of Pondicherry, Karnataka and Tamil Nadu states. Kerala has other rivers on its territory which provide the state with sufficient water, and Pondicherry, surrounded by Tamil Nadu, includes its claim in Tamil Nadu's. Therefore we can conclude that the main actors who make claims on the river water are Tamil Nadu and Karnataka, two states dependent on the river. The problem involves the 'equal' distribution of water between the actors in the dispute.

We call this a group-versus-group conflict because it concerns two federal states within the same political union, which are less likely to engage in any dispute or violent conflict than two independent nation-states. In fact, belonging to the same political unit should make the two states more interested in maintaining good relations. But rivers do not respect borders within or between countries, thus causing conflicts of interest between people concerned. In this case it is clear that the Tamil Nadu government represents a large farmer population living in the Cauvery delta, whose sole means of support is the highly water-consuming and labour-intensive rice cultivation, whereas the Karnataka represents a farmer group in the agricultural Mandyar district but also a growing population in the state's capital. This shows clearly that it is a group-versus-group conflict.

The farmers' organizations are active in this issue in both states, perhaps more so in Tamil Nadu than in Karnataka. These organizations have taken several initiatives and are naturally very important pressure groups influencing the state parties. But – at least in Tamil

Nadu – they are becoming disappointed that nothing is happening. In fact, they have declared that they would like the political parties to 'stop politicking the issue' (Ganapathi, 1993: 120). It is also widely believed that this simmering problem assumes larger proportions in drought years.

In fact, one could say that this water dispute is a dispute between the Tamils and the Kannadiga, the main ethnic groups of the two states. More or less serious violence erupts when new developments in the Cauvery case occur, the most striking case being the 1991 clashes between Tamils and Kannadiga around the border between the two states. The two groups have no historical or religious reasons to be hostile to each other. In fact, between the states there is a constant exchange of people, so you find many Kannadiga farmers living in Tamil Nadu and Tamils providing cheap and dependable labour in the rapidly expanding southern region of Karnataka. The ethnic groups have developed a hostility because they feel the other group is depriving them of such a vital resource as water. The groups are now experiencing a dispute which began over a hundred years ago. The differences in traditional irrigation systems, as well as the rapid growth in south Karnataka and the large farming population in the Tamil Nadu Cauvery delta, add to the unequal water usage. Karnataka denies having built dams without permission and accuses Tamil Nadu of wasteful water management. When water is scarce in Tamil Nadu, Karnataka is accused of taking water away from the Tamils. This seems to have developed into a standing accusation regardless of whether it is a drought year and Karnataka is short of water as well. The hostility between the two groups has escalated, and reached its most serious proportions in the violence in 1991.

Regarding the origins of the dispute over the Cauvery water we can conclude that the sharing of the water itself has caused the conflict in a long-term perspective, but the recent escalation has occurred because political actors have used the water issue to mobilize support for themselves or their own issues.

Concluding Remarks

From these cases we can conclude that the water issue, even though it is important in itself, has been used in these contexts as a tool by politicians to achieve their political goals, such as mobilizing support for a party or diverting attention from an internal power struggle among the party leadership. The water conflicts over the Ravi, Beas, Sutlej and Cauvery were further aggravated by the imposition of some rules and agreements from the centre at the time of the Emergency under the rule of Indira Gandhi. During the rule of the non-Congress parties at the centre after defeating Congress in the national elections, the water issue proved politically useful when the new government wanted to show its strength by taking new standpoints and initiating new water policies.

We have also seen from these three case studies that conflicts over a scarce resource like water can erupt on different levels: state versus state, state versus group and group versus group. The analysis of our second case study also suggests that group-versus-group conflicts can in the long run be transformed into state-versus-group conflicts.

Water is a vital resource to mankind, and even though it is a renewable resource, the demands of a growing population, rapid industrialization and the resulting urbanization, and an expanding agriculture are so marked that the existing water supply is not enough, and scarcity due to strong seasonal variations has become a problem. This is especially true for the countries in the poor developing world, which have weak state structures and lack the ability to deal with problems arising out of resource scarcities. Lack of education and blind ethnic loyalties also lead to politicization as well as ethnicization of the problem.

Water scarcity is no doubt a current and future threat to the fragile security of the developing world. Consequently, it is unwise to overlook the environmental problem – or rather, the problem caused by scarce resources like water – in making a security evaluation of a country or a region, especially in the developing world. In an interdependent and interconnected world, the conflicts in these developing countries might potentially spill over to destroy the peace and tranquility of the temperate developed region.

5

Mainland Southeast Asia:
Co-operation or Conflict over Water?

Joakim Öjendal

Introduction

When we look at the tranquil brown stream carelessly floating through mainland Southeast Asia towards the South China Sea, it is difficult to imagine what great importance the Mekong River has for a large number of people. But it is only in the dry season that the river is anything like tranquil. In August, when the monsoon arrives, the current is rapid and sweeps away any loose objects in its path. At this time of the year the river more clearly mirrors the economic and political turmoil it currently causes.

There are two things that make the situation of the Mekong River unique: first, it is a huge river almost totally unexploited on a large scale; second, a regional master plan on its proposed development was constructed *before* any major projects or conflicts had been initiated. This second feature is due to the Mekong Committee, a long-lasting regional co-operation body in mainland Southeast Asia, now reconstituted as the Mekong River Commission.

The Mekong River is often referred to as the greatest single natural resource of mainland Southeast Asia (MS, 1987: 1; MS, 1989: 39). The region it passes through is one of the poorest regions in the world. This fact highlights the contrast between present reality and future potential. Taken together, these features seem to indicate bright prospects for river basin development in the case of the Mekong.

It is no coincidence, however, that the river is so far unexploited. It is a herculean task to take on the complexities of river development, whether we are talking about irrigation, fishing, transport or

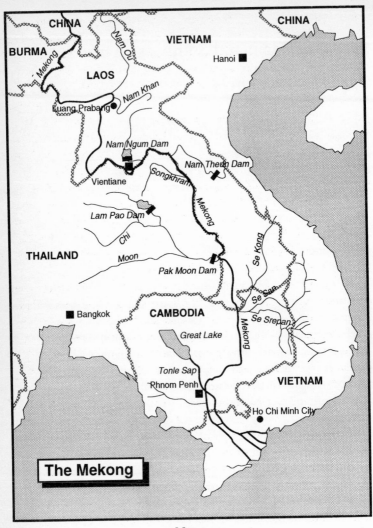

Map 5.1

power generation, or discussing politics, economics or ecology. A plethora of detailed plans, ambitions and critique exists (White, 1963; Sewell and White, 1966; MS, 1987; 1993; Statistical Publishing House, 1990; Ryder, 1993), but none of the major projects has received favourable enough assessment to move towards realization. Furthermore, the region is plagued with conflicts, and only recently, with the peace in Cambodia, is there 'enough peace' in the region for one seriously to start to believe in (or to fear) any major change in the present water regime. The peace and stability in the region are, however, fragile and cannot, at this stage, take any major shocks without endangering the promising development in regional co-operation and security. Even now there is some ominous tension over the proposed development schemes (*Chaipipat*, 27 March 1992; VNA, 14 March 1992; *The Nation*, 16 March 1992) and over the elusive moral and legal question of who has the right to the water, domestically (Mekloy, 1993) as well as regionally (Chongkittavorn, 1992: A2).

The question of sharing water between up- and downstream countries is still a generally unresolved and all too common source of conflict. In the Mekong case, the Helsinki Declaration of 1966 – which is an attempt to outline the legal rights to water usage – is commonly referred to. So is the Rhine agreement. Other attempts to find a legal instrument for dealing with this moral question have been made by the Mekong secretariat itself (MS, 1993b).

Adding to the horizontal problem of national conflicts (i.e. between nation-states) is the vertical problem of national development (between different needs on local and national levels): who will benefit from the possible changes in the water regime? Most people in the river basin are poor subsistence peasants totally dependent on access to water and with virtually no preparation for change. In Cambodia, for example, 90 per cent of the population live in rural areas, largely dependent on the annual flood from the river and harvesting only one crop a year. With an average annual rainfall of approximately 1,800 millimetres Cambodia does not experience any lack of water in absolute terms, but she cannot benefit in any way from the amount of water theoretically accessible. In general the level of education, the infrastructure and the degree of industrialization throughout the basin is low or very low, reinforcing dependence on the river and its tributaries.

So we have a string of contradictions in regard to the Mekong River development problem complex. First, not one mainstream project has yet been launched in the Lower Mekong Basin, but there are schemes and pre-feasibility studies for four mainstream projects and another three 'of international consequence'. Of these, two are singled out as interesting for the next round of negotiations (MS, 1987: 13f.). Second, the development of the river might serve as a catalyst for the region to overcome its conflictual history, but it might just as well turn into a nasty new regional conflict if it is not treated properly. Third, the peasants living in its basin suffer from lack of accessible water while there is still – seasonally – an abundance. Lastly, the ecological system – which is extremely sensitive, with some extraordinary phenomena – is not threatened only by river development schemes, but also by present overuse by farmers and fishermen. These contradictions all boil down to the ultimate paradox: *there is an immense pressure for change in the water regime, coexisting with terrifying insecurities connected to this very same change.*

I will try to highlight a number of the potential risks – i.e. the potential national conflict over water and the development problematic in Cambodia – with the situation described above, first by giving an overview of the physical features of the river, followed by the history of the Mekong co-operation and the regional political background. At this stage I put forward the concept *regional security*, which serves to explain the recent turmoil around the Mekong Committee. Before my conclusion I take a brief look at what to my mind are the three largest conflict risks associated with the struggle for water in mainland Southeast Asia.

The term 'mainland Southeast Asia' here means Vietnam, Cambodia, Laos and Thailand. 'The Mekong River' is short for the Mekong River Basin. It is widely agreed among the riparian countries to consider not only the river itself, but the drainage area as a whole. The focus is on the Lower Mekong Basin – that is, southwards from the tricountry juncture Burma, Thailand and Laos. The Mekong Committee, a regional co-operation body central in many aspects, was set up in 1957 and consisted of Thailand, Cambodia, (South) Vietnam and Laos. Its full name was 'The Committee for Co-ordination of Investigations of the Lower Mekong Basin'. In 1965 the statutes were amended to extend the authority of the Committee. This was also reflected in the change of name to 'The Committee for Co-ordination of Comprehensive Development of the Lower Mekong Basin'. The Committee is the deciding body, the Mekong Secretariat the executive body. The committee has recently been undergoing revision (see below).

About the Mekong River

Physical characteristics of the river basin[1]

The Mekong River carries 475 cubic kilometres of water a year. It is the tenth-largest river in the world measured in water flow, and by far the largest unexploited river in the world. At low flow it carries 1,600–2,000 cubic metres per second, which makes it the third in size in Asia after the Yangtze in China and the Ganges in India. It stretches 4,200 kilometres from Tibet to the Mekong Delta in Vietnam, 2,400 kilometres of which are in the Lower Mekong Basin. Its basin covers 795,000 square kilometres (more than six times the size of England). The total basin population is around 50 million, with an estimated GDP *per capita* of less than 200 US dollars per year. The birth rate and population growth are high throughout the basin; in Cambodia, for example, it reaches 2.8 per cent annually (IBRD, 1992: 8).

The Mekong River originates in Tibet, passes through the Yunnan province in China with its deep, inhospitable and thinly populated canyons, then strikes the Burmese border for a short while before it crisscrosses in and out of Thailand and Laos. At the violent and beautiful Khone Waterfalls it enters Cambodia rapidly before it slows up in central Cambodia. Finally, it discharges into the South China Sea through nine arms in the low-lying Mekong delta in the south of Vietnam.

The annual rainfall is somewhere between 1,000 and 3,000 mm, locally up to 4,000 mm, falling almost entirely during the rainy season, June to October, when the normally very reliable monsoon comes in over Southeast Asia. Of the four countries Laos contributes most water to the river, followed by Cambodia, Thailand, China, Vietnam and Burma in descending order. Of the lower basin, with its total of 607,000 square kilometres, 204,000 are covered by Laos (85 per cent of the country, 40 per cent of the basin), 182,000 by Thailand (23 per cent of the country, 20 per cent of the basin), 156,000 by Cambodia (86 per cent of the country, 26 per cent of the basin) and 65,000 by Vietnam (20 per cent of the country, 11 per cent of the basin). The monsoon is reliable but locally the rainfall is utterly unpredictable, notably so in northeastern Thailand.

The river carries a huge economic potential: the technical hydropower potential is estimated at some 37,000 MW and 150–180,000 GWh/year. This could be compared to Cambodia's total installed capacity of 85 MW (1993). The area suitable for irrigation is estimated at 6 million hectares; three times the total area under paddy cultivation in Cambodia. Bear in mind, however, that it is not clear how much of this it is socially and economically feasible to develop. What is clear is that fish is the major source of protein throughout the basin, and in many places transportation on the river – and its tributaries – is the only feasible way of moving.

The plan for the development of the Mekong River as of 1993

The most comprehensive source regarding the Mekong River development projects is the annual 'Work Programme', which gives a quick quantitative overview of the present plans (all figures from MS, 1993a).

This accounts for a total of 116 projects in the lower basin, of which 60 (52 per cent) are on a basinwide scale and 56 (48 per cent) on a national scale. The basinwide projects increased from 33 per cent in 1985 to 52 per cent in 1993, and it is the explicit ambition of the Mekong Committee to continue to increase the ratio of basinwide projects. Of the 116 projects mentioned, 40 per cent are already funded and under way in one guise or another. Another 196 million US dollars are required for the full funding of the 116 projects. Of the national projects Vietnam has 12, Thailand 8, Laos 14 and Cambodia 20. The remaining two non-basinwide projects are shared between two or three countries in the basin. Cambodia is, generally speaking, far behind in planning for river development. This is deliberately compensated for by the Mekong Committee.

The projects are divided into 'Policy and Planning', 'Technical Support', 'Resources Development' and 'Programme Projects'. Resources Development is the nucleus of the programme, containing categories such as 'Water Resources and Hydropower', 'Agriculture' and 'Fisheries'. The vast majority of projects are feasibility studies, information-gathering, human resources development, and the like. A limited number of projects cost around 3–8 million dollars, and one project (Kirirom 1 hydropower project in Cambodia, Project No. MKG/R.92003) reaches a budget in excess of 22 million dollars. This project is being delayed by security problems caused by the civil war in Cambodia.

It is obvious that we are dealing with a subject of major proportions and crucial importance for the people and states in the basin. Furthermore, this has to be dealt with in a region with a low degree of political stability, both between the states sharing the river and domestically. However, neither attempts to harness the Mekong River nor regional co-operation are novel phenomena; they have a long history. Let us take a look at them.

Historical Background to the Mekong River Co-operation

Preface to co-operation around the Mekong River

There were originally three major initiators for the Mekong project: the UN body ECAFE (Economic Commission for Asia and the Far East, based in Bangkok), the participating national governments, and the more elusive American interest to consolidate the non-Communist forces in the region. The latter contributed with authority within the UN system, and with a number of early studies of the prospects and potential of the Mekong River. Especially important was a reconnaissance tour in 1955 supported by the US Department of the Interior, the 'Wheeler mission' (UN, 1958) and, later, a study supported by the Ford Foundation (White *et al.*, 1962). The 'Wheeler mission' has a special role within the history of the Mekong Committee. It was led by General Raymond Wheeler, formerly chief of the United States Corps of Engineers, and it produced a road map that served as a catalyst for enhanced regional co-operation and acceleration of the pace of work with the Mekong River, both internally and externally for donors. It also explicitly encouraged the work of the Mekong Committee (Sewell and White, 1966: 20ff.).

The ECAFE involvement dates right back to 1949, when it was primarily interested in flood control and secondarily in water resources development (MS, 1989: 8f.). ECAFE encouraged its 'Bureau of Flood Control' to incorporate international rivers in its dual studies of technical problems and flood control. The Bureau recommended further studies of the basin (Bureau of Flood Control, 1952), but the region then experienced political turmoil, impeding immediate further action.

The ECAFE decision to widen the flood-control study to international rivers, the US interest of joining non-Communist forces (especially after the division of Vietnam), the joint interest of the riparian governments and the obvious international character of the river all pointed towards an institutionalized regional co-operative body. Thus, on 17 September 1957 the four riparians Thailand, Laos,

Cambodia and South Vietnam signed the statutes, and the Mekong Committee was born. Decisions were to be taken unanimously, and chairmanship was to rotate among the member states ('Committee for Co-ordination', 1957, Art. 2). The focus of the Mekong Committee activities would be: (1) data collection; (2) preparation of an overall plan; (3) planning and design of individual projects; (4) maintenance of existing projects; and (5) ancillary work (MS, 1989: 14). The committee was to concentrate on technical and co-ordinating activities, and was not invested with decision-making powers (even though it actually signed some agreements; see Convention on Power Supply between Thailand and Laos, 1965, in MS, 1989: 16). A big effort was made to try to give the Mekong Committee an independent position both from the UN system and from the member governments. Still it had to retain good relations with the UN system and, of course, legitimacy from its respective governments. The solution was that the committee was 'established by' the governments, but acted 'in response to decisions taken by the UN's ECAFE' (ibid.). This ambition was further underlined by the installation of the Executive Agent and his office (the Mekong Secretariat).

The early phase and the grand plans

Throughout the 1960s the project was imbued with great expectations and grand plans.

> I regard the Mekong river project as one of the most important and one of the most significant actions ever undertaken by the United Nations.... (U Thant, CBS Broadcast 1965, quoted in MS, 1989: 3)

The Mekong Committee annual report of 1961 outlines ten mainstream projects with a total capacity of 10,620 MW installed hydropower. Its plans exceeded 5.8 million hectares of irrigated land, and navigation would be improved by 1,720 kilometres. Added to this were projects for flood control and drainage.

The Mekong River development was, in retrospect, a hostage of the early reports and studies from the late 1950s and early 1960s. It brought the gigantism and the well-intended but naive reliance on technical solutions commonly bred by overoptimistic development thinking in the 1950s. It was stuck in the paradoxical situation of too large (overambitious single projects) and too little (regional integration) at the same time. It was too much engineering and not enough ecology and socioeconomic studies. This led to a situation where not much was achieved besides institutional strengthening and preparations for grand plans. The projects that had actually been achieved were not the grand ones, but the minor ones. Better overview and a more realistic approach were thus badly needed.

Maturation of the project?

This problem was addressed in 1970, when the '1970 Indicative Basin Plan' was published. It contained an attempt to compile and co-ordinate many large studies and had the ambition to outline plans to the year 2000. It was still a large plan that was presented, though, containing a number of mainstream dams requiring tens of billions of dollars investment over more than twenty years. There was, however, a broadening of the development concept, and socioeconomic and ecological studies were given a higher status. The improvement was not a major breakthrough for the 'softer parts' of development thinking, but it was at least tangible. In the mid-1970s approximately 210 MW of power were generated by projects initiated within the framework of the Mekong Committee and 212,000 hectares were irrigated, of which the major part was in Laos and – in particular – in Thailand (MS, 1989: 40 ff.). There was a huge discrepancy between the original hope for a quick completion of the plans and the actual result so far. It can partly be sought in somewhat naive development planning, but even more so in the civil wars raging in Cambodia, Laos and Vietnam (and to a minor extent in Thailand), where the Communists were slowly gaining the upper hand. With the arrival of the Khmer Rouge in Cambodia the committee was thrown into severe crisis. During 1975 and 1976 its work was virtually nonexistent.

The Regional Politics of the Development of the Mekong River

Regional political background to the Mekong River project

The Mekong River project is closely related to the temperature of the political relations in the region – initially so in regard to the intense global Cold War fought there, but during the 1980s increasingly dependent on internal development in step with ongoing conflict resolution. This is not to say that the conflicts over water lessened with the waning Cold War. It is, however, to say that the nature of the conflict changed, and that disputes might be more 'solvable' regionally. What follows is a brief attempt to see how the political relations in the region reflect co-operation around the Mekong River.

Decolonization and Communist success

1954 was the year of formal independence for the Indochinese states Cambodia, Laos and (North and South) Vietnam. It was also the year of the birth of SEATO (Southeast Asia Treaty Organization), the US-inspired regional security organization which served as a bulwark against Communism. Finally, the mid-1950s was also the period when the proposition on the Mekong River Project was launched and formulated.

Thailand was formerly a solid supporter of the USA, as were Laos and South Vietnam. The two latter regimes were not in full control in the country due to Communist rivalry for power. In Cambodia Prince Sihanouk was so far firmly in power, but with an anti-US/pro-Chinese policy in the making. North Vietnam was led by Ho Chi Minh and the nationalist/Communist regime. The Geneva Conference of 1954 divided Vietnam and indirectly led Cambodia and Laos into a long-lasting civil war.

The Communist insurgencies in South Vietnam, Laos and Cambodia gained increasing momentum throughout the 1960s, fuelled by the constantly degenerating leadership in the three countries. By the beginning of the 1970s it was already obvious that the Communists were gaining the upper hand. With the American withdrawal following the Paris Agreement of 1973, the fall of the three regimes was merely a question of time.

ASEAN (the 'Association of the Southeast Asian Nations', consisting of Thailand, Malaysia, Indonesia, Singapore, the Philippines and – from 1984 – Brunei) was created in 1967. Its statutes spoke of economic and cultural co-operation, but the underlying agenda focused on regional security with an anti-Communist watchdog role – externally and internally. With the Communist takeover of Indochina in 1975 the organization was alarmed and, following the failed attempt at regional reconciliation, the Cold War reproduced itself in the Southeast Asian region. It displayed a bipolar structure with the two major contenders being Thailand and Vietnam, thus coinciding with the two major rivals for water in mainland Southeast Asia.

Ancient rivals in regional co-operation

The Thai–Viet rivalry is not a modern phenomenon. Since the collapse of the Khmer Empire in the fourteenth century the two have ended up on different sides of many conflicts, latent or manifest (see Turley, 1985, 1987; Viraphol, 1985). Now, most recently, the struggle over water is one of the most alarming ones.

Three peaks of tension between Thailand and Vietnam can be discerned in the modern era: in 1975, right after the victory of the Communists in Cambodia and Vietnam; 1978/79, due to Vietnamese membership of COMECON and the overthrow of Pol Pot in Cambodia; and in 1984/85, stemming from a major Vietnamese offensive in Cambodia to wipe out the Khmer Rouge guerrilla forces.

The first peak of tension brought the work of the Mekong Committee to a standstill, and the committee's worst crisis so far. When the first wave of mistrust between Thailand and its now Communist members waned, they picked up discussions on how to proceed under present circumstances. Cambodia was marginalized, and marginalized itself, due to hostile attitudes to international co-operation in general and Thailand and Vietnam in particular. The result, in January 1978, was that the Mekong Committee was re-created in an interim form (the Interim Mekong Committee, IMC) containing only three of the necessary four members. This had repercussions in two major areas: the regional co-operation around the Mekong, kept up since 1957, survived in spite of strong regional tensions. On the other hand, any major project had to be postponed (notably all mainstream projects) due to the fact that Cambodia was not a partner in the co-operation and major decisions had to be taken in consensus to be fully valid.

The new construction got off to a bumpy start. On Christmas Day 1978 Vietnam began a large-scale invasion of Cambodia which led to the overthrow of the Pol Pot regime. In just a few months' time the Vietnamese army pushed all the way through Cambodia to the Thai border. Ostensibly fulfilling the Thais' worst-case scenario with a militarily expanding Vietnam, the Mekong Committee held the pressure; a source of some pride within the secretariat (Oram, personal interview, 12 April 1991). The work, however, slowed down considerably, and only in autumn 1980 did it pick up to anything like efficiency. This firmness in institutional co-operation was a breakthrough for the longstanding ambition to promote regional stability.

The third peak of tension occurred during the Vietnamese offensive against the Khmer Rouge guerrillas and bases in Cambodia in 1984/85. The offensive was successful to the extent that it obliterated the Khmer Rouge bases in Cambodia; it was less successful in that the guerrillas fled into Thailand to seek refuge. The Vietnamese made some attempt to follow the Khmer Rouge which led them close to, or even into, Thai territory; Thailand replied on a high military level. This event, arguably the most serious direct contact between Thai and (the unified) Vietnam military forces in post-world-war Southeast Asian history, did not seriously disrupt the work of the Mekong Committee.

The conclusion seems to be that in spite of escalating conflict, the Mekong Committee did not disintegrate as it had partly done before. Thus we can discern a confidence-building process at work over river co-operation. Confidence-building is a key to successful future river management.

De-ideologization and the Cambodia conflict

Throughout the 1980s, Vietnam successfully carried out a reform programme, Doi Moi. Doi Moi has liberalized Vietnamese society and created a market-orientated economy not too different from that of many other East or Southeast Asian countries (de Vylder and Fforde, 1988; Ljunggren, 1992). Cambodia and Laos have followed suit (Ljunggren, 1992). One implication of this programme is that the ideological regional Cold War has collapsed, and mutual perceptions of threat have decreased. This opens up the way to increased co-operation between ASEAN and Indochina in general, and between Thailand and Vietnam in particular.

The work of the Mekong Committee during this period was seriously hampered by the absence of Cambodia. As a result many minor projects and, especially, many feasibility and pre-feasibility studies were conducted. Data and competence were thus compiled in ample measure for what had originally been perceived as the 'real' development of the Mekong River: the mainstream projects.

Cambodia was not welcomed back because of ASEAN's (and especially Thailand's) refusal to recognize the Heng Samrin/Hun Sen government as lawful. It became quite clear that the Interim Mekong Committee (IMC) would not be able to carry out its task effectively without Cambodia, and equally clear that the Cambodia conflict had to be solved before Cambodia could re-enter the Interim Mekong

Committee. The statutes for the Interim Mekong Committee stated that the Mekong Committee would resume its existence 'once all members of the latter Committee [the Mekong Committee] have decided to participate in that organization' (IMC, 5 January 1978, art. 3). Cambodia would thus automatically be readmitted into regional river co-operation once it had a legitimate government.

The political solution of the Cambodia conflict (the content of which is beyond the scope of this essay; see Kiernan, 1991; UN, 1991) was signed in October 1991, and a 'free and fair election' was conducted in May 1993. It was recognized by all major parties to the conflict; thus the road was open to renewed co-operation in the Mekong Committee. Before we discuss the modern development of water, security and regional co-operation, let us take a closer look at these concepts.

As we have seen, it seems that the old set of conflicts has basically disappeared. The former principal conflict emanated from the Cold War, fixing the conflict lines and the status quo. The new emerging set of conflicts is more related to national interest within the region. Let us take a closer look at how one can approach the question of security on a regional level, followed by an overview of the different national interests.

Regional security as an approach to understanding the Mekong River Development

Hopes have been pinned to a regional approach to security problems in the Third World for a long time – not least by the UN, which stated this in its Charter as the first measure to be taken when international peace and security are endangered (Article 33: 1). Strengthening the regional security umbrella was also an open ambition in the shaping of the original Mekong Committee (White, 1963: 49 ff.). The regional approach to security arrangements and conflict resolution is maintained, and recently emphasized, within the UN system – of which the Mekong Committee is an offspring (UN, 1992: 119).

Also outside the UN system there is a rich collection of literature focusing on the region as a vehicle for conflict resolution and development.[2] The *interdependence idea* is well acknowledged and successfully applied in the case of Europe. The basic idea is that different states should be so dependent on each other that none of them can afford to resort to violence to solve conflicts. This idea suits the Mekong region well; a river containing a large number of common projects would certainly serve as a brake on outbreaks of violence. It could well be argued that the idea of the common Mekong development project has on several occasions restrained states from diplomatic and political confrontation. The problem remains, however, the asymmetry of up- and downstream states.

Another idea is that the increased level of co-operation will decrease 'the image of the enemy' cultivated by some thinkers (Jervis, 1976; 1978). The assumption is that working together will build confidence, which will be further enhanced when the projects are successfully managed together. This will thus create a positive spiral. The ambition is to reach a certain level where a country 'can afford' to invest trust in the region and be confident that it will pay off. Ultimately a level of mutual confidence will be reached which has been labelled 'a security community' (Jervis, 1982).

Economic development (economic growth plus social development) would also stabilize the region, and the Mekong River project definitely has this potential. It is often stated that the legitimacy of all regimes in this region hinges upon the capacity to generate economic growth.

The Mekong security problem also fits well into the concept of a security complex. Buzan (1991) argues that some regions are locked into a lasting security relationship, and countries in a region can be tied to each other whether they want to be or not. Mainland Southeast Asia is such a region, sharing the Mekong and thereby being forced into a common project interacting with the security problem.

Finally, the Cambodia conflict has given ASEAN a reputation for being capable of solving – or at least containing – conflicts (Alagappa, 1993). It has also underlined the necessity of having regional arbitration, 'good offices' and regional support for any agreement. After the waning Cold War, we have simultaneously seen calls for an expansion of ASEAN to the Indochinese states (Nguyen, 1993; Hoang, 1993) as well as worries about the actual sustainability of ASEAN (Buszynsky, 1992; Alagappa, 1993). Instead, there has been a tendency to form subgroupings, for example Thailand–Cambodia–Laos–Vietnam. The underlying rationale for this latter movement would be Thailand's desire to be the gateway to an opening Indochina and the Indochinese countries' need for a good broker for integrating into the world market. Thus we have both the case and the need for a mainland Southeast Asia subregion.

It is in this light that we must approach the recent development of the Mekong River project. To sum up: the ending of the Cold War releases regional initiatives; the evolution within ASEAN and Indochina points towards increased integration in the mainland Southeast Asian subregion; and the tension over development of water resources requires a certain amount of regional co-operation. In this situation the Mekong Committee has an important role to play.

New Tensions and Diverging National Interests?

Modern Mekong history

In the wake of an ostensibly successful conflict resolution in the Southeast Asia region following the agreement on the Cambodia conflict, the prospects for consensus around the future development looked bright. The two major obstacles – the ideological competition and the Cambodia conflict – were removed. New dynamics are, however, at play which focus – among other things – more concretely on the struggle for water resources and diverted national interests. Let us first make an inventory of the national interests before we discuss recent developments.

Thailand's interest

Thailand has experienced more than a decade of high economic growth, and faces rapid modernization. It aspires to a status as a Newly Industrialized Economy. The ambition highest on the Thai agenda is to continue this development. This rapid industrialization has some serious implications for the Mekong River Project. Three features deserve mention. First, Thailand needs electricity badly. Until the year 2001 the increase in firm electricity demand is expected to be close to 10 per cent annually (Kositchotethana, 1993: 23). The oil bill is already high, and all available hard currency is needed to carry on the modernization, especially urgent infrastructural investment, including improved education. Furthermore, Thailand faces an overall power constraint, since the expansion of need outstrips the plans for new power plants. EGAT (Electricity Generating Authority of Thailand) faces harsh criticism for not being able to keep up with the growing need (*The Nation*, 26 December 1992: A1).

Second, there is a great need for fresh water – for drinking, and for agriculture as well as industrial use (Pornpong, 1993: A4). The scarcity of water in Thailand frightens planners as well as ordinary people, and is a very tense topic. Who has the right to the water is an inflamed debate in Thailand (Mekloy, 1993: III, i). This is emphasized by the drought and the more than usually irregular rainfalls in the last few years. Irrespective of other pros and cons, large dams are viewed by the authorities as the only way of securing access to water. As Prime Minister Suchinda observed: 'You have to choose. It is either the environment or people dying of starvation' (*Bangkok Post*, 2 May 1992). He also said: 'but as a prime minister, people's well-being must come first' (*The Nation*, 5 May 1992).

Third, even though Thailand has experienced economic success on a national scale, the northeastern part – the Korat Plateau – has been neglected, and remains as poor as ever. This has created serious imbalances such as unwanted concentration of economic activity, urbanization and production bottlenecks. There is also a risk that the marginalization of a large part of the population will lead to political and social instability (MS, 1987: 18). Furthermore, the region faces high population growth, ecological degradation, temporary drought and permanently unreliable rainfall. Outright starvation is lurking around the corner.

It is claimed that there is a preliminary version of a gigantic 'one generation scheme' for diverting water from the Mekong for irrigating the Korat Plateau, the Khong–Chi–Moon project (Ryder, 1993). According to this version, between 9 and 30 per cent of the dry-season flow would be diverted from the Mekong River in the last phase of the Khong–Chi–Moon project (*ibid*.: 3). The controversial and furiously debated Pak–Moon Dam is generally viewed as the first in this major scheme. There is no final decision on the entire plan, but there is a preliminary parliamentary decision to continue (*ibid*.). Considering the stress caused by lack of water and electricity, and lack of Korat Plateau development, it seems difficult for the Thai authorities to back down from some kind of major engagement of this kind. There is also another huge scheme under debate – the Kok–Ing–Yom–Nan project – a diversion from the Mekong River serving the northern part of Thailand. No details about this scheme have been officially published.

Thus, in general, the Thais favour the building of large-scale dams in order to improve power generation, but they need to capture water from the basin for domestic use, and they need to launch an ambitious development scheme for the Korat Plateau. Thailand is comparatively cash-rich and has some engineering competence, which means she is relatively independent. The conclusion is that there is a narrow-logic argument for Thailand to disregard the Mekong co-operation, especially if it is perceived as restraining rather than supporting. Of course this would have serious implications for regional security and integration, and will thus be avoided as far as possible, but one cannot any longer take Thai participation for granted.

Laos's interest

Laos is a small, mountainous and ethnically divided country with a low degree of industrialization and a low level of education. It is forced in the short term to concentrate on development derived from natural resources: the forest and the Mekong. Laos is home to the river for the longest stretch in the lower basin, contributes the major part of the water, and has the greatest hydropower potential. In other words, the renewable water resource used for hydropower generation is Laos's most promising export good and the sector with the highest potential. The Mekong River project is well viewed by the potential donor, so Laos will probably receive the much-needed assistance for construction both from fellow members of the committee and through external donors. For a number of years Laos has been approaching Thailand which presently, as we have seen, has a huge need for power which will grow even greater in the future. There are old agreements between the two regarding the transfer of power, and new ones are under consideration or even newly signed (Manibhandu, 1993: A1).

Laos is also a landlocked country, and as such it is in need of improved transportation of bulk goods. The Mekong is a theoretically possible way of sailing from the South China Sea to Kratieh in central Cambodia for ocean-going vessels during the rainy season. North of Kratieh there is a major physical obstacle: the Khone Waterfalls on the Laos–Cambodia border. Even though this obstacle is not likely to be overcome for large vessels in the near future, improved transportation possibility within the country is of great interest to Laos. In spite of the waterfalls the Mekong has a huge potential to be an effective transportation route for Laos to the South China Sea.

Cambodia's interest

Cambodia has not only been outside the Mekong Committee for fifteen years, but has also been almost totally internationally isolated. As a result of this and of the civil war it has lagged behind in research in and preparation for development of water resources. Cambodia has a large potential for hydropower, as well as for irrigation, fisheries and improved navigation, but there are no major hydropower stations, irrigation structures are scattered and small-scale, fish catches are in decline and navigation capability is limited. 'One of the problems in water development in Cambodia is that the needs are so great in so many areas that it is almost impossible to know where to start.' (Niny, personal communication, 3 June 1993).

It is quite clear, however, that in the short term basic economic structure must be the platform for development. The peasants need the annual flood to water their rice paddies and the fish catch must be kept at least at the present level. As a result of these imperatives the ecological balance must be maintained. Cambodia would also benefit greatly from flood control (the heavy rains in 1991 and 1994 caused a lot of physical destruction). Preparation for change in the water regime is extremely scanty among Cambodian peasants (Öjendal, 1993), and potential for disrupting the productivity in the fishing sector is high due to sensitive ecological systems (Hubble, 1993; IBRD, 1992: 6).

In the long term hydropower would be a most welcome relief for the Cambodian hard-currency deficit, and even a good source of export income through sales to both Thailand and Vietnam (cf. Laos). Irrigation is another priority. Currently only one rice crop a year is harvested in large parts of Cambodia, compared to two or three in many parts of mainland Southeast Asia. Lack of irrigation capacity is the major obstacle to a drastic increase in rice production where self-sufficiency is the number one goal. Cambodia used to be the country in Southeast Asia with the largest surplus *per capita* in the 1960s. It should be acknowledged, however, that besides the water problem, poor soils, lack of fertilizer, mine problems, an uncertain security situation and uncleared forest are other serious constraints to increasing rice production in Cambodia.

A third priority is to increase the fish catch; it has been deteriorating due to overcatch and degraded ecology, especially in the Ton Le Sap Lake (Nilsson, 31 August 1992; IBRD, 1992: 6). A barrage between the Ton Le Sap Lake and the Mekong River could be one of the first major activities on the Mekong River project in Cambodia. It would also serve as a flood-control measure.

There is a broad consensus among the Cambodian experts on the Mekong River that water development must, at least in the short and medium term, focus on rural development (Khiet, personal communication, 31 March 1993; Niny, personal communication, 31 March 1993).

Vietnam's interest

Along with the Doi Moi, a craving for rapid economic development has come to Vietnam. The success of Doi Moi rests to a large extent on the increase in agricultural production. Since 1988, when parts of Vietnam were close to starvation, it has become the third-largest rice exporter in the world. The most dynamic part of Vietnam in this respect is the Mekong Delta, where up to 50 per cent of the rice is cultivated, and even though this region has experienced a dramatic increase in production in the period 1986–93, it is still regarded as the agricultural region in Vietnam with the biggest untapped potential. In 1989 the Mekong Delta yielded 8.9 million tonnes, corresponding to 47 per cent of total paddy production in Vietnam. The paddy yielded in the delta is rising more quickly than in other parts of the country and it is safe to say that it claims a larger part now. Between 1986 and 1989 paddy under cultivation rose 6.7 per cent, productivity (yield/ hectare) rose 17.8 per cent and total production 25.4 per cent. Corresponding figures nationwide are 3.7 per cent, 14.9 per cent and 18.8 per cent respectively (General Statistical Office, 1991: 62 f.).

In the footsteps of Doi Moi – with its focus on foreign investments and acceptance of individual consumerism – the need for electricity is also rising sharply; well over 10 per cent annually from 1986 onwards. This need causes the pace to increase rather than decrease (General Statistical Office, 1991: 28).

Vietnam has two distinctly different parts covered by the Mekong Basin: the western central highlands and the Mekong Delta. These two parts have different needs from – and make different contributions to – the river development which, to some extent, coincide.

The central highland is a barren land (rainforest or highland savannah), thinly populated, with high rainfall and desperate poverty. From here a number of tributaries discharge into the Mekong (then into Cambodia, to return to Vietnam in the delta), notably the upper Se San River and the Sre Pok River. The area has a great potential for hydropower (1,630 MW in the Se San basin alone – IMC, 1991: 18 f.), and a number of projects have been studied for a long time (e.g. the Yali Falls I and II, Ry ninh, and the Pleikrong). The Yali Falls project is potentially the first major project in the new era, since it is economically feasible and well studied, and a relatively small number – in Mekong terms – of people must be resettled: around 3,000. This would increase much-needed power-generating capacity, stimulate economic development in the central highlands, and serve as a flood moderator for Cambodia and Vietnam. The latter is perhaps the major Vietnamese interest, reminding us of the second, and more important, part of Vietnam that is directly affected by the Mekong River, the delta.

The delta is sensitive to two things: too much and too little water from the Mekong. Since agricultural production in the delta is the nucleus of the Doi Moi development strategy, the Vietnamese interest in the Mekong river is specifically aimed to secure and improve the agricultural and fishing productivity of the delta. Too much water is perhaps the most immediate threat, but also the easiest to avert.

Flooding caused by heavy rainfall damages large agricultural tracts every year. The delta is a low-lying area which is very difficult to protect against the floods. It has to be done further up the river – for example, by dams on tributaries in the central highlands in Vietnam or in Cambodia (the 'barrage' mentioned above). The problem of too little water is possibly the more serious in the long run; the delta faces regular salt-water intrusion from storms in the South China Sea, high tides or low water level in the Mekong. The intrusion caused by the two former is exacerbated when the latter occurs. Salt-water intrusion disrupts the soil, decreases the harvest and causes unbearable living conditions. In the rainy season, July to November, the problem is limited, but it is much more serious when the water level is low, in April/May. This situation will become acute if any major portion of the river's water is diverted upstream during the dry season.

All these potential problems have somehow to be accommodated when plans to change the present water regime proceed. This started a period of repositioning between the riparian countries *vis-à-vis* each other, and a redefinition of how the co-operation would be managed.

Recent developments: conflicts over Cambodia's readmittance

It was widely assumed that the absence of Cambodia would be terminated when there was a regime in Phnom Penh that was recognized by Bangkok. Thailand signed the Paris Peace Agreement for Cambodia, including the leadership arrangement in the SNC (National Security Council). Discussions on the Mekong River were quickly transferred to the correct authority in Cambodia (Alfsson, personal communication, 17 February 1993). The Mekong Secretariat was also extraordinarily quick in their administrative treatment of the new situation in Cambodia; it was already in the workplan for 1992. So far so good. Thailand would host a meeting in February 1992 in Chiang Mai, northern Thailand. The meeting would transfer chairmanship from Thailand to Vietnam, and confirm the readmittance of Cambodia into the Mekong Committee.

The meeting was, however, surprisingly and hastily called off by the Thais, who seemed to have changed their position on the readmittance of Cambodia into the Mekong Committee. Instead they presented a proposition whereby Cambodia's admission would be connected to the admission of China and Burma. Thailand called for a new meeting, but this time the Vietnamese, who did not approve of the Thai manoeuvring, felt that they were being pushed around, and declined to come. Vietnam did not particularly approve of the Thai proposition, and especially not its coupling to Cambodia's admittance.

To shed some light on this sequence we have to go back to the statutes of the Mekong Committee and Interim Mekong Committee respectively. The original Mekong Committee was quite clear that the water was a common resource and that its destiny could be decided only in consensus. The Interim Mekong Committee, however, was less clear on this point, and in general a less common project, triggering national rather than regional initiatives. Thailand viewed a new position where Cambodia, Vietnam and, possibly, Laos would veto the Thai plans. If China and Burma were to be involved, new statutes would have to be created, and certainly consensus on decisions on water use would not be applicable. Furthermore, Burma could be expected to side with Thailand – so would China to some extent, and China would certainly be critical of Vietnam. All in all this would put Thailand in a better position to the one she would have in a renewed Mekong Committee. One could suspect that the concrete reason for Thailand to oppose a return to unanimous decisions between the four original Mekong Committee countries on the use of water is its plans to use the water in the Korat Plateau (or elsewhere) in a way and/or on a scale that they could not expect the others to agree upon.

Status quo

Thailand pursued its demand on Chinese and Burmese participation, a claim that neither Cambodia nor Vietnam opposed in substance, but refused to tie to Cambodian readmittance. In this they were supported by the Interim Mekong Committee statutes which allowed Cambodia back automatically when it broke its international isolation. These conflicting perspectives led to a complete deadlock. Through a number of meetings during 1992 (Bangkok, Hanoi, Hong Kong) the situation did not improve, and Mekong co-operation faced its worst crisis since the mid-1970s. Even with mediation by the UNDP the situation did not unlock until a fateful meeting in Kuala Lumpur, 14–16 December 1992. At this meeting it was only the pressure from the donors (including the UNDP) that saved the Mekong Committee from break-down. Large sums of money have been invested in the committee over the years, and it was in none of the donors' interests to see the co-operation break down at this stage; on the contrary, they wanted, finally, to be able to see some rapid progress as a dividend on the hundreds of millions invested in preparation for future development.

Conflict resolution and a new start

> If joining the Committee means the loss of Thai sovereignty [veto rights by downstream countries], we can go it alone. It is the three Indochinese countries which will benefit from joining the committee in the future. (Thai Deputy Foreign Minister, quoted in *Chaipipat*, 19 March 1992)

Thailand claimed that the thirty-five-year-old statutes – formed in a totally different context – were preposterous, and demanded re-negotiation. Cambodia and Vietnam thought that Thailand was not playing fair when she broke the statutes because they no longer suited her. Thailand had the upper hand, though, being upstream, being far richer, and having a potential co-operation with China and Burma in the making. Thailand also considers – as we have seen above – a conflictive alternative: to continue with her plans for water development outside the co-operation of the Mekong Committee.

The UNDP intervened, took over the chairmanship temporarily, and found a senior UNDP official knowledgeable in water, international law and well acquainted with the Mekong River project (Dr Redozowics). He toured the region in early 1993, discussed the situation at a number of meetings, and asked for 'national position papers'. He compiled them and came up with a proposition for new statutes for the Mekong River co-operation. The proposition was discussed during autumn 1993 and a large part of 1994.

A tentative agreement was reached in late 1994, and formally came into effect in April 1995. The new body, The Mekong River Commission, is politically upgraded and the solution stresses information, continuous contacts between the riparians and adherence to international law, without giving any veto right to any riparian state. It shows a case of initially successful conflict settlement rather than the harmonization of diverse underlying interests. Let us take a closer look at two areas with high risk potential.

Two Special Features of the Mekong River Development

I will touch upon two cases that carry a high risk and/or promises of high return. I have called them 'development problems in Cambodia' and 'The Thai–Vietnamese rivalry'. Both have been mentioned before in the text, but deserve somewhat closer scrutiny.

Development problems in Cambodia

The first problem is of a vertical nature: how will Cambodia cope with the Mekong project? The country is in desperate need of rural development. The Mekong project has been attracting propositions for large-scale solutions, potential donors usually favouring medium- to large-scale projects, and development in Cambodia has both a historical and a modern tendency to revolve around Phnom Penh rather than the rural areas (Curtis, personal communication, 1 September 1992). How can this be dealt with without causing imbalances and social disorder in Cambodia? The problem can be divided into two parts: how will the Cambodian state come to terms with the external influence, and how will the link between rural needs and national economic strategy be established?

Cambodia is an unusual case with extreme development problems. Within a period of twenty-five years it has faced civil war, carpet bombings, genocide, occupation by a foreign country, mass flights and international economic embargo. Thus the country is far behind other countries in the region in most sectors of development. Almost 90 per cent of the population live in rural areas, the industrial sector is very small – 15 per cent of GDP in 1991 and decreasing – and no major relief in this respect can be seen in the near future (IBRD, 1992: 7, 13). GDP *per capita* is around 160 US dollars. Economic growth and development has to be generated mainly in the agricultural sector, and since the country is cash-stripped, any major investment has to come from abroad. This situation underlines the precarious position of the Cambodian state.

An empirical study by this author, interviewing fifty families, shows that reliance on water from the Mekong by ordinary villagers is very high. There is very limited preparation for change. Irrigation is certainly possible, but the actual damming of the water is only a minor problem; secondary and tertiary irrigation structures are nonexistent, so is the money for investment in, and knowledge about, irrigated agriculture at grassroots level. Not one of the tradesmen interviewed regarded their work as tenable without the Mekong annually reaching at least two-thirds of its highest level. The peasants, who are in a large majority, need the annual flood in order to grow their rice in the traditional way.

Furthermore, the villagers have very little contact with the authorities. There is a political administration down to village level, but there are few channels for the ordinary people up to province level, not to speak of the difficulties of reaching the national decision-making level. There is no local or provincial democratic system (yet), there are very few Cambodian NGOs working on rural development, and there is no tradition of popular resistance in Cambodian society; even less so after the last decades of genocide and protracted civil war.

Thus on the one hand the rural population is the backbone of Cambodian society, and agriculture is the sector where development has to take place. On the other hand rural people are voiceless and extremely vulnerable to change, especially to change without their participation.

'The Cambodians have been without resources for so long that now they say yes to everything' (Curtis, personal communication, 1 September 1992). Cambodia is the heartland of the Mekong River development project, and the Mekong River Basin (encompassing 86 per cent of its territory) means everything to Cambodia.

Now, in the 1990s, it seems as if nobody 'can afford' to let the river remain untouched. On the contrary, the pace of construction is accelerating. Consequently, development plans are abundant and aid money is available on a scale that Cambodia has never experienced before, especially in co-operation with the Mekong Committee, drawing on their good reputation for planning, technical and executive ability. The development plans aim at economic growth, which is urgently needed, but economic growth in this respect might not be the same as economic development. So, on the one hand we have desperately needed resources ready to enter the country in technically well-planned projects, but on the other we have a lack of knowledge and resources on how these can be utilized in a productive as well as a socially stabilizing manner.

Thai–Vietnamese rivalry

The other case study is of a horizontal nature. Vietnam and Thailand are old rivals; both have ambitions to be major regional powers, and both have embarked upon rapid modernization and economic growth strategies. The Mekong River puts them ostensibly in a zero-sum game where one loses when the other wins. How can this potential conflict be turned into rewarding co-operation?

Let us take a closer look at the details of these seemingly incompatible interests. The Thais have, arguably, grand plans for the development of the Korat Plateau. There are few figures and great secrecy around these plans, which were integrated with the programme co-ordinated by the Mekong Committee at an early stage. Since then responsibility has been taken away from the regional co-operation body and placed under domestic Thai authorities. The first part of the scheme would encompass 100,000 hectares of irrigated paddy, which would produce 247,000 tonnes of paddy and 46,000 jobs. One dam – the Pak–Moon Dam – is already under construction despite heavy protests from the villagers who will be negatively affected (Traisawasdichai, 1992). As mentioned above, a large portion of the water in the dry-season flow could be diverted in the Pak–Chi–Moon project alone in its final phase. This would, arguably, reduce the low flow to around 1,000 cubic metres per second, compared with the 2–3,000 cubic metres per second that the Mekong Secretariat is calculating (1987: 10).

Another grand project, Kok–Ing–Yom–Nan, would finally end up in the Chao Phya (the river passing through Bangkok), which would considerably ease the lack of water in the Bangkok area (Mekloy, 1993: III, 1).

The Thai authorities claim that the risks outlined by critics of the project are exaggerated. They claim that there is no significant diversion of water, and that the projects(s) are carried out with Thai money for Thai regional development, and are thus of no concern to others. Often the future is presented as a choice between exploitation of the river's water and starvation for the Thai peasants in the area.

The direct economic cost to Vietnam of any serious diversion of water from the mainstream is difficult to estimate – except that it is high. The major problem is salt-water intrusion in the delta. Qualified investigations into this problem are conducted (see 'Studies of Salinity Intrusion' phases I, II and III, MS, 1992). It should also be noted, for the future, that this extremely populated area is one of the most sensitive areas in the world to an anticipated future sea-level rise due to the greenhouse effect.

The present salt-water intrusion affects 2.1 million hectares of land and 15 million people. It hits rice cultivation, and thereby the very important Vietnamese rice export industry and future plans for expansion. To continue this nightmare scenario, we can conclude that it is not only a *zero–sum game*, but a *negative-sum game*. The former would be a situation where Thailand increases rice production at the expense of Vietnam, or vice versa; while the latter would be a situation where increased Vietnamese production not only reduced Thai production (or vice versa), but also world market prices, thus doubly reducing the benefit from export sales. To add to this gloomy picture we can note that the Thais – with a capability of harnessing huge masses of water in large dams – would gain political–economic leverage over Vietnam, quite possibly amounting to virtually irresistible pressure.

The problem is not, however, intractable; it all depends on how the rivals perceive each other. *If* there were a great deal of trust between the two, an ideal situation could be created and there would instead be a *plus–sum game*. There is abundant water in the rainy season, and lack of water in the dry season. Masses of water could be dammed – and used in Thailand if desired – during the rainy season, and there would still be enough for a modest flood downstream and to fill the dams and release the water in the dry season. The Thais could use water for the Korat Plateau – as long as they made sure that they returned it to the mainstream. The Vietnamese (and the Cambodians) would gain doubly: the floods would decrease and the water flow during the dry season would increase. This formula, however, requires a certain degree of trust in each other, and trust is not an abundant commodity in mainland Southeast Asia so far.

There is, however, one aspect in this dam-building scenario that has been treated rather superficially: the river as a vulnerable ecological system.

The Ultimate Constraint?

The Lower Mekong River Basin as an ecological system

This overview has focused on development and security aspects of the proposed development of the Mekong River. Before we draw our conclusion we must, however, take a quick look at the river as an ecological system and the possible threats emanating from any major constructions.

There is massive criticism against the development plans for the superficial ecological thinking they exhibit (Lohmann, 1990; Ryder, 1993; Hubble, 1993). The issue displays a seemingly never-ending story of chain reactions, unwanted side-effects and threats to unique ecological systems which, in the second round, will negatively affect the livelihood of the bulk of the people living in the basin. Large dam constructions frequently face harsh criticism for their ecological destructiveness (Goldsmith and Hildyard, 1986; Pearce, 1992; Ryder, 1993) but also recently for low profitability in economic terms, and doubts about their lifespan (Adams, 1992).

As for varied species of fish, the Mekong River is one of the richest in the world (surpassed only by the Amazon and Zaire Rivers). This richness is severely endangered by dam-building, which impedes fish-migrating possibilities and decreases the number of rapids, which are claimed to be 'the centres of biodiversity in rivers akin to coral reefs in the oceans' (Ryder, 1993: 8).

The ecological system around the Ton Le Sap Lake in Cambodia is created by the extraordinary circumstance that this tributary reverses its flow when the Mekong is flooding. If dams are constructed, there will certainly be no major flood (except in years of far higher than normal rainfall), and the Ton Le Sap will no longer reverse its flow. Nobody today can tell what would happen to the fishery in the lake and its surroundings, and what would happen to agricultural land which historically always has been enriched with nutritious deposits, if the water regime were changed.

Every year approximately 70,000 hectares are flooded by the Mekong River. This annual flooding plays a pivotal role in transferring water and fish to inland fisheries. 'Creeks, marshes, inundated forests and ponds in the lower Mekong region are filled with rainwater or floodwater on a seasonal basis and are as important for family fishing as the rivers and shallow lakes' (Ryder, 1993: 8).

This restraint on dam construction is to be taken seriously. Starting from a virtual zero level, this is being increasingly done now, even though the work on ecological safeguarding could still be much re-inforced. 'Nature has always changed, now it is man that changes nature. That is inevitable, but let us try to do it as mildly as possible' (Harrison, personal communication, 8 June 1993).

What is to be done with a virgin river in the 1990s?

In the 1960s there would not have been much hesitation about what to do with the Mekong River, but we hope we have learnt a few things during the last three decades. First, large dams are not un-problematic; neither politically/economically nor socially/ecologically. Second, economic development is not a linear process, it is not a technical problem and it is definitely not as easy as it might look at first glance. Third, water is becoming an ever scarcer resource with an increasing economic and political importance. Or – to put it another way – water is no longer a 'free good' available in abundance. It is a resource that will be competed for like many other natural resources. The only difference is that this resource – water – is urgently necessary for the livelihood of all people.

The first point leads us to the conclusion that we must think twice before starting to construct any mainstream dams on the Mekong River – for both political and sustainability reasons. The second en-courages us to be a little less deterministic on which direction we are heading in and what 'development' is. It also tells us to be attentive to the implications of any major changes in water regime in terms of national and regional security. The third, finally, forces the countries sharing the Mekong River to find a formula for co-operation across national borders and establish a sustainable understanding on how a limited resource, water, can be shared.

The co-operation around the Mekong River has the advantage that it is well established; there is as yet no absolute water scarcity, and the region has a high potential. Let us hope that these advantages are enough for a positive development for the river basin and its inhabitants.

Notes

1. In the absence of other information the figures here are taken from a number of the Mekong Secretariat studies, notably Interim Mekong Committee, 1987; MS, 1989; MS, 1992; MS, 1993a,b.

2. For the integrationist approach, see Cantori and Spiegel (1970). For regional 'regimes' see Deutsch (1957); Hosti (1967); Jervis (1982). For a view closer to the realities of international relations, see Haas (1970) and Buzan (1991) (the idea of any special notion of the concept of 'region' is, of course, basically incompatible with the strict realist school). For contributions specifically discussing the regional approach to peace in Southeast Asia, see Ayoob (1986); Buzan (1988); and Alagappa (1993).

Looming Water Crisis:
New Approaches Are Inevitable

Malin Falkenmark and Jan Lundqvist

The Challenge

Against a background of current trends in the South in terms of escalating population- and development-driven water demands, constraints in terms of storage sites and financing possibilities, and expanding and intensifying water pollution, the authors claim that present water management strategies are vastly insufficient and need fundamental revision. Regulative and administrative mechanisms are inflexible and inefficient, reliance on market mechanisms is often less than realistic in many Third World countries, and negotiating platforms for settlement of water conflicts are poorly developed.

Perceptions have to be modernized, based on rainfall over a river basin as the basic resource; a new respect for water must replace present utilitarian views founded on a mechanical, disconnected view; a new professionalism must be introduced whereby the fact that water is a finite, vulnerable and multifunctional resource is properly acknowledged.

Strategies must pay proper attention to land/water linkages: land use has to be adapted to hydroclimatic constraints; non-polluting land use has to be aimed at; the possible impacts of land-use changes on water partitioning must be duly acknowledged. Water management should include local water allocation in a framework of regional water resources conservation, where water is used in the most worthwhile manner, and criteria must be found for priority selection between conflicting water functions and upstream–downstream claims.

Almost existential issues such as the conflict between food self-reliance and urban/industrial development have to be carefully analysed, and consequences for other world regions in terms of food import expectations and dependence on exterior food financing as compared to risk for large-scale migration must be identified. The conventional idea of 'think globally – act locally' does not make sense when it comes to water, since it overlooks the regional level in between – the very level where river-basin management for water sharing has to take place. A new globally valid water ethic is urgently needed to guide such water sharing.

The present predicament: low awareness, weak institutions and arbitrary water allocations

Awareness of the significance of water for human well-being, for virtually any development activity and its relation to environmental problems, has come gradually and partially. At the Stockholm Conference on the Environment in 1972 water was given a low profile, although there was a call to improve drinking water and sanitation around the world. Some years later, in 1977, the first UN Conference on Water in Mar del Plata, Argentina, marked a concern for water issues. In retrospect, the impact has been meagre. In the Brundtland Commission Report from 1987, 'Our Common Future', for instance, the role of fresh water is largely ignored. Twenty years after the Stockholm Conference, at the UNCED meeting in Rio in 1992, water was put more firmly on the agenda. However, it was dealt with in a sectorized manner and with no discussion about the significant differences between hydroclimatological zones in terms of preconditions for overall development and environmental stability and care.

This does not mean that water has been a non-issue. In terms of investments and public concern, a lot of attention has been devoted to it. Massive investments have been made in irrigation systems since the 1960s, and the 1980s were earmarked as the International Drinking Water and Sanitation Decade, which could be seen as the most tangible outcome of the Mar del Plata meeting. A significant feature of the policies that formed the background to these developments was a lack of a realistic and proper perception of water as a finite, mobile and vulnerable resource.

Water was looked upon as a ubiquitous commodity which should be made readily available according to some rather arbitrarily formulated requirements. Response to these requirements was facilitated by a belief that technical arrangements could make it all possible. The perception of drinking water as a social service – something that citizens have an indisputable right to request governments to supply – probably springs from the necessity of water for life and, indeed, human dignity. From there it is not very far to argue that the right to water should not and cannot be questioned. It has been taken for granted that this necessity of life should be free, or almost free. In principle, the same attitude was taken to irrigation water, which was provided very liberally.

Water policies in recent decades were thus focused on the task of augmenting supply, and formulated from pressing social issues. Irrigation offered an opportunity to alleviate mass hunger and famine. Improved water supply to households held the promise of reducing heavy tolls in terms of human suffering from disease and premature deaths, and lessening the drudgery of water fetching. In this perspective, activities in the water sector are commendable, and progress has been made. Viewed against the costs and efforts, performance is not univocally undisputed. Health improvements are much less than initially expected, and many of the irrigation schemes built during recent decades are beset with well-known problems of low efficiency and environmental consequences in terms of salinization, waterlogging, and so on.

Apart from poor overall performance, there are other circumstances which signal that prevailing strategies for water management need revision. A concern for management of water resources under increasing scarcity and societal stress, including financial constraints and with due consideration to the functioning of ecosystems, is a key challenge. Many countries in the South are currently in the process of formulating comprehensive frameworks for water resources management. These efforts are supported by major international organizations. The World Bank, for instance, recently issued a comprehensive policy paper where its new objectives for the water sector are specified (IBRD, 1993). FAO has established an International Action Programme on Water and Sustainable Agricultural Development (IAS-WASAD). Corresponding activities are found in WMO, UNDP, UNICEF, UNESCO and UNEP. Today they are participating in special programmes related to water resources in a large number of countries. In addition, several bilateral agencies have marked a strong concern in the sector.

In this chapter we will concentrate our attention on a few of the challenges and obstacles that need to be dealt with in efforts to improve water resources management:

1. First and foremost, water management must be based on the recognition that water is a finite and vulnerable resource, and that the preconditions for its accessibility, development and use vary with hydroclimatological conditions. The environmental preconditions for development are thus significantly different in countries located in the dry climate tropics as compared to, for instance, the temperate zone.

2. As a result of a standardized supply-orientated approach, a weak and partly inappropriate institutional structure has evolved. Few countries, if any, have a well-functioning system for allocating water between competing demands and needs; there are no routines for financing the ever-increasing costs related to supply and maintenance, and so on.

3. A third serious obstacle to proper water resources management is the separation of rights from responsibilities and respect. 'Water rights' imply a legal status or an order that is not supposed to be questioned. It also implies that the 'rights' can be translated into amounts of water; who should get it on a priority basis, and so on. Formulated as the 'right to water', it has a moral connotation and is frequently associated with drinking water. It is taken for granted that all people should be guaranteed this vital water as part of their human rights. No responsible person would deny anybody this basic necessity of life. Contrary to the fairly established perception of 'rights', however, there is a much weaker understanding of what responsibilities and reciprocal obligations should be associated with moral or formal rights. Responsibilities are seldom specified although, for instance, many countries subscribe to the Polluters Pay Principle. Obligations on those who receive drinking water are even less clear. A mechanical perception of rights and responsibilities is a logical outcome of a strictly utilitarian view of development and the environment. In complex and dynamic situations, development objectives tend to be disconnected from an environmental ethic. Respect for water's life-giving qualities, not only its immediate utilitarian potential, is a basic precondition in efforts to achieve sustainable development.

These three points pinpoint the failure to promote a proper awareness of water as a scarce and precious resource of significant value with many competing uses and functions. In areas and during seasons where water becomes inadequate in relation to overall needs and demands, which is increasingly the situation in many countries in the world, the necessity of improved management becomes manifest.

Criteria which provide guidance for how to develop, allocate and re-allocate limited water resources between competing needs and demands, and how best to use and dispose of them, are therefore of great importance. An institutional structure and proper tools and instruments to implement the criteria are required, and a shift from a supply-orientated approach to one where sharing of common water resources forms the context in which these criteria must be designed and politically decided. There is no escape from the fact that anything near a sustainable development requires long-term views and a committed political will *vis-à-vis* water and other resources.

Facing unheard-of difficulties

During the last half-century or so, and particularly during recent decades, the records for water development works and distribution systems have been extraordinary, by any standard. Yet these efforts to improve the situation by a large number of agencies, together with local efforts, fall short of achieving stated objectives, let alone solving the problems. Around a billion people are estimated to be without safe water supplies, and close to double that number, about 1.7 to 1.8 billion, do not have access to adequate sanitation. Household needs are often assumed to be around twenty-five to forty litres per person per day. This modest amount of water for survival and human dignity was the target to be achieved during the International Drinking Water and Sanitation Decade (the 1980s). As already indicated, this objective was not achieved.

Staggering as these figures are, it is more challenging to ponder over the amounts of water required to produce the food, biomass and other necessities of a decent life. Whereas a few litres a day are a basic minimum for survival, at least a tonne per day on average is required to produce the food needed for a reasonable diet (Clarke, 1991). Calculations carried out by colleagues at FAO suggest higher figures, or between 3 and 6 tonnes of water per person per day. The more non-vegetarian food is consumed, the more water will be required.

The need and demand for water will continue to grow. The combination of the needs of those who do not have the political or economic power to articulate their requirements, together with demands by other groups, raises important policy issues. The perpetuation of poverty and population increase in resource-scarce areas will mean a large number of people with very limited power to get access to water or control its development and allocation. The need of these groups of people for water, among other things, may have to be catered for through programmes where survival and the satisfaction of basic human needs are the realistic goals rather than the achievement of a self-generating development. The notion of 'sustainable development' in this context seems, indeed, awkward. Other groups will, through their purchasing power or political position, be able to demand an increasing share of the water that is actually accessible for distribution.

The challenge is not, however, related only to a distinction between needs and demands. A more compelling problem is that conventional approaches to augment overall supplies meet with difficulties which were basically unheard of until recent times. The situation is now characterized by a virtual impossibility to increase supply for one user or one sector without repercussions on the supply to others. Some of the reasons for this are presented below.

There is no more water

First of all, the available water resources are simply limited. In principle, the amount of water that can be made accessible for various purposes and to various groups of people is determined by precipitation falling over the catchment areas where water is required. The amount varies from year to year and between seasons. Apart from these fluctuations, which are quite significant in the South and may extend over long periods, the amount is virtually fixed. It is at the same level today as it has been historically, and future generations will have to make do with the same amount. On a *per capita* basis, the availability is thus reduced in proportion to population increase.

Withdrawals at one site during one period will inevitably have an impact on possibilities of augmenting supply elsewhere and in the future. This is especially noticeable in terms of groundwater exploitation. The total amount of groundwater is indeed huge, but contrary to surface water resources, replenishment is a slow process. Lifting of groundwater therefore often reduces the groundwater capital. The rates at which groundwater is withdrawn exceed the rates at which nature replenishes the stocks in many areas and countries (ICWE, 1992; Gleick, 1993; Sahagian *et al.*, 1994).

The notion of water as a finite resource should be kept separate from the problems of water scarcity. Scarcity of water is to some extent a relative concept. As will be discussed further below, inappropriate technology, and lack of proper pricing, in combination with inadequate institutions, will rapidly result in overuse by some and lack of access to water for others.

Another important reason is that the most accessible and appropriate sites for construction of dams and reservoirs have already been taken into use. The costs of building additional storage facilities and conveyance systems are soaring. Attempts to recover costs have so far enjoyed little progress (see, for instance, IBRD, 1993). Return to expenditure in the irrigation sector, which has been a major engine behind water development, is questioned. Tighter financial conditions do, of course, also contribute to a revision of previous policies. One result is that investments in additional irrigation facilities have been substantially reduced during the last decade or so.

Environmental concerns

Water development and allocation is not only a quantitative problem. With an intensified use of water, pollution becomes rampant. Dilution of waste water in streams and other water bodies, which used to be the 'natural' way to neutralize a threatening degradation of water quality, does not work in densely populated areas or in areas where most of the available water is 'used' for one purpose or another. Nature's recovery processes are being overtaken by the anthropogenic assault. The application of pesticides and other chemicals in agriculture and in health programmes, and the growth of industries with few or no purifications of emissions, contribute to accumulation of pollutants that are picked up by streams, wells and coastal areas. The signs of a degradation of the natural environment and the health hazards, especially for urban residents, are obvious.

The hard facts are amplified by vocal environmental movements. Many of the contemporary projects are questioned, and thus the adequacy and validity of the 'business-as-usual' approaches.

A Look Ahead

Multiple water functions call for a management revolution

Earth is the only planet in the solar system where liquid water can exist at all, and thus where life as we know it is possible. Water's vital role in the biosphere is linked to at least five central functions:

- the health function: clean water is essential for human health;
- the habitat function: the health of aquatic ecosystems is essential for fish/seafood supply, and a major determinant of biodiversity;
- the two production functions: (a) biomass production, necessary for the supply of food, fuelwood and timber; (b) societal production, since industrial development has traditionally been 'lubricated' by easy access to water;
- the two carrier functions: as a carrier of solutes and silt, water is active in generating environmental problems by its erosive force and the disturbances that follow from water's mobility in the global water cycle;
- the psychological function, which makes water bodies, water views, fountains, etc., fundamental human preferences.

All these parallel functions make water management a complex issue. Traditionally, management generally prioritizes specific functions, paying less attention to others. Principally, each function has its own stakeholders. This is mirrored also in the administrative system, where different functions are generally managed under different ministries. As long as water resources are not under any particular stress, this management model has worked well enough in the past. As the stress on water increases, however, the challenge becomes one of satisfying as many functions as possible without conflict. What will be needed is nothing less than a management revolution (Chitale, 1993).

Incompatible claims for water

Access to safe and adequate provision of water and arrangements for its disposal remain a tremendous bottleneck to development and, indeed, a hindrance to human dignity and well-being. Before we proceed, let us have a look at water development during this century and sketch a scenario of what is likely to come. Figure 6.1 illustrates the increase in water withdrawals to three main sectors during this

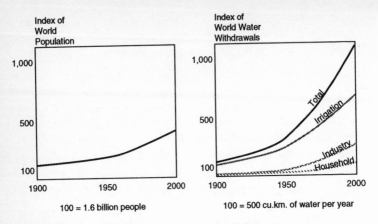

Figure 6.1   Water Withdrawals are Growing Faster than Population

Comparison between population growth (left) and growth of water withdrawals on a global level (right), for the years 1900 to 2000. Since both diagrams start with 1900 levels of population and water withdrawals at the index value 100, the faster growth of water consumption is quite evident. (For figures on world water withdrawals, see Shiklomanov, 1993; and Biswas, 1992.)

century. Comparison is made with the increase in population during the same period. Most of us are probably accustomed to seeing an exponential curve showing the unprecedented population increase during this period. However, compared to the water withdrawal curve, the population increase seems fairly modest. During this century the supply of water to various sectors of society has increased about two-and-a-half to three times faster than the population growth.

In the future, the pattern of needs and demands on water is likely to change considerably. Apart from an overall increase, we may expect to see changes that can be grouped into three geographical configurations and are likely to be found in large parts of the world. We may foresee that upstream use will expand at the expense of downstream use, and urban supplies will be favoured at the expense of rural provisions. Finally, the increase in population is to a large extent in areas where overall water availability is quite limited and uncertain.

The incompatible claims for additional water in upstream and downstream positions are evident in many basins. About 40 per cent of humankind depends on water flowing in basins shared by two or more countries. An additional number of basins cross state boundaries where political and legal systems vary, and long-term rights to water between upstream and downstream interests are not clarified, let alone guaranteed. The amount of water available in a basin originates to a large extent in the head reaches of the system. This is the case, for instance, with the Nile, where some three-quarters of the water comes from the catchments of the Blue Nile and Atbara in Ethiopia (see further Hultin, Chapter 1).

The upper Nile river countries now have ideas to utilize more of the water that is accessible within their borders. In the 1960s, preparations were made to utilize water from the Blue Nile system to expand irrigation in Ethiopia. In a report by the US Department of the Interior (1964) it was, for instance, suggested that about 433,000 hectares of land could be irrigated, for which twenty-six reservoirs would be required. Currently, reconnaissance studies carried out by the consultancy firm WAPCOS indicate that a much larger area in Ethiopia could be irrigated by withdrawing water from the Blue Nile. Similarly, some years ago, the FAO made a study of Uganda where it was estimated that the irrigation potential was substantial. As compared to the current requirement of some 0.2 million cubic metres per day, the irrigation potential, if fully developed, would mean a withdrawal of 11 million cubic metres per day, or close to 16 per cent of the Nile flow (Entebbe Report, 1993). To what extent these ideas and suggestions are realistic remains to be seen.

Reallocation from rural to urban supply?

For several decades, rural development has been a key feature in development efforts in the South. Water supply schemes for irrigation and other purposes have been an important component of that strategy. Moris (1987) aptly describes the policies behind irrigation expansion as a 'privileged solution', indicating that donors and governments invested large amounts of money in costly irrigation schemes with scant attention to performance. Today, the vision of rural development is blurred and expansion of irrigation facilities has been substantially reduced. Scarcity of funding, long gestation periods and a lack of visionary rural development models contribute to a more complex picture.

Parallel with this change in policy contents, there are significant shifts in the context in which it is shaped. The balance between rural and urban populations will change so that the minority of urban dwellers will gradually become a majority at the beginning of the next century. Local sources of water to supply these expanding city needs and demands are increasingly insufficient or are becoming so polluted that they are unsuitable for use. Supply to the burgeoning cities must therefore be arranged by reallocating water that used to be allotted exclusively to rural areas. This kind of diversion is a noticeable feature in many countries.

It is likely that a reallocation from rural to urban supply will be facilitated by the gradual build-up of political support by urban dwellers. Besides the political and economic motivations, the woeful living conditions in rapidly growing cities will promote more efforts to support the urban poor, perhaps at the expense of the rural poor.

Sharing common water resources

Projections about growing demands and need for water raise questions about technological options. It is sometimes argued that contemporary technology enables us to transfer water from surplus to deficit areas, and also to reuse and recycle it almost indefinitely. On the 'water planet' where only a tiny fraction of all water is used (2.5 per cent of all water is fresh water, and out of this much less than 1 per cent is withdrawn (Engelman and LeRoy, 1993), it may sound quite defensive and overly pessimistic to predict a mounting water scarcity problem.

Currently available technologies play a significant role in terms of supply, treatment, and so on. But in terms of finding means and ways of feeding the growing population with food and biomass, for which substantial amounts of water are needed, the technological potential is much less clear as compared to technological developments in the industrial sector and also in the tertiary sector.

The main task in the foreseeable future will therefore be how to share common water resources available in a catchment area between upstream and downstream users, between various sectors, between rural and urban areas, between preservation of the functioning of ecological systems and more direct tangible needs, and so on. Inter-basin transfer of water from surplus to deficit areas is partly an extension of the same basic question. But long-distance transfer of water is progressively expensive. A tradeoff is soon reached where it makes more sense to import the required food and possibly other necessary items rather than importing water. In other areas it is likely that people will move to areas where resources are less scarce (Döös, 1994).

Sharing common, finite resources raises questions about the relative significance of water for various functions in society and in the environment. How should variations in hydroclimatic preconditions be reflected in societal goals? What are the rationale and criteria for (re)allocating finite water resources between growing and competing needs and demands? What are the policy issues and instruments?

Environmental Preconditions for Development

Putting the landscape in focus

Hitherto water management has been addressing rather straightforward issues: water supply, waste water treatment, reservoirs, hydropower units, and so on. Perceptions have been utilitarian, and dominated by engineers and ecologists. The provision of water has been seen as a technical issue – even in water-scarce countries where one would have expected water availability to guide land-use planning. In polluted lakes and semi-enclosed seas, water was for decades seen as a victim of pollution, with less attention to the fact that water itself was indeed the 'crook' that brought the pollution as a consequence of the integrity of the water cycle.

With rapidly rising demands, due to more and more tricky competition situations, these simplistic ideas will not be good enough. Managers have to accept that they will have to learn to handle complexity. Water is needed for many parallel uses, it has many parallel functions in both nature and society, and society gets disturbed in many different ways by water-related problems. The general public as well as politicians need a basic understanding of man's dependence on the water cycle on this planet, and the media will have to be relied upon to provide this understanding.

The first thing needed is a modernized set of water concepts so that this complexity can be handled. Concepts like water resources, water consumption, water supply, and so on, have to be improved so that their meaning becomes completely clear and unambiguous. For example, water consumption is today used both for water use in general, and for the fraction of that water that is in fact literally consumed in the sense of vanishing from the local water system by returning to the atmosphere. This is what the hydrologists in the former Soviet Union called irretrievable losses. Similarly, water supply tends to be used in two senses: on the one hand it refers to natural water availability from the water cycle; on the other for the technical supply system, bringing water to a society to satisfy needs in households, industries, and so on.

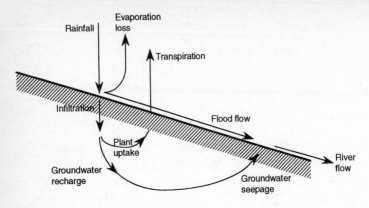

Figure 6.2 The Different Paths of Water over and through the Ground
Rainfall over the landscape is divided into two main branches: a vertical branch of
return flow to the atmosphere, and a semi-horizontal branch recharging aquifers
and rivers.

As already indicated, realistic principles for water sharing have to
be developed. But to do this we need a new mental image. Principles
are needed by which the water passing a certain point in a river system
should be allocated between local stakeholders, but also principles by
which those water needs can be matched with parallel needs further
down the river system. In other words, we have to start thinking not
of water resources in general, but of water in relation to the landscape
through which it is continuously moving. This makes the landscape a
useful starting point, since it is the scene for human activities. We
need an easily understandable mental image of the water moving
through that landscape, above and below the ground from the water
divide down to the mouth. Principally, that water is available for use
while it passes through the landscape. But the upstream uses influence
the amount, the seasonality and the quality of the water available to
the downstreamers, and therefore the opportunities and problems
related to water-dependent land use there.

People participating in the environment/development dialogue also
need to understand the integrity of the water cycle itself, and where
and when the circulating water is available for use. In a certain locality
we need to know the fraction of the potentially available amount, that
is, the water passing by, which is in fact available so that it can be
easily 'harvested' and put to use, and by what means a larger fraction
of the overall amount can be mobilized. A large part may, for instance,

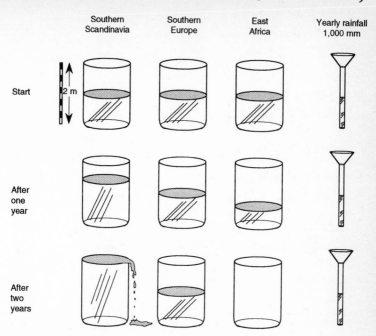

Figure 6.3 Evaporation Takes Its Toll of the Rains

Whether 1,000 mm of annual rainfall is little or much depends on the 'thirstiness' of the atmosphere (evaporative demand), here demonstrated by three water barrels, each 2 m high and starting with 1 m of water. They are left for two years in three different hydroclimates, all with 1,000 mm of annual rainfall but with different evaporative demands: southern Scandinavia with 500 mm/year; southern Europe with 1,000 mm/year; and East Africa with 1,500 mm/year.

pass by rapidly as floods, whether flash floods or seasonal floods. That water can be harnessed only after storage in reservoirs.

We also need to increase our understanding of how the rainfall to a particular landscape is divided between two main branches: the vertical branch returning water to the atmosphere, and the horizontal branch of water passing through aquifers and rivers towards the sea (Figure 6.2). We may call the water actually consumed in biomass production the *green water*, that is, the water in the root-zone, accessible to plant roots. The surplus left to recharge the horizontal branch forms groundwater and river runoff – this water we may think of as the *blue water* available for human use in society.

With these perceptions the basic resource is the rainfall over the basin, which is principally partitioned between the return flow to the

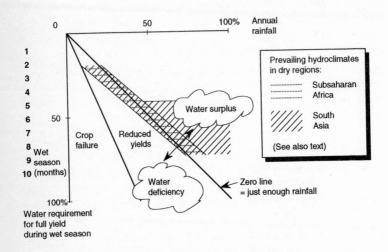

Figure 6.4   Will There Be Enough Rain?

Is the rainfall large enough to allow full crop yields to develop during the wet season? The diagram shows annual precipitation on the horizontal axis against cropwater requirements for full yields, both divided by the annual evaporative demand during the wet season on the vertical axis. The zero line indicates conditions where the rainfall is equal to the evaporative demand. Beyond the zero line there is a water surplus left to recharge aquifers and rivers. Below it, only reduced crop yields or even total crop failure is the outcome.

atmosphere and the runoff. The consumption of green water for biomass production through plant transpiration is in one sense a loss, but can be seen as a 'productive loss'. There may also be purely non-productive losses in terms of evaporation from moist surfaces in the landscape.

Non-negotiable hydroclimatic constraints

If sustainability is to be taken as more than a buzz word, it must mean that life should be organized without destroying vital life-support systems, in particular fresh water, on which every living being critically depends, and land fertility, on which biomass production – including the food supply of the world population – depends. The crucial importance of water for plant growth and socioeconomic development implies that water availability limits land-use options in a certain locality. The basic water resource for activities in a certain landscape is rainfall. The potential usefulness of precipitation is limited, however, by the thirstiness of the atmosphere (the so-called evaporative demand or potential evapotranspiration). This is demonstrated in Figure 6.3, which clarifies whether 1,000 mm of annual rainfall is little or much: where evaporative demand is only 500 mm per year, it is a huge amount (Falkenmark and Rockström, 1993). Where this demand is 1,500 mm per year, it is not much at all.

Having understood that water availability limits water-dependent land use, a worthwhile question to ask is what societal demands can in fact be met within existing biophysical constraints? Does the precipitation in fact allow crop yields to develop fully? In other words, does the rainfall produce enough green water to satisfy the evaporative demand of the crops during the growing season? Another question concerns the situation during drought years. A third is whether there is any surplus water left to recharge aquifers and rivers with blue water, and whether that surplus is large enough to support water-dependent land-use activities like industry or irrigated agriculture.

The diagram in Figure 6.4 shows whether different combinations of precipitation and evaporative demand during the growing/wet season allow full crop yields, and/or produce a surplus of blue water. It shows annual precipitation on the horizontal axis, and on the vertical axis the evaporative demand during the wet season. Along the diagonal zero line in the middle, rainfall is just equal to the evaporative demand during the wet – i.e. growing – season.

In a place where the two climate co-ordinates meet to the *left* of the zero line, rainfall is not enough to allow a full crop yield to develop. The result is reduced yields. The 'minus 50 per cent line' indicates what is often thought of as the minimum soil moisture allowing even reduced yields. On the left side of that line, there will be total crop failure unless the crops are being drought-proofed by adding extra water to the root-zone. In a certain locality, falling to the *right* of the zero line, there is a rainwater surplus beyond the evaporative demand during the wet season. This surplus will form blue water and recharge aquifers and rivers. In other words, there is extra water available in the landscape that can be collected and put to social use.

True water scarcity as a predicament

Two regions where the above questions are particularly relevant are Sub-Saharan Africa and South Asia. These are the regions where crop production increase has not kept pace with population growth during the past twenty-year period: in both these regions crop production has remained at around 2,100 calories per day, with widespread malnutrition as a result (FAO, 1993a). FAO predicts that neither region will be able to increase production much beyond this level. At the same time these are the two regions left behind in demographic development – that is to say, fertility still is four children per woman or even more, and population grows more rapidly than in any other world region.

Where does the gradient zone in Sub-Saharan Africa between the desert and the rainforest fall in Figure 6.4? Could problematic hydroclimatic conditions be part of the reason why that particular region has been left behind? The grey area in the diagram indicates the prevailing climatic conditions in that zone. The width of the grey area includes year-on-year rainfall fluctuations. This means that seven out of ten years will fall within the grey area, but extreme dry years will fall outside on the drier side. In the wooded savannah zone, for instance, during average years there will be rain allowing full crop yields, but during drought years there will be reduced yields.

The fact that the gradient zone in Sub-Saharan Africa is located so close to the zero line clearly demonstrates the *extremely vulnerable conditions*. A standard measure to protect agriculture from crop failures would therefore be to store water surplus from good years to bad, so that it can be made available for drought-proofing purposes.

Besides the Sub-Saharan gradient zone, the diagram also indicates the general climatic conditions that tend to dominate in large parts of the monsoon zone in South Asia. The drier parts of that region do in fact have a similar hydroclimate to the African gradient zone. Only where the wet season is five months or longer may the rainfall be high enough to make floods a serious climatic complication.

What this schematic analysis indicates is in fact that the region with the most rapid population growth and a stagnating food production is at the same time a region of extreme vulnerability due to hydroclimatic constraints. It is interesting to note that FAO, in the study on food prospects up to 2010 just referred to, assumes a crop production increase of some 3 per cent per year – equivalent to a green revolution. It should be noted that not even such a rapid increase in production would allow any improved nutrition; that is, local food supply systems would remain unable to satisfy the local populations: the *per capita* calorie level would stay practically unchanged. The migration patterns to be expected, as indicated by Döös (1994), may therefore indeed manifest themselves during the next decade.

What we have seen is that water may be scarce in several ways in parallel: scarcity of green water, constraining crop production, and scarcity of blue water, constraining socioeconomic development, at least along the lines practised in the water-rich parts of the world. The droughts form an additional mode of water scarcity which will escalate problems with both green and blue scarcity. And finally, the soil surface may be vulnerable through a tendency towards crust formation. In such a case rain cannot infiltrate, green water scarcity develops and plant growth collapses. Instead, rains form rapid flash-floods, with severe erosion, followed by downstream sedimentation and inundations. As has been shown in a recent article (Falkenmark and Rockström, 1993) there is a striking congruence in Sub-Saharan Africa between the map showing the twenty countries suffering from severe famine during the 1984–5 drought, and the maps showing these four modes of water scarcity. Thus, it seems that the famine is closely linked to the water scarcity, something which makes evident sense when drawing conclusions from the diagnostic diagram in Figure 6.4.

The hydroclimatic predicament of Sub-Saharan Africa and South Asia which emerges from the above discussion raises the fundamental question whether these regions could achieve the goal of self-sufficiency in food production in accordance with what their politicians are currently aiming at. The emerging question, rather, is how large this level might be. The environmental preconditions thus reveal some fundamental choices that will have to be made in the near future: if non-negotiable hydroclimatic constraints do not allow large enough food production due to true water scarcity, the question is, should complementary water supplies be imported to these regions, or should they import food from other regions? The question is indeed what would be the best possible use of the water that is available to the region, and what socioeconomic production might be most effective in order to earn enough foreign income to be able to pay for the imported food.

There may also be imported runoff

But besides the rainfall over an area, there may also be rivers passing through that bring imported water originating from rainfall over upstream parts of the river basin. Several countries in fact receive most of their waters through rivers which originate in other upstream countries. Botswana, Bulgaria, Cambodia, the Congo, Egypt, the Gambia, Hungary, Luxembourg, Mauritania, the Netherlands, Romania, the Sudan and the Syrian Arab Republic all receive 75 per cent or more of their water resources from upstream countries (FAO, 1993b).

The role that such 'imported' runoff may play in a country's or region's water management depends on many factors. A key question is whether or not the imported water is easily accessible. Differences in this respect may be illustrated by comparing Botswana and Egypt. The basic similarity is that only some 5 per cent of the overall blue-water availability is endogenous, whereas 95 per cent is exogenous. Egypt's whole socioeconomic development has been based on the water imported with the Nile, which passes right through the inhabited strip of the country and is therefore extremely easily accessible.

In the case of Botswana, on the other hand, the exogenous water is brought by three main international rivers: the Limpopo, entering from South Africa; the Okavango, entering from Angola/Namibia; and the Zambesi, bringing water from Zaire, Angola, Namibia and Zambia. Although Botswana is extremely water-rich in relation to overall blue-water availability, its self-image is that of a country with a chronic water scarcity. The reason is that the entering rivers are not seen as accessible for use: the Limpopo has already been exploited in South Africa; the Okavango is seen as 'untouchable' in view of the extremely well respected aquatic ecology of the delta; and the Zambesi has to be shared with six other states upstream and downstream.

In other words, there may be different types of constraints on imported river water:

- physical constraints, related to the geographic position of the entering rivers in relation to the country (passing right through as opposed to passing along the periphery as the two extremes);
- political constraints, related to the difficulties of reaching agreement on shared use of international rivers with the other river-basin countries;
- ideological constraints, related to different alternative uses of the river water (the river's function as valuable habitat versus water source for purposes of societal production).

In the case of the Nile, the physical constraints are very low; and political constraints have been manageable in the past – as long as the interest in water withdrawals from upstream countries have remained limited. In the case of Botswana, physical constraints are active for all three rivers. Political constraints complicate the use of the Zambesi's water, and ideological constraints limit the use potential of the Okavango water.

There is also another problem involved: imported water is a much less reliable resource than the water originating from rainfall over a country. There is a risk that intensified biomass production upstream within forestry or agriculture will send more water back to the atmosphere, leaving less blue water to feed the river. This is the predicament of Egypt, which is in fact the victim of the upstream countries in the sense that socioeconomic development there may very well involve more water consumption in the real sense, depleting Egypt of part of the resource which has hitherto constituted the very lifeline of this country.

Coping with Land/Water Interactions

A two-way relationship between land use and water

We have seen that land use is deeply dependent on water availability: water scarcity may constrain land-use options through the risk of crop failures and water supply problems caused by a growing population and a growing industrial sector. Rice can be grown only where there is plenty of water. When there is not enough water in the root-zone (scarcity of 'green water'), plant production stops altogether. For optimal crop yields, there has to be enough green water to satisfy the water requirements of the crop as defined by the evaporative demand of the atmosphere. A city can continue to function only as long as water is being supplied to the water-dependent urban functions, in particular water for households, hospitals and industries. The city of Bulawayo (Zimbabwe) was very close to evacuation during the 1992 drought. There was just a metre or so left in the drinking water reservoir when the rains returned.

The integral nature of the water cycle is combined with the opposite relationship between land use and water: land use has an impact on water. Most of the water in aquifers and rivers has earlier passed through the ground, and carries the chemical and hydrological history of that journey. Land use influences not only the quality of the water passing on to downstream parts of the river basin but also the flow and the seasonality of that flow. This is because land use, and the manipulations of soil and vegetation that go with it, influence essential determinants of water flows and pathways through a landscape, above and below the ground (Falkenmark and Mikulski, 1994). Land use also involves waste handling and output of chemicals to the atmosphere, the land and the water bodies, polluting the water circulating in the cycle.

In view of the close interconnection between land use and water conditions in general, the land/water dichotomy reflected in the land-use chapters of Agenda 21 is heavily misleading (Falkenmark, 1993). It can be stated that land-use decisions are often – due to the effects of land use on water – water decisions as well. Proper management therefore demands that land and water management be integrated, at least in the sense that land-use management has to have a water component, and water management has to have a land-use component. For example, to protect against water quality deterioration, efforts must also focus on land-based pollution sources.

Adapting land use to hydroclimatic constraints

It is evident from the above that – at least in vulnerable areas – hydroclimatic and hydrographic constraints have to be taken into account in land-use planning. Without access to household water, inhabited areas have no future. Industrial areas also depend on water supply for water-dependent industrial processes. And successful agricultural yields are critically dependent on access to protective irrigation during drought periods.

Basically, the combination of rainfall and evaporative demand during the wet season should guide preferred cropping patterns. In water-scarce regions, the possibility of drought-proofing the crop production has to be co-ordinated with other uses of the water passing through the landscape (municipal uses, industry). In other words, the water has to be shared between upstream and downstream users, and between different sectors of society.

Turning back to the diagnostic diagram (Figure 6.4), there are different ways to cope with the water constraints it indicates:

- where the wet season is short (less than some 2.5 months) there is always the risk of crop failure; there is no surplus, forming blue water (unless the land is degraded); the evident livelihood pattern is pasture;

- between 2.5 to 5 months of erratic wet-season rainfall implies vulnerable agriculture with particular risk of crop failure during dry years; limited amounts of blue water are recharged during wet years; crops have to be drought-resistant; and the way to collect extra water is by rainwater harvesting;

- between 5 and 7 months of wet season endangers crops during occasional extreme drought years; the availability of blue water is still limited; and rainwater harvesting remains a viable form of water collection;

- between 7 and 9 months of wet season means that occasional crop failure is still a risk; the amount of blue water now allows runoff collection for protective irrigation.

Aiming at non-polluting land use

In water-scarce regions it is particularly essential that the passing water be carefully protected from quality deterioration from waste-producing land use which makes the water unusable for water-dependent activities in the region. In other words, land use has to be managed to avoid unwise waste-handling and other polluting activities that might expose the water to quality degradation.

Water's role as a carrier of solutes and silts through the landscape is well-known. Much has been written already about erosion of vulnerable landscapes and the downstream sedimentation and inundations which tend to go with it. Water as a unique solvent, chemically reactive and in continuous movement, transports excess nutrients, pesticides, and so on, to groundwater aquifers and rivers, causing eutrophication and oxygen depletion in the surface waters.

Water partitioning awareness

Vegetation changes influence the water partitioning between the 'green' return flow to the atmosphere and the surplus left to recharge aquifers and rivers. There are two partitioning points in the soil profile: the upper, between overland flow and infiltration into the ground; and the lower, between plant uptake and surplus recharging aquifers, later to feed the river further down in the landscape. The outcome of vegetation changes may be quite different where both partitioning points are involved, and where only the root-zone partitioning is active (Sandström, 1995). In Australia, deforestation has resulted in reduced water consumption as transpiration and increasing groundwater recharge, and in flat areas in waterlogging. The lower partitioning point seems to be the active one. The way to mitigate that problem has been careful afforestation to increase the return flow to the atmosphere.

The Australian experience is well documented, but in areas where the upper partitioning point is also active, the result of deforestation would have been different. When the soil permeability to rainwater changes, the surface runoff changes, with altered possibilities for the rain to infiltrate. The effect on groundwater formation from deforestation/afforestation varies with soil permeability, topography and precipitation pattern, among other things. The call for afforestation as a panacea for mitigating land deterioration addresses this particular partitioning point.

The impact of vegetation change must also be seen in relation to alternative land use. If deforestation is followed by a denuded landscape, very little rainwater may infiltrate through surface soil and groundwater recharge may be less as compared to the situation when trees help to make soils permeable for rains to infiltrate and percolate. If, on the other hand, deforestation is followed by 'a well-managed grassland', which is often the case in Australia, then the grass will arrest erosion and will also allow rains to infiltrate. In large parts of Third World countries where population pressure is high, hydroclimate is more extreme and land management is beset with various shortcomings, 'well-managed grasslands' are rare. It is much more common to see degraded and denuded lands.

Cities are part of river basins

In water-stressed areas, cities can no longer be treated as isolated islands, just bringing water from remote sources with little attention to other water needs in the river basin. The city has to be seen in its landscape context, since it is linked to the rest of the basin by the water passing downstream from the water divide. In this situation, cities with different locations tend to expose different problem profiles. For example, the typical problems suffered by cities near the water divide, like Lusaka in Zambia, is groundwater overexploitation as the city grows. Also, groundwater pollution easily develops under the city. In Third World cities in the foothill area – for example, Bandung on Java – inundations from silty floods generated by poor land use in the upstream regions may be typical. Further downstream in the river valley, pollution from upstream cities would also be added to this problematic. Closer to the delta region, problems with salt-water intrusion tend to develop. One example is Dakar, where a dam has even been built to stop the salt wedge of sea water from entering the river and disturbing irrigation in the downstream parts of the river valley. In cities close to the sea, groundwater overexploitation quickly produces salinity intrusion in the coastal groundwater aquifers. Examples are the aquifers along the Mediterranean coast in Israel and downtown Bangkok, where land subsidence has followed as an additional problem.

With city growth comes an escalating water demand. Once the possibility to supply cities with further amounts of water at an acceptable cost is limited, one important alternative is to try to retard the often almost uncontrolled city growth that is going on at present in many Third World countries – in other words, to reduce urban migration from rural push. Much more interest should be taken in the dilemma of Third World metropolises. The present tendency to introduce water tariffs is merely to buy time by trying systematically to reduce any ongoing water wastage.

Framework for Water Management in Times of Scarcity

Water is not ubiquitous

Growing competition for finite water resources, together with the soaring costs of developing, distributing and treating them, are changing the context of water management. Under these conditions it is a fallacious misconception to perceive water as a ubiquitous commodity that is free to use and to pollute. But the conditions under which water is accessible and used do vary. An important distinction is between rainwater, which is readily available in localities where it falls, and water made available through some man-made infrastructure. Rainfed agriculture, like most ecosystems, depends on rainwater. During periods without rain, and for most activities other than rainfed agriculture and the like, the dependence on some kind of arrangement for collecting, storing, withdrawing and conveying water is necessary. Generally speaking, the need for water supply arrangements increases in accordance with growing needs and demands.

Whereas rainwater is an open-access resource, and is usually perceived as a common good, the water supplied through man-made infrastructures is not. The likelihood that external interests or agencies will influence the use of the rains seems negligible, although it is not without relevance. If land use in an area is intensified so that a larger share of the rains falling over it is used, for instance in connection with afforestation programmes, comparatively less water may be available for alternative downstream uses. Moreover, the use of land and water has a potential impact on water quality. Any use of rainwater is thus likely to have repercussions on the quantity and/or quality of the water which can be made available in society. The question 'who owns the rains?' is therefore relevant. In practice, it is difficult to deal with this issue directly. It is, however, an essential question in efforts to integrate land and water management, as discussed above.

Water resources management must therefore be based on a recognition that water is both a finite and a vulnerable resource which performs several significant functions in society and in the environment. It represents a great value to a wide array of users, although 'value' may have various prefixes – economic, health, symbolic, religious, and so on. Policies must recognize the various functions of water, as defined earlier, and the linkages to land processes and ecosystems. Criteria for water allocation and use are urgently needed so that available resources may be used in the most worthwhile manner.

Water functions and allocation mechanisms

During recent decades, policymakers' attention has been concentrated on two functions of water: health and production in terms of irrigation. Currently, the significance of water in industrial development is emphasized, whereas habitat and carrier functions are still poorly formulated, and an adequate policy is still lacking. But perhaps more importantly, there are only vague ideas on how to value the *relative* significance of the various functions. Where water is scarce and thus insufficient to guarantee that all functions are properly fulfilled, the uncomfortable questions of priority and choice will come up. Should limited water resources be allocated, on a priority basis, in efforts to achieve food self-sufficiency? Or should industrial demands be given priority? And how should ecological aspects be considered and valued?

Institutions which have been assigned water management tasks have rarely been expected to ask this type of question. Management has been organized in a sectoral manner with negligible cross-sectoral co-ordination. Decision-making, accountability and loyalty have been directed upwards in the central Ministry.

Existing institutional structures and routines are therefore ill-equipped to handle hard choices in terms of allocation priorities which, as discussed above, are increasingly the realities in quite a number of countries in the South as well as the North. They also pose serious challenges within international river basins. The choices are, generally speaking, most problematic between food production and urban-industrial sectors, and between upstream and downstream areas in large basins. In principle and in practice, there are three principal mechanisms to deal with the challenges of allocating water to the most worthwhile use, each one with associated pros and cons.

One is the political and administrative procedure, with its associated regulatory instruments to arrange supplies, which has been the dominant approach in the past. As discussed in the introductory sections, it paid scant attention to resource aspects, supplies became very costly and allocation was inefficient. By focusing on technical supply issues, and comparatively less on how water was actually used and disposed, expectations of additional quantities of water were left to develop more or less unchecked. Subsidies and lax control in allocation and in the actual use of water resulted in overuse and misuse on the part of some consumers, whereas others became the victims of this imperfect allocation mechanism. The task now is to identify an alternative approach which is better suited to deal with the problems that have evolved and those which will be there tomorrow.

In the current debate, there is a strong plea for demand management and the use of economic incentives to achieve improved water management. Much hope is vested in market mechanisms as a means of achieving a better allocation of water in the sense that each additional unit of water should be demanded and used where it will give the highest value in return. In addition, the cost of supplying the water demanded should ideally be reduced if its development and distribution are taken care of by actors in a market, as compared to arrangements made by the political and administrative system. From a resource perspective, a demand-management approach is promising, since it is assumed to reduce overconsumption and thus makes relatively more water available for functions which would otherwise be without water.

A demand-management approach may be seen as a principle, and the actual design of arrangements to implement it may vary from country to country. A 'free market' as a mechanism for the development, allocation and disposal of water represents one extreme interpretation of how to operationalize demand management. In theory it has a lot of advantages: it promotes efficiency, it will transfer management to the most important stakeholders, namely the users themselves; it will not be hampered by stiff bureaucratic control and regulations, and so on (see, for instance, Winpenny, 1994).

Although it is reasonable to assume that market mechanisms would help to improve at least some parts of water management, there are some important circumstances which have to be taken into account. First of all, the development and distribution of water presume a physical infrastructure. This is very different from an ordinary market situation, which is a non-geographical, non-spatial and non-visible arrangement. Once a certain storage and conveyance system is built, a certain logic in the allocation of water is being created. Since water is a bulky commodity, it cannot easily be transferred between various potential users without considerable cost. This represents a quite different situation from that of most other commodities traded on a market.

A well-functioning water market simply does not exist in most cases, and it does not develop overnight and without cost. Arguments in favour of a market tend to assume that the preconditions for a free and perfect market are there, or that they will easily develop. Apart from the physical complications mentioned above, there are structural impediments that have to be overcome. In most regions in the South, the legal status of rights to draw water – which is an essential condition for the proper functioning of a market – is uncertain. Ownership or right to water may be vested in the state, it may be a common good, and where private ownership exists, it may be circumscribed. Equally important, the required easy access to information, which is another precondition for a well-functioning market, hardly exists. The so-called transaction costs – the time and effort required to inform and establish contracts, etc. for actors on a market – could be quite high.

Nevertheless, water marketing does play quite an important role in development and distribution in some areas – for instance in groundwater marketing in a number of states in India, and also in Bangladesh (Shah, 1993). Well-developed water markets also operate in Chile (Gazmuri, 1994; and John Briscoe, personal communication). As a supplement to public supplies, water marketing is quite common, particularly in terms of water vending to households and to some extent in the industrial sector. Water markets are also a noticeable feature in Colorado in the USA.

A third principal option is to promote a negotiating process whereby various stakeholders meet with the intention of defining goals, reaching a settlement on pricing, and sharing responsibilities related to water management (Karin Kemper, personal comm.). This process should thus include an identification of the various obligations related to water management. Compared to the two mechanisms presented above, the 'negotiation model' is less clear. Probably the French River Basin Management approach is the best example in this connection (Cheret, 1993). This system has been in existence in France since the beginning of the 1960s. Management is carried out mainly as a collaboration between two levels of actors. Six river-basin agencies are responsible for technical and long-term planning, monitoring, financial calculations, operation and maintenance, and so on. The other main bodies are six committees where the stakeholders – farmers, industrial representatives, municipalities, and others – meet and negotiate about their contributions, goals of the organization, fees, investments, and so forth.

An important feature of the third option is that the organization is built within a river-basin framework. The establishment of River Basin Authorities has repeatedly been recommended by commissions who have worked on water management problems. In practice, only a few of them are working according to their objectives. The best-known example is the Tennessee Valley Authority in the USA. Another is the Murray River Commission in Australia. Neither has attracted any important followers in its respective country, and the tasks performed within these organizations are limited. In the TVA the task is hydropower, while for the MRC irrigation is a major issue. The French model is interesting, since it covers the entire country.

Water rights and wrongs?

Economic and other incentives are obviously needed as part of a strategy to improve water management. The tendency to take certain 'rights to water' through some rather arbitrary regulatory arrangement for granted does not function where the costs of developing, distributing and treating water are soaring, and abuse is common. What is more, rights to water, combined with substantial subsidies, are generally not enjoyed by those who most urgently need them. Water rights are, of course, an essential guarantee for the proper functioning of a

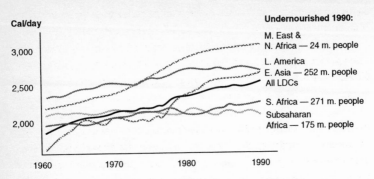

Figure 6.5   Crop-production Increases and Numbers of
Undernourished on a Regional Basis

Crop-production increase *per capita* in different world regions 1960–1990, according
to FAO 'Agriculture towards 2010'.

society, but when rights become separated from responsibilities and
are coupled with subsidies to better-off sections of a community, there
is an obvious risk that the request for the maintenance of 'water
rights' will lead to 'water wrongs'.

Rights and responsibilities are part of the regulatory arrangements,
but they can also be translated into economic and other incentives
and sanctions. Since economic considerations do play an increasing
role in the debate about water management, it is important to discuss
the extent to which economic calculations should be the basis for
how to value water, and to what extent they may contribute to a
desirable allocation between competing demands and needs. Since the
relative return on additional inputs of water varies between sectors
and localities, an allocation made on a 'free market' might change the
access to water quite markedly as compared to the present situation.
It would also mean a substantial increase in the price to many consumers. Apparently, a water policy must include economic as well as
social and environmental considerations. Since needs and demands for
water are not very well correlated with the economic performance of
various sectors, there must be some regulatory arrangements whereby
water may be allocated on a priority basis to certain functions, regardless of economic considerations.

Today, there is a general consensus that top priority should be
given to the provision of drinking water, but the level of subsidy may
vary. Although a substantial share of the world population continues

to be dependent upon unsafe and far-from-home sources of water, the commitment among the international donor community, as well as among national governments, to improve the situation in this sector remains strong. This was recently demonstrated by the Ministerial Conference on Drinking Water and Environmental Sanitation (IRC, 1994) and earlier in Agenda 21.

A much less clear picture emerges with regard to allocation between food production – that is, how much water should be allocated to irrigation – and other sectors, primarily in the expanding cities and conurbations. The actual situation is that agriculture is not able to compete economically for limited water resources. Most urban sectors can afford to pay more for water, since the return per unit used in urban/industrial sectors is significantly much higher. It is also likely that the gestation period is much shorter for returns on investments made in water supplies to urban sectors as compared to rural supplies. Comparisons of the economic return on investments in additional water supplies in food production and in urban/industrial sectors clearly suggest that it makes sense to divert some water from the low-value, low-efficiency and highly subsidized irrigation sector.

Many countries are therefore finding themselves in a situation where the agricultural sector will have to give up a certain portion of the water on which it has been accustomed to rely and to see this water being reallocated to expanding cities. In addition, the farmers in irrigation schemes are now expected to pay more for the water they used to receive at a very subsidized rate and/or are facing new regulations which will require that they pay for the pollution of water bodies. All this is happening at a time when irrigated agriculture is expected to produce 'more out of less'. Over the next thirty years, an estimated 80 per cent of the additional food supplies required to feed the growing world population is supposed to come from irrigated farming (IIMI, 1992).

Comparisons between the two alternatives often overlook two important circumstances. One is that industry, and to some extent households, could recycle and reuse water. For food and biomass production this is not a relevant concept. The amounts of water which are needed to grow crops and trees will return to atmosphere and must, for all practical purposes, be regarded as consumed or 'lost'. It will return as precipitation, but we cannot be sure when, where and how. It may return as damaging downpours, it may be too late during the season or outside the areas where it is required. For food production, which consumes the largest fraction of all water available, this 'non-negotiable fact' assumes significant proportions when we consider water requirements over time. Crops do not take days off. Their water requirement is biologically determined, and cannot be postponed to the next day or the next week. If water does not reach crops during critical stages of growth, the result is inevitably reduced yield or crop failure.

For the sector consuming the largest amounts of water, the conditions are thus quite different as compared to, for instance, industrial production. Apart from the impossibility of recycling and reusing water and the need for proper timing of supply, it is important to recognize that improvements in efficiency are not possible to the same extent in biological production as in mechanical, industrial production. To produce a kilo of rice or any other crop, about the same amount of water is required today as previously, and will in principle continue to be the same in the future. There are differences between various crops and hydroclimatic conditions, but generally speaking, biologically and hydroclimatologically determined water requirements cannot be manipulated in the same way as in manufacturing plants. Data from industrial water use in industrialized countries illustrate that water requirements may be cut quite significantly (Postel, 1992).

Another important circumstance is related to the basic-need character of food. In large parts of the tropics, where availability of water is limited and rainfall is erratic, and food production is thus problematic, the attainment of national food self-sufficiency becomes very difficult. Politically, the goal of food self-sufficiency has a high priority all over the world. The alternative to self-sufficiency through domestic production is, of course, to import. From a water perspective, this makes sense for those countries where it is much more expensive and problematic to import the large volumes of water required to produce the food needed than to import the food directly. But there are two limitations to such a strategy. If more and more countries choose to import food, overall food production will be reduced and the potential in the remaining food-producing areas may soon be exhausted. The other limit has to do with economic and political contexts. Food imports have to be paid for by somebody – by those importing or by others. If exports from the food-importing countries are weak, then the 'trade' will depend on the goodwill of donors or other external bodies. Assuming that population growth continues, there are, however, no more alternatives, apart from hunger and the mass exodus of people from food- and water-deficient areas.

A New Reverence for Water Is Needed

Think basinwide, act locally

The centralized approach in the water sector may be seen as part of a general bias towards global perspectives on the environment and development. In the rhetoric about development strategies, there is increasing reference to the global level and to the local level. Notions such as 'think globally, act locally', which was coined in the 1960s, and the more current 'global village' illustrate this odd combination, which leaves a big gap. The urge to 'think globally and act locally' does, however, have a lot of appeal and seems to encapsulate the essence of a moral required in a world where we all depend on each other.

These expressions do illustrate the fact that many challenges are global in character, and what is done in any one place is linked to global processes. Global warming can be interpreted as the consequence of the increased amounts of greenhouse gases in the atmosphere, mainly CO_2, which, among other things, is the result of burning fossil fuels by humans. Similarly, the thinning of the ozone layer may be explained as the result of joint human activities in a large number of local places. In practice, and for the majority of humankind, the links between local activities and global consequences are not that direct. There are many circumstances in between which stimulate, regulate and may control the global impact of local action. The combination of a global vision and local actions is therefore hard to comprehend; perhaps more interestingly, it bypasses significant levels in the decision-making and action-taking hierarchy. One may also wonder what kind of local actions are performed by those who think globally. And how will it help those who do act locally – the farmer or the drawer of water – if they think globally?

The experience with community participation, which has been a key concept in connection with drinking water and sanitation projects, illustrates this point. Proper community participation assumes that activities and institutions at local level are co-ordinated, and have a mutually agreed objective and strategy with those at higher levels. But it is not the lack of global vision which is causing the weak and slow implementation of the community participation principle. Rather, it is difficulties in creating fruitful interactions in the decision-making at regional and national level.

Paying attention to the two opposite geographical levels may mean that the significance of the levels in between is overlooked. As Chitale (1993) commented 'Globalization of new concerns may unknowingly lead to the overshadowing of the earlier priorities'. For resource management, and particularly with regard to water resources management, the most relevant levels are the catchment or river basin on the one hand, and hydroclimatic zones on the other, as discussed above. Thinking of water globally may lead to the idea that it is plentiful. The very uneven distribution over comparatively small areas and between short periods of time is not a distinguishing trait of a global picture. Moreover, the differences between warm and temperate regions require an understanding of the zoning of Earth into various hydroclimatological regions.

Even national figures tend to show a distorted and false picture. As an example, India and Great Britain have about the same population density per land area and about the same amount of water *per capita*. In 1990, in fact, India had more water *per capita* than people in the UK (Engelman and LeRoy, 1993). But there are few who would argue that water scarcity is an issue of the same magnitude in the two countries.

Due to the bulkiness of water and its comparatively low economic value, cross-basin transfer is not a viable option in most cases. There are examples of long-distance transfers, and plans exist for additional projects. But owing to very heavy costs and to political disagreements about the redistribution of water, it is obvious that the river basins rather than the global setting will remain the main arena where common water resources will be developed and have to be shared.

Call for a water ethic

In the glaring light of the challenges which humankind faces today and in the future, there is a need for a change of attitude to environmental conditions for development, and a new professionalism with regard to water resources and their management. Water is already a significant constraint on a decent livelihood and progress in large parts of the world. If current population increase trends and pollution, and so on, continue unchecked, the scenario for living conditions for millions and millions of people are, indeed, gloomy. And water problems are certainly playing a crucial role in most scenarios.

This represents a tremendous challenge which calls for joint efforts based on a common water ethic as part of a wider concern for the environment. The life-giving qualities of water tend to be hidden behind the concern for more immediate tangible management aspects such as the supply of household water, conveyance to various users, and so on. The combination of a visionary water ethic and skills among various groups of society must be included in a strategy to improve water management. The plea for a water ethic has been eloquently voiced by Postel (1992). Other prominent colleagues have displayed the shortcomings of conventional approaches in resource management (see, for instance, Chambers, 1993; Daly and Cobb, 1989).

The significance of water for our well-being, let alone our very existence, has echoed in poems and in religious texts and rituals. In a historical and cross-cultural perspective, no other part of bountiful nature has received the same attention. Apart from praise for its divine characteristics, water has also been guarded by secularized custodians. The development and use of water has been of great concern to kings, communities and individuals alike. A famous statement by Parakrama Bahu I (1153–86 AD), through whom Sri Lanka reached the high-water mark in the harnessing and use of water resources, illustrates this concern: 'not even a little water that comes from the rain must flow into the ocean without being made useful to man'.

The combination of a respectful attitude to water and a pragmatic, and, notably, despotic and hierarchical approach to its management has been a distinguishing trait in the evolution of cultures and societies throughout history. Respect and reverence for water led to the building of sophisticated hydraulic arrangements. Presumably, the ethical connotations facilitated the building of these systems, and also their operation and maintenance. In contrast to the prevailing attitude today, the utilitarian approach was not founded on a mechanical and disconnected view of nature, but linked to an environmental ethic. With reference to contemporary debate, it is relevant to note that the social institutions, together with a set of clear incentives and sanctions vis-à-vis water management, were part of the prevailing culture, and integrated with overall development objectives of society.

The perception of water and the approach to the management of this resource have changed significantly, particularly during recent decades. The sense of respect is very much weaker, and water is reduced to a physical object. Arrangements to augment supply and distribution have increasingly become a profession alongside the evolution of other professions intended to deal with other issues in society. As of recent times, water – or rather, the lack of water – has become a problem whose solution requires technical and organizational arrangements, but hardly any other qualifications.

This is not an attempt to downgrade the significance of professionalism, nor the relevance of technical and hydraulic skills to proper water management. Our concern is related to the concentration of attention on certain skills at the expense of an empathy for the social and environmental context in which (water) development takes place.

The objective of water projects is not to build a dam or to install a pump. It is to ease the burden and drudgery of those who have to draw water from unsafe and far-away sources. It is to improve health, boost production, stabilize income, maintain the functioning of life-support systems, and so on. Sustainable development presumes that all of these objectives be considered in some parallel manner. The concern for the multifunctional value of water has so far been neglected. There is a need for a new professionalism which does not lead to another generation of compartmentalization, nor to a lingering disregard for the linkages between resource endowments, environmental conditions and livelihood situations.

Bibliography

Abed, George, 1990, *The Economic Viability of a Palestinian State*, Institute for Palestine Studies, Washington, DC.

Adams, W.M., 1992, *Wasting the Rain*, London: Earthscan.

Alagappa, M., 1993, 'Regionalism and the Quest for Security: ASEAN and the Cambodian Conflict', *Journal of International Affairs*, 46, 2 (Winter).

Alfsson, C., employee of UNTAC and ESCAP, interview, 17 February 1993, Phnom Penh, Cambodia.

Anderson, Ewan W., 1988, 'Water: The Next Strategic Resource', in Starr and Stoll (eds), 1988, pp. 1–22.

Ayoob, M. (ed.), 1986, *Regional Security in the Third World: Case Studies from Southeast Asia and the Middle East*, London: Croom Helm.

Bari, Z., 1977, 'Syrian–Iraqi Dispute over the Euphrates Waters', *Quarterly Journal of International Studies*, New Delhi, 16, 2 (April), pp. 227–44.

Baskin, Gershon (ed.), 1993, *Water: Conflict or Cooperation, Israel/Palestine Issues in Conflict Issues in Cooperation*, Israel/Palestine Center for Research and Information, Jerusalem, II, 2, First published 1992, revised 1993.

Batutu, H., 1981, 'Some Observations on the Social Roots of Syria's Ruling, Military Group and the Causes for its Dominance', *The Middle East Journal* 35, 3, pp. 331–44.

Baxter, Craig, 1989, 'The Struggle for Development in Bangladesh', *Current History* 88, 542, pp. 437–44.

Benvenisti, Meron, 1984, *The West Bank Data Base Project: A Survey of Israel's Policies*, Washington, DC: American Enterprise Institute for Public Policy Research and West Bank Data Base Project.

Benvenisti, Meron, 1986, *The West Bank Data Base Project – 1986 Report: Demographic, Economic, Legal, Social and Political Development in the West Bank*, Jerusalem: The Jerusalem Post Press.

Benvenisti, Meron, Z. Abu-Zayed and D. Rubinstein, 1986, *The West Bank Handbook: A Political Lexicon*, Jerusalem: The Jerusalem Post Press.

Bertocci, Peter J., 1986, 'Bangladesh in 1985: Resolute Against the Storms', *Asian Survey* 26, 2, pp. 224–34.

Beschorner, Natascha, 1992, 'Water and Instability in the Middle East', *Adelphi Paper* 273, London: Brassey's for the International Institute for Strategic Studies.

Biswas, Asit K., 1992, 'Water for Third World Development: A Perspective from the South', *International Journal for Water Resources Development*, 8, 1, pp. 3–9.

Biswas, Asit K., 1993, 'Management of International Waters: Problems and Perspectives', in El-Habr (ed.), 1993, pp. 167–88.

Biswas, Asit K. and Habib N. El-Habr, 1993, 'Environment and Water Resources Management: The Need for a New Holistic Approach', in El-Habr (ed.), 1993, pp. 117–25.

Blyn, George, 1966, *Agriculture Trends in India, 1891–1957: Output, Availability, and Productivity*, Philadelphia, PA: University of Pennsylvania Press.

Briscoe, J., World Bank, personal communication.

Brock, Lothar, 1991, 'Peace Through Parks: The Environment on the Peace Research Agenda', *Journal of Peace Research*, 28, 4, pp. 407–23.

Brown, Lester, 1977, *Redefining National Security*, Worldwatch Paper 14, Washington, DC: Worldwatch Institute.

Brown, Lester, 1994, 'Facing Food Insecurity', in Brown (ed.), 1994, pp. 177–97.

Brown, Lester (ed.), 1994, *State of the World 1994* (Worldwatch Institute), New York: W. W. Norton.

Bulloch, J. and A. Darwish, 1993, *Water Wars: Coming Conflicts in the Middle East*, London: Victor Gollancz.

Bureau of Flood Control, 1952, *Preliminary Report on Technical Problems Relating to Flood Control and Water Resources Development of the Mekong – an International River*, Bangkok.

Buszynsky, L., 1992, 'Southeast Asia in the Post-Cold War Era: Regionalism and Security', *Asian Survey*, 32, 9, September, pp. 830–47.

Butterfield, J. and S. Madi, 1989, 'South Lebanon, the Forgotten Occupation', *Middle East Philanthropic Fund (MEPF) (Boston) Newsletter*, 2, 1 (Spring).

Buzan, B., 1988, 'The Southeast Asian Security Complex', *Contemporary Southeast Asia*, 10, 1, pp. 1–16.

Buzan, B., 1991, *People, States and Fear: An Agenda for International Security Studies in the Post-Cold War Era*, Hemel Hempstead and New York: Harvester Wheatsheaf.

Buzan, B., G. Rizvi *et al.*, 1986, *South Asian Insecurity and the Great Powers*, London: Macmillan.

Cantori, L.J. and L.S. Spiegel, 1970, *The International Politics of Regions: A Comparative Approach*, Englewood Cliffs, NJ: Prentice Hall.

Central Bureau of Statistics, 1989, *Statistical Abstract of Israel, 1989*, Jerusalem.

Central Bureau of Statistics, 1993, *Statistical Abstract of Israel, 1993*, Jerusalem.

Chaipipat, Kulachada, 1992a, 'Thailand Wants New Group to Probe Mekong Problems', *The Nation*, Bangkok, 19 March.

Chaipipat, Kulachada, 1992b, 'Strong Distrust Delays Cooperation on Mekong', *The Nation*, Bangkok, 27 March, p. A2.

Chambers, R., 1993, *Challenging the Professions: Frontiers for Rural Development*, London: IT Publications.

Cheret, I., 1993, *Water Management in France*, First Annual Conference on Environmentally Sustainable Development, 30 September and 1 October 1993, ESD and The World Bank.

Chitale, M. A., 1993, *Barriers to the Development and Management of Water Resources*, Stockholm Water Prize Laureate Lecture, Stockholm Water Symposium 1993.

Chongkittavorn, K., 1992, 'VN Expects Fair Mekong Policy', *The Nation*, Bangkok.

Choudhury, G. W., 1968, *Pakistan's Relations with India 1947–1966*, London: Pall Mall.

Clarke, R., 1991, *Water: The International Crisis*, Cambridge, MA: MIT Press and London: Earthscan.

Cohen, Saul, 1986, *The Geopolitics of Israel's Border Question*, Tel Aviv University, Jaffee Center for Strategic Studies, Jerusalem: The Jersualem Post Press, and Boulder, CO: Westview Press.

Collins, Robert O., 1990, *The Waters of the Nile: Hydropolitics and the Jonglei Canal, 1900–1988*, Oxford: Clarendon Press.

Committee for Co-ordination of Investigations of the Lower Mekong Basin, 1957, Bangkok (statutes for the original Mekong Committee signed 17 September 1957 in Bangkok).

CSE (Centre for Science and Environment), 1991, *Floods, Flood Plains and Environmental Myths* (State of India's Environment: A Citizens' Report), New Delhi: CSE.

Curtis, G., employee of UNTAC, country expert, interview 31 March 1993, Phnom Penh, Cambodia.

Daly, H. and J. B. Cobb Jr, 1989, *For the Common Good*, Boston, MA: Beacon Press.

Dam, N., 1980, 'Middle Eastern Political Clichés: 'Takriti' and 'Sunni' Rule in Iraq; 'Alawi' Rule in Syria', *Orient* 1, pp. 42–57.

DANIDA, 1993, East African Water Resources Seminar, 24 to 29 May, Entebbe and Copenhagen.

Davis, Uri, 1987, *Israel: An Apartheid State*, London: Zed Books.

Davis, Uri, Antonia E.L. Maks and John Richardson, 1980, 'Israel's Water Politics', *Journal of Palestine Studies*, IX, 2 (34), pp. 3–31.

Deutsch, Karl W. *et al.*, 1957, *Political Community and the North Atlantic Area*, Princeton, NJ: Princeton University Press.

Döös, B. R., 1994, 'Environmental Degradation, Global Food Production, and Risk for Large-scale Migrations', *Ambio*, 23, 2, pp. 124–30.

Duna, Cem, 1988, 'Turkey's Peace Pipeline', in Starr and Stoll, 1988.

El-Habr, Habib N. (ed.), 1993, *(International Journal of) Water Resources Development* (Special issue, Environment and Water Development: Some Critical Issues), 9, 2.

Elmusa, Sharif, 1993, 'Dividing the Common Palestinian–Israeli Waters: An International Water Law Approach', *Journal of Palestine Studies*, XXII (87), 3, (Spring), pp. 57–77.

Engelman, Robert and Pamela LeRoy, 1993, *Sustaining Water: Population and the Future of Renewable Water Supplies*, Washington, DC: Population Action International.

Entebbe Report, 1993, East African Water Resources Seminar, 24–27 May,

Ministry of Foreign Affairs, Copenhagen.

Environmental Protection Service, 1988, *State of Israel, The Environment in Israel*.

Falkenmark, Malin, 1989a, 'The Massive Water-Scarcity Now Threatening Africa – Why Isn't it Being Addressed?', *Ambio*, 18, 2, pp. 112–18.

Falkenmark, Malin, 1989b, 'Middle East Hydropolitics: Water Scarcity and Conflicts in the Middle East', *Ambio*, 18, 6, pp. 350–52.

Falkenmark, Malin, 1989c, 'Vulnerability Generated by Water Scarcity', *Ambio*, 18, 6, pp. 352–3.

Falkenmark, Malin, 1990, 'Global Water Issues Confronting Humanity', *Journal of Peace Research*, 27, 2, pp. 177–90.

Falkenmark, Malin, 1993, *Follow-up of Agenda 21. Towards Integration of Land Use and Water Management*, Guest Lecture, Stockholm Water Symposium 1993.

Falkenmark, Malin, Hans Ackefors and Lars Kristoferson, 1988, *Perspectives of Sustainable Development: Some Critical Issues Related to the Brundtland Report*, Stockholm Studies in Natural Resources Management, No. 1, Stockholm: Sundt Offset.

Falkenmark, Malin and Gunnar Lindh, 1993, 'Water and Economic Development', in Gleick (ed.), 1993, pp. 80–91.

Falkenmark, Malin, Jan Lundqvist and Carl Widstrand, 1990, *Water Scarcity – An Ultimate Constraint in Third World Development*, Tema V, Report 14, University of Linköping: Department of Water and Environmental Studies.

Falkenmark, Malin and J. Rockström, 1993, 'Curbing Rural Exodus from Tropical Drylands', *Ambio*, 22, pp. 427–37.

Falkenmark, Malin and Zdzislaw Mikulski, 1994, 'The Key Role of Water in the Landscape System. Conceptualization to Address Growing Landscape Pressures', *GeoJournal*, 33, 4, pp. 355–63.

FAO, 1993a, *Agriculture: Towards 2010*, Doc. C 93/24, Food and Agriculture Organization, Rome.

FAO, 1993b, *Yearbook*, Food and Agriculture Organization, Rome.

Farouk-Sluglett, M. and P. Sluglett, 1990, *Iraq since 1958: From Revolution to Dictatorship*, London and New York: I.B. Tauris.

Fukui, Katsuyoshi and John Markakis (eds), 1994, *Ethnicity & Conflict in the Horn of Africa*, London: James Currey.

Ganapathi, V., 1993, 'Cauvery Water Dispute: No Cheer Yet: Farmers Unhappy in Tamil Nadu', *Frontline*, 10 September, p. 120.

Gazmuri, S., 1994, 'Chilean Water Policy', Short Report Series on Locally Managed Irrigation, No. 3, IIMI, Colombo.

General Statistical Office, 1991a, *Economy and Trade of Vietnam 1986–1990*, Ministry of Trade, Hanoi.

General Statistical Office, 1991b, *Statistical Data of the Socialist Republic of Vietnam*, Statistical Publishing House, Hanoi.

Ghazi, Falah, 1990, 'Arabs versus Jews in Galilee: Competition for Regional Resources', *GeoJournal*, 21, 4, pp. 325–36.

Gleick, Peter H., 1992, *Occasional Paper Series of the Project on Environmental Change and Acute Conflict*, A Joint Project of the University of Toronto and the American Academy of Arts and Sciences, No. 1, (September), pp. 3–28.

Gleick, Peter H., 1993, 'An Introduction to Global Fresh Water Issues', in Gleick (ed.), 1993, pp. 3–12.

Gleick, Peter H. (ed.), 1993, *Water in Crisis: A Guide to the World's Fresh Water Resources*, Oxford: Oxford University Press.

Goldsmith, E. and N. Hildyard (eds), 1986, *The Social and Environmental Effects of Large Dams*, Cornwall: Wadebridge Ecological Centre.

Golubev, Genady N., 1993, 'Sustainable Water Development: Implications for the Future', in El-Habr (ed.), 1993, pp. 127–54.

Grinter, L.E. and Y.W. Kihl (eds), 1987, *East Asian Conflict Zones*, London: Macmillan.

Guhan, S., 1993, *The Cauvery River Dispute: Towards Conciliation*, Madras: Kasturi & Sons.

Gupta, Dipankar, 1985, 'The Communalising of Punjab, 1980–1985', *Economic and Political Weekly*, 20, 28, pp. 1185–90.

Haas, M., 1970, 'International Subsystems: Stability and Polarity', *American Political Science Review*, 64, 1, pp. 98–123.

Hansen, A. H., 1966, *The Process of Planning: A Study of India's Five Year Plans 1950–1964*, Oxford: Oxford University Press.

Hansson, Göte, 1989, 'Ethiopia', *Macroeconomic Studies*, 1, Stockholm: SIDA, The Planning Secretariat.

Harrison, J., Senior Officer, Mekong Secretariat, interview 21 January 1993, Bangkok, Thailand.

Harrison, Paul, 1993, *The Third Revolution: Population, Environment and a Sustainable World*, Harmondsworth: Penguin.

Heiberg, M. and G. Øvensen, 1993, *Palestinian Society in Gaza, West Bank and Arab Jerusalem: A Survey of Living Conditions*, FAFO Report 151, Oslo.

Heller, Mark, 1983, *A Palestinian State: The Implications for Israel*, Cambridge, MA: Harvard University Press.

Heller, Mark and Sari Nusseibeh, 1991, *No Trumpets, No Drums: A Two-State Settlement of the Israeli–Palestinian Conflict*, New York: Hill & Wang.

Hoang Anh Tuan, 1993, 'Why Hasn't Vietnam Gained ASEAN Membership?', *Contemporary Southeast Asia*, 15, 3, December, pp. 280–91.

Holsti, K.J., 1967, *International Politics: A Framework for Analysis*, Englewood Cliffs, NJ: Prentice Hall.

Homer-Dixon, Thomas F., Jeffrey H. Bouthwell and George W. Rathjens, 1993, 'Environmental Change and Violent Conflict', *Scientific American*, February, pp. 38–45.

Hubble, P., 1993, *Antithetical Perceptions of Developemnt and Environment: Village People and the State in Rural Thailand*, York University (MSc), Toronto.

IBRD (International Bank for Reconstruction and Development; the World Bank), 1992, *Cambodia – Agenda for Rehabilitation and Reconstruction*, The World Bank, East and Pacific Region Country Department I.

IBRD, 1993, *Water Resources Management: A World Bank Policy Paper*, Washington, DC.

ICWE, 1992, *International Conference on Water and the Environment: Development Issues for the 21st Century*, 26–31 January 1992, Dublin.

IIMI, 1992, *Developing Environmentally Sound and Lasting Improvements in Irrigation Management: The Role of International Research*, International Irrigation Management Institute, Colombo.

IMC (Interim Mekong Committee), 1978, *Declaration Concerning the Interim*

Committee for Coordination of Investigations of the Lower Mekong Basin, Vientiane.

IMC, 1987, *Perspectives on Mekong Development*, Bangkok.

IMC, 1991, *Preparing for New Challenges: Annual Report 1991*, Bangkok.

Ing Khiet, Minister of Energy (from August 1993), interview 30 and 31 March 1993, Phnom Penh, Cambodia.

International Law Association, 1966, *Helsinki Rules on the Uses of the Water of International Rivers*, Helsinki.

IRC, 1994, *Ministerial Conference on Drinking Water and Environmental Sanitation: Implementing UNCED Agenda 21*, 19–23 March, Noordwijk, International Reference Centre, The Netherlands.

Israel Information Service Gopher, November 1991a, *Background: Water, Israel and the Middle East*, Information Division, Israel Foreign Ministry.

Israel Information Service Gopher, November 1991b, *Multilateral Tasks: Round 3 – Update*, Information Division, Israel Foreign Ministry.

Israel Information Service Gopher, 27 January 1992, *Multilateral Issues: Water in the Middle East*, Information Division, Israel Foreign Ministry.

Israel Information Service Gopher, 24 November 1992, *Multilateral Talks: Structure and Progress – Update*, Information Division, Israel Foreign Ministry.

Israeli–Jordanian Informal Draft Agenda, Washington DC, 27 October 1993, *Journal of Palestine Studies*, XXII (86), 2 (Winter), pp. 142–3.

Israeli–PLO Declaration of Principles on Interim Self-government Arrangements, Washington DC, 13 September 1993, *Journal of Palestine Studies*, XXIII (89), 1 (Autumn), pp. 115–21.

Israel's Central Bureau of Statistics, 1994, Jerusalem.

Jaber, Raghda, 1989, 'The Politics of Water in South Lebanon', *Race and Class*, 31, 2, pp. 63–7.

Jain, S. N. *et al.*, 1971, *Interstate Water Disputes in India*, Bombay: Tripathi Pvt. Ltd.

Jervis, R., 1976, *Perception and Misperception in International Politics*, Princeton, NJ: Princeton University Press.

Jervis, R., 1978, 'Cooperation Under the Security Dilemma', *World Politics*, January 1978, pp. 167–214.

Jervis, R., 1982, 'Security Regimes', *International Organization*, 36, 2, pp. 357–78.

JMCC (Jerusalem Media Communication Centre), 1989, *Bitter Harvest: Israeli Sanctions against Palestinian Agriculture during the Uprising – December 1987–March 1989*, Jerusalem: JMCC.

JMCC (Jerusalem Media Communication Centre), 1993, *Israeli Military Orders in the Occupied Palestinian West Bank 1967–1992*, Jerusalem: JMCC.

Jørgensen, B., 1991, 'Ethnic Dimensions of Regional Security: The Case of South Asia', in Ohlsson (ed.), 1991, pp. 106–31.

Kaarsholm, Preben and Jan Hultin (eds), 1994, 'Inventions and Boundaries: Historical and Anthropological Approaches to the Study of Ethnicity and Nationalism', *International Development Studies, Occasional Paper No. 11*, Roskilde: I.D.S. Roskilde University.

Kahan, David, 1987, *Agriculture and Water Resources in the West Bank and Gaza (1967–1987)*, Jerusalem: The Jerusalem Post Press.

Kally, Elisha, 1986, *Water Supply to the West Bank and Gaza Strip, Interim Report*, The Armand Hammer Fund for Economic Cooperation in the Middle East,

Tel Aviv University.

Kally, Elisha, 1991/92, *Options for Solving the Palestinian Water Problem in the Context of Regional Peace*, Israeli–Palestinian Peace Research Project, Working Paper Series No. 19, The Harry S. Truman Research Institute for the Advancement of Peace, Hebrew University, Israel.

Khalil, S., 1989, *The Republic of Fear: Saddam's Iraq*, London: Hutchinson Radius.

Kienle, E., 1990, *Ba'th v. Ba'th: The Conflict between Syria and Iraq 1968–1989*, London and New York: I.B. Tauris.

Kiernan, B., 1991, *The Making of the Paris Agreement on Cambodia, 1990–91*, Paper presented at the Indochina Project Conference, Kauai, 18–20 December 1991.

Kolars, J., 1986, 'The Hydro-Imperative of Turkey's Search for Energy', *Middle East Journal*, 40, 1 (Winter), pp. 53–67.

Kolars, John, 1990, 'The Course of Water in the Arab Middle East', *American–Arab Affairs*, 33 (Summer), pp. 66 f.

Kopytoff, Igor, 1987, 'The Internal African Frontier: The Making of African Political Culture', in I. Kopytoff (ed.), *The African Frontier. The Reproduction of Traditional African Societies*, Bloomington: Indiana University Press, pp. 3–84.

Kositchotethana, 1993, 'Electricity Demand Seen to Rise 12.1%', *Bangkok Post*, 1 March 1993.

Kramer, Mark N., 1987, 'Soviet Arms Transfers to the Third World', *Problems of Communism*, September–October, pp. 52-68.

Kumar, P. *et al.*, 1984, *Punjab Crisis: Contexts and Trends*, Chandigarh: Centre for Research in Rural and Industrial Development.

Lesch, Ann Mosley, 1992, *Transition to Palestinian Self-Government*, Report of a Study Group of the Middle East Program Committee on International Security Studies, American Academy of Arts and Sciences, Cambridge, MA. Published in collaboration with Indiana University Press, Bloomington and Indianapolis.

Lindgren, Göran, 1990, 'World Data in Figures', *Research Information*, No. 5, Uppsala: Uppsala University, Department of Peace and Conflict Research.

Ljunggren, B., 1992, *Market Economies under Communist Regimes: Reform in Vietnam, Laos and Cambodia*, PhD Dissertation, Southern Illinois University.

Lohmann, L., 1990, 'Remaking the Mekong', *The Ecologist*, 20, 2, London, pp. 61–6.

Lowi, Miriam, 1992, 'West Bank Water Resources and the Resolution of Conflict in the Middle East', *Occasional Paper Series of the Project on Environmental Change and Acute Conflict*, A Joint Project of the University of Toronto and the American Academy of Arts and Sciences, No. 1 (September), pp. 29–60.

McCaffrey, Stephen C., 1993, 'Water, Politics and International Law', in Gleick (ed.), 1993, pp. 92–104.

Mageed, Yahia Abdel, 1993, 'Environmentally Sound Water Management and Development', in El-Habr (ed.), 1993, pp. 155–65.

Manibhandu, A., 1993, 'Thais Ready to Host Talks on Four-Way Cooperation Pact', *Bangkok Post*, Bangkok, p. A1.

Maoz, M. and Avner Yaniv (eds), 1986, *Syria under Assad: Domestic Constraints and Regional Risks*, London and Sydney: Croom Helm.

Markakis, John, 1987, *National and Class Conflict in the Horn of Africa*, African

Studies Series 55, Cambridge: Cambridge University Press.

Markakis, John, (ed.), 1993, *Conflict and the Decline of Pastoralism in the Horn of Africa*, London: Macmillan.

Markakis, John, 1994, 'Ethnic Conflict and the State in the Horn of Africa', in Fukui and Markakis (eds), 1994, pp. 217–37.

MEED (Middle East Economic Digest), 1991, January.

Mekloy, P., 1993, 'Whose Water?', *Bangkok Post*, Bangkok, p. III,1.

Misra, K. P., 1978, 'The Farakka Accord', *The World Today* 34, 2, pp. 41–4.

Moris, J., 1987, 'Irrigation as a Privileged Solution in African Development', *Development Policy Review* 5, pp. 99–123.

MRG (The Minority Rights Group), 1985, *The Kurds*, Report No. 23 (revised), London: Expedite Graphic Limited.

MRG (The Minority Rights Group), 1987, *The Armenians*, Report No. 32 (revised), London: Expedite Graphic Limited.

MS (Mekong Secretariat), 1970, *Indicative Basin Plan*, Bangkok.

MS (Mekong Secretariat), 1987, *Perspectives on Mekong Development*, Bangkok.

MS (Mekong Secretariat), 1989, *The Mekong Committee: A Historical Account (1957–89)*, Bangkok.

MS (Mekong Secretariat), 1992, *Studies of Salinity Intrusion in the Mekong Delta*, Ho Chi Minh.

MS (Mekong Secretariat), 1993a, *Work Programme*, Bangkok.

MS (Mekong Secretariat), 1993b, *Preparatory Organizational and Legal Studies*, Bangkok.

Naff, Thomas, 1991, Lecture held at a seminar on Peacekeeping, Water and Security in South Lebanon, in London, 4 October, arranged by Centre for Lebanese Studies, Oxford.

Nash, Linda, 1993, 'Water Quality and Health', in Gleick (ed.), 1993, pp. 25–39.

Nguyen Nhan Quang, Programme Officer Vietnam National Mekong Committee, interview 7 June 1993, Hanoi, Vietnam.

Nguyen Vu Tung, 1993, 'Vietnam–ASEAN Cooperation in Southeast Asia', *Security Dialogue*, 24, 1, pp. 85–92.

Nijim, Basheer K., 1990, 'Water Resource in the History of the Palestine–Israel Conflict', *GeoJournal*, 21, 4, pp. 317–23.

Nilsson, L., environmentalist at the Mekong Secretariat, interviews 31 August 1992, 21 January 1993, and 9 June 1993.

Ohlsson, Leif (ed.), 1989, *Case Studies of Regional Conflicts and Conflict Resolution*, Göteborg: Padrigu Papers.

Ohlsson, Leif (ed.), 1991, *Regional Conflicts and Conflict Resolution. Case Studies II*, Göteborg: Padrigu Papers.

Ohlsson, Leif (ed.), 1992, *Regional Case Studies of Water Conflicts*, Göteborg: Padrigu Papers.

Öjendal, Joakim, 1993, 'Interview Survey in Kratieh Province', May, unpublished.

Oram, R., Information Officer, Mekong Secretariat, interview 2 April 1991, Bangkok.

Pankhurst, Alula, 1992, *Resettlement and Famine in Ethiopia: The Villagers' Experience*, Manchester: Manchester University Press.

Pearce, Fred, 1991, 'Africa at a Watershed', *New Scientist*, 23 March, pp. 34–41.

Pearce, Fred, 1992, *The Dammed: Rivers, Dams and the Coming World Water Crisis*,

London: The Bodley Head.

Persson, S., 'Kongedømmet i Jordan: De palestinske elitenes rolle', *Internasjonal Politikk*, 1–2, pp. 37–59.

Ploss, Irwin and Jonathan Rubinstein, 1992, 'Water for Peace', *The New Republic*, 7, 14 September, pp. 20–22.

Pornpong, S., 1993, 'Bt88 Bn Budget Approval to End Water Shortage', *The Nation*, Bangkok, p. A4.

Postel, Sandra, 1984, *Water: Rethinking Management in an Age of Scarcity*, Worldwatch Paper 62, Washington, DC: Worldwatch Institute.

Postel, Sandra, 1989, *Water for Agriculture: Facing the Limits*, Worldwatch Paper 93, Washington, DC: Worldwatch Institute.

Postel, Sandra, 1992, *Last Oasis: Facing Water Scarcity*, (The Worldwatch Environmental Alert Series), New York: W. W. Norton.

Postel, Sandra, 1994, 'Carrying Capacity: Earth's Bottom Line', in Brown (ed.), 1994, pp. 3–21.

Precoda, Norman, 1991, 'Requiem for the Aral Sea', *Ambio*, 22, 3–4, pp. 109–14.

Pugh, Deborah, 1990, 'Egypt Finds Water Beneath its Sea of Sand', *New African*, October.

Rabo, A., 1986, *Change on the Euphrates: Villages, Townsmen and Employees in Northeast Syria*, Stockholm: Akademitryck.

Rahmato, Dessalegn, 1988, 'Settlement and Resettlement in Mettekel, Western Ethiopia', *Africa: Rivista trimestrale di studi e documentazione dell'Instituto Italo-Africano*, XLIII, 1, pp. 14–34.

Ramana, M. V. V., 1992, *Inter-state River Waters in India*, Madras: Orient Longman Ltd.

Renner, Michael, 1989, *National Security: The Economic and Environmental Dimensions*, Worldwatch Paper 89, Washington, DC: Worldwatch Institute.

Reuger, Sara, 1993, 'Controversial Waters: Exploitation of the Jordan River', *Middle Eastern Studies*, 29, 1 (January), pp. 53–90.

Roberson, B. A., 1986, 'South Asia and the Gulf Complex', in Buzan and Rizvi, 1986, pp. 159–80.

Rose, Norman, 1986, *Chaim Weizmann: A Biography*, New York: Penguin.

Rowley, Gwyn, 1990, 'The West Bank: Native Water-resource System and Competition', *Political Geography Quarterly*, 9, 1, pp. 39–52.

Ryder, G., 1993, *An Introduction to the Potential Environment Effects of the Khong–Chi–Mun Diversion Project on The Lower Mekong Basin*, Bangkok.

Sahagian, D. L., F. W. Schwartz and D. K. Jacobs, 1994, 'Direct Anthropogenic Contributions to Sea Level Rise in the Twentieth Century', *Nature*, 367, 6.

Saleh, Hassan Abdul Kadir, 1990, 'Jewish Settlement and Its Economic Impact on the West Bank', *GeoJournal*, 21, 4, pp. 337–48.

Sandstrom, K., 1995, 'Forests and Water – Friends or Foes? Hydrological Implications of Deforestation and Land Degradation in Semi-arid Tanzania', Linköping Studies in Arts and Science, Linköping.

Sayigh, Y., 1982, *The Arab Economy: Past Performance and Future Prospect*, New York: Oxford University Press

Schiff, Ze'ev and Ehud Ya'ari, 1990, *Intifada: The Palestinian Uprising – Israel's Third Front*, New York: Simon & Schuster.

Schulz, M., 1989, 'The Palestinian–Israeli Security Complex. Inconciliatory

Positions or Regional Cooperation?', in Ohlsson (ed.), 1989, pp. 112–47.

Sen, S. R., 1962, *The Strategy for Agricultural Development and Other Essays on Economic Policy and Planning*, New York: Asia Publishing House.

Sewell, D. and G. White, 1966, 'The Lower Mekong – An Experiment in International River Development', *International Conciliation*, 558, New York.

Shah, T., 1993, *Groundwater Markets and Irrigation Development: Political Economy and Practical Policy*, Bombay: Oxford University Press.

Shalev, Aryeh, 1980, *The Autonomy – Problems and Possible Solution*, Center for Strategic Studies, Paper 8, Tel Aviv.

Shawwa, Isam R., 1993, 'The Water Situation in the Gaza Strip', in Baskin (ed.), 1993, pp. 23–36.

Shiklomanov, Igor A., 1993, 'World Fresh Water Resources', in Gleick (ed.), 1993, pp. 13–24.

Shiva, V., 1991, *The Violence of the Green Revolution*, Penang: Third World Network.

Shuval, Hillel, I., 1987, 'The Development of Water Reuse in Israel', *Ambio* 16, 4, pp. 186–90.

Shuval, Hillel, I., 1992, 'Approaches to Resolving the Water Conflicts between Israel and Her Neighbors – A Regional Water-for-Peace Plan', *Water International*, 17, pp. 133–43.

Shuval, Hillel, I., 1993, 'Approaches to Finding an Equitable Solution to the Water Resources Problems Shared by Israelis and the Palestinians in the Use of the Mountain Aquifer', in Baskin (ed.), 1993, pp. 37–84.

Si Niny, Permanent Secretary of the National Cambodian Mekong Committee, interviews 18 August 1992 and 3 June 1993, Phnom Penh, Cambodia.

SIPRI Yearbook 1991, *World Armaments and Disarmament*, Oxford: Oxford University Press.

Sorensen, J., 1993, *Imagining Ethiopia: Struggles for History and Identity in the Horn of Africa*, New Brunswick, NJ: Rutgers University Press.

Springborg, R., 1981, 'Baathism in Practice: Agriculture, Politics, and Political Culture in Syria and Iraq', *Middle Eastern Studies*, 17, 2, April, pp. 191–209.

Springborg, R., 1986, 'Infitah, Agrarian Transformation, and Elite Consolidation in Contemporary Iraq', *Middle East Journal*, 40, 1, Winter, pp. 33–52.

Starr, Joyce R., 1991, 'Water Wars', *Foreign Policy*, 82, Spring, pp. 17–36.

Starr, Joyce R. (ed.), 1983, *A Shared Destiny: Near East Regional Development and Cooperation*, New York: Praeger.

Starr, Joyce R. and Daniel C. Stoll, 1988, 'Water for the Year 2000', in Starr and Stoll (eds), 1988.

Starr, Joyce R. and Daniel C. Stoll (eds), 1988, *The Politics of Scarcity: Water in the Middle East*, Boulder, CO and London: Westview Press.

Statistical Publishing House, 1990, *Mekong Delta – Its Location and Potentialities*, Hanoi.

Swain, Ashok, 1993, 'Conflicts over Water: The Ganges Water Dispute', *Security Dialogue* 24, 4, pp. 429–39.

Swamy, P. M. and S. Rai, 1993, 'Jaya's Subtle Game: The Lady Exploits Tamil Insecurity', *India Today*, 15 August, p. 15.

Tamimi, Abdel-Rahman, 1991/92, *Water: A Factor for Conflict or Peace in the Middle East*, Israeli–Palestinian Peace Research Project, Working Paper Series, No.

20, Arab Studies Society, Jerusalem.

Taubenblatt, Selig A., 1988, 'Jordan River Basin Water: A Challenge in the 1990s', in Starr and Stoll (eds), 1988, pp. 41–52.

'TN Admits Giving Wrong Data on Cauvery', *Indian Express* (New Delhi), 17 February 1994.

Traisawasdichai, M., 1992, 'Environment Group Charges Egat with Breach of Dam Pact', *The Nation*, Bangkok.

Triulzi, Alessandro, 1994, 'Ethiopia: The Making of a Frontier Society', in Kaarsholm and Hultin (eds), 1994, pp. 235–45.

Turley, W., 1985, *Confrontation or Coexistence – the Future of ASEAN–Vietnam Relations*, Institute of Security and International Studies, Bangkok.

Turley, W., 1987, 'Thai-Vietnamese Rivalry in the Indochina Conflict', in Grinter, L.E. and Y.W. Kihl (eds), *East Asian Conflict Zones*, London: Macmillan.

Ullman, R. H., 1983, 'Redefining Security', *International Security* 8, 1, pp. 129–53.

UN, 1958, *Programme of Studies and Investigations for Comprehensive Development of the Lower Mekong River Basin*, UN documents TAA/AFE/3, 22 April.

UN, 1991, *Agreements on a Comprehensive Political Settlement of the Cambodia Conflict*, United Nations, 23 November 1991.

UN, 1992, *Handbook on the Peaceful Settlement of Disputes between States*, New York.

UNFPA (United Nations Fund for Population Activities), 1991, *Population and the Environment: The Challenges Ahead*, New York: UNFPA.

UNFPA, 1992, *The State of World Population 1992*, New York.

US Department of the Interior, 1956, *Reconnaissance Report – Lower Mekong River Basin*.

US Department of the Interior, 1964, *Land and Water Resources of the Blue Nile Basin, Ethiopia*, Bureau of Reclamation.

Viraphol, S., 1985, 'Thailand's Perspective on Its Rivalry with Vietnam', in Turley, 1985.

VNA (Vietnam News Agency), Foreign Ministry Spokesperson on the Mekong Committee, 14 March 1992, 92.114, Hanoi.

de Vylder, S. and A. Fforde, 1988, *Vietnam: An Economy in Transition*, Stockholm: SIDA.

Wallensteen, Peter (ed.), 1988, *Peace Research: Achievements and Challenges*, Boulder, CO and London: Westview Press.

WCED, 1987, *Our Common Future*, World Commission on Environment and Development, Oxford University Press.

White, G. F., 1963, 'The Mekong River Plan', *Scientific American*, 208, 4, Chicago, pp. 49–59.

White, G. F. *et al.*, 1962, *Economic and Social Aspects of Lower Mekong Development*, Bangkok.

Widstrand, C. (ed.), 1980, *Water Conflicts and Research Priorities*, Oxford: Pergamon Press.

Winpenny, J., 1994, *Managing Water as an Economic Resource*, London: ODI.

Wolf, Aaron and John Ross, 1992, 'The Impact of Scarce Water Resources on the Arab–Israeli Conflict', *Natural Resources Journal* 32, 4 (Fall), pp. 919–58.

Wood, Adrian and Michael Ståhl, 1990, *Ethiopia: National Conservation Strategy, Phase One Report*, International Union for the Conservation of Nature

(IUCN).

World Bank, 1987a, *Ethiopia: Recent Economic Development and Prospects for Recovery and Growth*, Report No. 5929-ET.

World Bank, 1987b, *Ethiopia – Agriculture: A Strategy for Growth, A Sector Review*, Report No. 6512-ET.

Yaniv, Avner, 1987a, *Deterrence Without the Bomb: The Politics of Israeli Strategy*, Lexington, MA and Toronto: Lexington Books.

Yaniv, Avner, 1987b, 'Syria and Israel: The Politics of Escalation', in Ma'oz and Yaniv (eds), 1987, pp. 157–78.

Index